Haunthenticity

Tracy McMullen

HAUNTHENTICITY

Musical Replay and the Fear of the Real

Wesleyan University Press Middletown, Connecticut

Wesleyan University Press
Middletown, CT 06459
www.wesleyan.edu/wespress

Manufactured in the United States of America
Designed by Mindy Basinger Hill
Typeset in Minion Pro

Library of Congress Cataloging-in-Publication Data

Name: McMullen, Tracy, author.

Title: Haunthenticity : musical replay and the fear of the real / Tracy McMullen.

Description: Middletown, Connecticut : Wesleyan University Press, [2019]

Series: Music/culture | Includes bibliographical references and index.

Identifiers: LCCN 2018036452 (print) | LCCN 2018042824 (ebook) | ISBN 9780819578549 (ebook) | ISBN 9780819578525 (hardcover : alk. paper) | ISBN 9780819578532 (pbk.)

Subjects: LCSH: Popular music—History and criticism. | Authenticity (Philosophy) | Tribute bands (Musical groups)

Classification: LCC ML3470 (ebook) | LCC ML3470 .M444 2019 (print) | DDC 781.6409—dc23

LC record available at https://lccn.loc.gov/2018036452

5 4 3 2 1

The Publisher gratefully acknowledges the support of the Endowment of the American Musicological Society, funded in part by the National Endowment for the Humanities and the Andrew W. Mellon Foundation.

THIS BOOK IS DEDICATED *to all of my teachers and students.*

Thus has the cage betrayed us all, this moment,
our life, turned to nothing through our terrible attempts to insure it.

James Baldwin | "Everybody's Protest Novel" (1949)

CONTENTS

ACKNOWLEDGMENTS

It would appear that it takes a village to keep Tracy going. Some people have had a heavier load than others (Drebs comes to mind . . . you know who you are). I attempt now to acknowledge and thank that village. I can only hope I'm a decent villager in turn to my family, friends, and colleagues. Life is challenging in our modern world, as I think this book articulates. I thank those who have helped me along the way.

At the turn of the millennium I was earning an MM in jazz saxophone performance and an MA in composition at the University of North Texas. UNT gave me tremendous fodder for thinking about music, the past, race, gender, and jazz in the university system. I appreciated my talented and kind friends there, many of whom I still see: Eliza, Jiyeon, and Ryan McGillicuddy with whom I now have Maine in common; Tito Charneco, Jeff Fort, Nikki D'Agostino, Lily Maase, Erin Costelo, Kevin Patton, Maria del Carmen Montoya, Tom Blancarte, Paul Tynan, Fred Samson, Jangeun Bae, and Justin Svrcek. I had wonderful professors at UNT from whom I continue to learn: Mike Steinel, Fred Hamilton, John P. Murphy, Jim Riggs, Paris Rutherford, Dan Haerle, Neil Slater, Butch Rovan, and the late Phil Winsor. Joe Klein hipped me to the music department at the University of California, San Diego, for which I am forever grateful. Not least, performing in the inimitable Cary Richards Orchestra offered a bounty of insight and energizing ire.

My work on the Glenn Miller reenactment and on Wynton Marsalis began while I was earning my PhD in critical studies/experimental practices (CS/EP) in the Department of Music, University of California, San Diego. UCSD was very supportive, and I thank the department for funding my research travel to Yale University to interview Thomas Duffy and to examine the Yale Band archives. I benefited from the intellectual and artist brilliance of the faculty, including

Jann Pasler, David Borgo, Mina Yang, Andy Fry, Nancy Guy, Miller Puckette, Shahrokh Yadegari, Ed Harkins, Mitchell Morris (visiting from UCLA), and Lisa Lowe. I would especially single out two faculty members: my dissertation adviser, Anthony Davis, whose creative, insightful, and original thinking stimulated new ways of understanding my research, and professor of visual art Norman Bryson, who met with me regularly to discuss drafts of my work. Being able to converse with Norman regularly made it difficult to leave UCSD, and I miss his wit and dazzling intelligence tremendously. The CS/EP program encouraged the integration of artistic and scholarly endeavors, and my experiences as a musician and composer inspired my scholarship both directly and indirectly. Being able to play regularly as a duo with bassist Mark Dresser deepened my practical understanding of jazz and improvisation. Just trying to hang somewhere in the outskirts of his musical universe must have laid down some decent karma for my next jazz lifetime. I was also able to play with Anthony Davis, including a recording of my music with him, Mark, and others. And then there's George Lewis. George had effectively departed for Columbia University in my first year at UCSD. Living in his house, however, made contact inevitable! Thank you, George, for taking an interest in my work, writing so many letters of recommendation, and connecting me with other scholars and artists in the way that you do. I am grateful to have you as a colleague and friend. My cohorts from UCSD continue to inspire me every day with their creative and intellectual work and their continued friendship. I resort to listing names, but I've been fortunate to visit many of them around the world and share wonderful times. I hope to remain in touch with them all. Thanks to Cristyn Magnus, Tildy Bayar, Gascia Ouzounian, Steve Willard, Michelle Lou, Jason Robinson, Marianthi Papalexandri-Alexandri, Juliana Snapper, Lauren Wooley, Sean Griffin, Carolyn Joan Lechusza Aquallo, Alan Lechusza, Jeff Kaiser, Guy Obrecht, Alex Khalil, James Ilgenfritz, and Nick DeMaison. Although Ben Piekut followed George to Columbia, I met him at UCSD and he has been a helpful interlocutor and editor over the years. Other UCSD graduates and folks from San Diego who have offered me wisdom, friendship, and music include Dana Reason, Charlie Kronengold, Ellen and Bob Weller, Allison Johnson, Jason Stanyek, P. D. Magnus, Nathan Hubbard, Marcos Fernandes, Al Scholl, Scott Walton, and the Trummerflora crew. UCSD's departments of Visual Arts and Music are incredibly inspiring, creative, and vibrant places, and I feel blessed to be part of that family.

I benefited from a postdoctoral fellowship with the Improvisation, Community, and Social Practice research initiative (now the International Institute for Critical Studies in Improvisation [IICSI]) in 2007–2008. In *Haunthenticity*, I describe Replay as the performance of zero contingency; it is the opposite of improvisation. My next book will start where this one leaves off: with improvisation in jazz as an antidote to Replay. Therefore, all of my thinking on improvisation informs this book. Many IICSI scholars have supported my work and stimulated my thinking over the years, including Ajay Heble, Ellen Waterman, Gillian Siddall, Frédérique Arroyas, Georgina Born, Eric Lewis, and Ingrid Monson. Deborah Wong, Robert O'Meally, and Desmond Manderson have been particularly influential. I was able to associate with Pauline Oliveros over the course of my work with IICSI, and I learned a tremendous amount from her, including "don't take the bait" or get caught in a "tape loop" of thought! Performing a duo improvisation set with her at University of California, Davis, was one of my performance career highlights. I miss her. Lisa Barg has been a great colleague and dear friend. Thanks for coming to the Musical Box with me, for insight and advice (scholarly and otherwise), and for the good times in Montreal with David Brackett, Sophie, and Fred that I trust will continue! I thank bill bissett and Melissa Walker for their continued friendship and poetry that traces back to that year in Guelph. Pete Williams has been a great friend and colleague whom I met in Guelph. In that same circle of now longtime friends, Kara Attrep, Rob Wallace, and Sam are now a second family to me, and I thank them for inviting Auntie Tracy into their fun, smart, and loving world!

I returned to my roots in the Bay Area in 2009 to adjunct in the Music and the Gender and Women's Studies departments at University of California, Berkeley. Inspiring and generous colleagues in both departments stimulated and encouraged my work, including Ben Brinner, Jocelyne Guilbault, Myra Melford, Charis Thompson, Paola Bacchetta, Mel Chen, Minoo Moallem, Barbara Barnes, Jennifer Ring, and especially Trinh T. Minh-ha. The Beatrice Bain Research Group offered a place for my research during this time. I want to thank my good friend T. Carlis Roberts. T. is now an associate professor of music at UCB and has been an extremely supportive friend and colleague during my job search and beyond. Bountiful thanks, T. Other Bay Area friends who have supported me over the years include Sue Crosman, Steve Israels, Dave Mihaly, Annelise Zamula, Bill Noertker, Jon Birdsong, Mike Richards, Hadley Loudon, David Rinehart, Cati Laporte, and especially Sean Regan, with whom I've enjoyed productive conversations for, well, a really long time. Trumpeter Marina Garza started me on my educational journey by introducing me to the University of North Texas. I'm happy to count longtime women-in-jazz advocates and stellar musicians Ellen

Seeling and Jean Fineberg as friends. Aimee Norwich has helped to ground me for many years as a fellow wisdom seeker. The Tibetan Nyingma Institute in Berkeley got me on my right path, lo these many years ago. This book is in part dedicated to the memory of Frances Strassman, whom I met there and whose wisdom directly guided me for twenty years. Sylvia Gretchen, Pema Gellek, Lama Palzang, and ultimately, Tarthang Tulku, have given me indescribable support. Finally, I must thank my longtime friend from our days on The Farm, Geoff Minter. I could not be more appreciative to have you as a fellow traveler through this fascinating life. More than anyone I know, you never forget to be fascinated.

I spent a magnificent year in Los Angeles as a Provost's Postdoctoral Scholar in the Humanities at the University of Southern California. I thank Mina Yang, again, who had moved to USC and became my postdoc adviser. Mina was a great mentor to me, serving on my dissertation committee and then working with me at USC. She also had a great "in-law bungalow" behind her house in Hollywood, where I happily resided. Thanks also to Karen Tongson, J. Jack Halberstam, and Alice Echols for insightful discussions, and to my creative writing friends Lucinda Jenney, Chase Winton, Barbara Williams, Rebecca De Mornay, Jack Grapes, and Margie Goodspeed. Margie read some drafty writing, and I thank her for her cogent criticism from a nonacademic writing perspective.

I arrived at Bowdoin College in 2012, and it has been a wonderful place to work. I was supported with a teaching release to focus on research in 2012–2013, travel funding to attend Jason Moran's "In My Mind" performance in Washington, DC, and college-sponsored writing retreats. Dean and fellow music scholar Cristle Collins Judd was an early mentor there and an inspiration. My colleagues in the Music Department are the best a person could ask for, including Robby Greenlee, Vin Shende, George Lopez, and Frank Mauceri. Marceline Saibou has been my "writing BUDDY," a term she finds exceedingly American but goes with it anyway. I thank Mary Hunter and Michael Birenbaum Quintero for their lucid feedback on drafts, and Mary especially for her mentoring. She helped shepherd me as a junior faculty member new to Bowdoin and a Californian new to New England. I am also grateful for productive discussions with faculty and staff in other departments, including Susan Faludi, Russ Rymer, Hanetha Vete-Congolo, Dana Byrd, Arielle Saiber, Aaron Kitch, Samia Rahimtoola, Guy Mark Foster, Liz Muther, Abbie Killeen, Carrie Scanga, Madeleine Msall, Charlotte Daniels, Ya Zuo, Charlotte Griffin, Dan Stone, Jack O'Brien, and Bridget Spaeth. I've especially learned from working with Judith Casselberry, whose work and thinking overlap with mine and whose brilliance I can only wish did as well. I'm also especially grateful to Brian Purnell and Leana Amaez for their ceaseless intelligence and warmth. Tess Chakkalakal has been a wonderful colleague and a supportive friend. A special thanks to Theater Studies professor Sarah Bay-Cheng, who read the introduction and chapter 3 and gave invaluable feedback. I was fortunate to find another scholar so interested in performance and reenactment in my own backyard. I look forward to continued productive conversations.

I am part of a large community of scholars in the jazz and popular music fields, and friendships and conversations with them have nurtured this book. I thank Bernard Gendron for a couple of great Maine dinners and for an eminently valuable discussion on how to write that introductory chapter! Tammy Kernodle, Norma Coates, Maya Gibson, Christina Baade, Monica Hairston O'Connell, Lara Pellegrinelli, Kristin McGee, Yoko Suzuki, Scott Deveaux, Gayle Murchison, David Ake, Aaron J. Johnson, Gabriel Solis, Vijay Iyer, and Steve Waksman have all offered wise and lucid conversations over the years. I thank Jason Moran, Sébastien Lamothe, Thomas Duffy, and Steph Paynes for their illuminating interviews. My editors at Wesleyan University Press, including series editors Deborah Wong and Sherrie Tucker, Marla K. Zubel, Mary Garrett, and copyeditor Elizabeth Forsaith have been fantastic. The anonymous reviewers offered unstinting and exceedingly helpful criticism and insight. Thanks especially to Suzanna Tamminen, who helped steer this book to its completion. Maine has been a wonderful new home for me and my musical and spiritual life. Andrew Roseman, Tyler Heydolph, Mark Tipton, Peter McLaughlin, Sam Sherrie, Tom Porter, Ryan Blotnick, Gay Pearson, John Clark, Sherrie Phair, and Flash Allen have been fantastic musical compatriots. Tracy Davis, Steve Gilbert, Peter Comas, Jan Piribeck, Gina Mastroluca, Bridget Spaeth (again), Kiki O'Connell, Jeb Enoch, Julie Taylor, Michelle Laughran, Shirsten Lundblad, Soozie Large, Donna Chamoff, Donna Giroux, Philip Frey, Meg Pachuta, Holly Howard, Kay Sullivan, Kathleen Beecher, Khenpo Jigme, and Khenpo Choephel are of immeasurable support, as I hope they know. Thrangu Rinpoche is my "Big Teacher" to whom this book is dedicated.

I want to thank my family, Mike McMullen, Kate and Joe Caciari, Barb McMullen, Debbie and Eleanor Gagus, Grace and Walt Krawza, Ruth Ann and Jim Kinneer, Marg and Jim Fetsko, Patty Ettestad, Carol, Sue, Lynn, Debbie, Lori, Ken, Walt, Jim Jr., Chris, and Tony. My father, Bill McMullen, died of pancreatic cancer in 2014. I thank him for encouragement and inspiration, especially in my adult life. My mom, Kate, has supported me throughout my life, and I thank her for the skills and confidence I have developed based on her instructions and encouragement. She was my first teacher, to whom I dedicate this book. Karen Saarela has been a friend for so long that she belongs in the family paragraph. Thanks, Karen, for being there for me, then and now. I also want to remember my partner, Robert Freeberg, who died in 2008 while I was in Canada on a postdoctoral fellowship. My research took a strong turn toward the topic of loss in the wake of that event. His kindness, generosity, intelligence, quirkiness, and talent have continued to be an inspiration to me. As another important teacher in my life, this book is dedicated to him.

Above all I want to thank the venerable Dr. Sherrie Jean Tucker. Sherrie agreed to be my codissertation adviser with Anthony Davis, even though she was at the University of Kansas and I was at UCSD. This was extra work for her with no recompense whatsoever, yet I have never received even one molecule of that impression from her. She guided me in my dissertation, wrote innumerable letters of recommendation for me while I was on the job market beginning in 2008 (economic downtown, anyone?), bought me dinners at conferences (and drinks—thanks, too, to Tami Albin for her generosity and virtuosic humor!), and has continued to inspire my scholarship ever since (WWSD—what would Sherrie do?). Everyone who knows Sherrie knows what a generous, ethical, and thorough scholar she is. And how smart! She is not only a model scholar, but a model human being for so many people. I am in the front of that line. I owe her champagne dinners for the rest of my life. Thank you, Sherrie!!

ABBA the Concert is a label owned by 21st Century Artists. Often other ABBA tribute bands, such as The Visitors, will perform tours marketed as ABBA the Concert. For this reason, various band names may appear on websites that display the ABBA the Concert logo.

Haunthenticity

INTRODUCTION

Haunthenticity

Repetition and Identity Compulsion in Cultural Production

The spectre . . . emerges out of a fear . . . [of] freedom.

Slavoj Žižek, "The Spectre of Ideology"

FANTASY: IN THE BEGINNING (YOU ARE THERE)

The black stage lights up with a deep blue glow. On the right, keyboardist Tony Banks materializes out of the darkness, surrounded by his electric pianos and mellotron; drummer Phil Collins appears, looming behind a mountain of drums that fill the back of the stage. On the left, guitarist Steve Hackett comes into view, seated, as usual, while bassist Mike Rutherford wields his double neck slightly behind him and closer to the drums. Banks attacks his RMI electric piano, alternating between rapid arpeggios of minor, major, and suspended chords, the piercing tones of rock as operatic overture. Three large screens line up horizontally in the background, clicking through scenes from 1970s New York. The deep blue light turns to a brighter green when the drums and bass enter, emphasizing the new major key as the light returns to blue. Peter Gabriel, who has been standing backstage right, begins to move. In a black leather jacket, white shirt, and jeans, face darkened with brown makeup, he leans heavily into the microphone. His reedy, slightly nasal, somewhat clenched voice intones the syllables as the band crescendos: "and the laaaaaaaaaaaamb . . . lies doooooooooown . . . on

Broaaaa-ah-aaahdway." He is the main character, Rael, in Genesis's progressive rock opera *The Lamb Lies Down on Broadway.* Gabriel leaps to center stage, where the machine-produced fog wafts around his feet. The auditorium vibrates with Collins's crisp drumrolls, muscular tom patterns, and theatrical cymbal crashes. An intricate bass countermelody weaves against the unrelenting keyboard arpeggios. Gabriel's body jerks to the stabbing rhythm of the lyrics. The audience roars its excitement.

The audience being three hundred concertgoers in Club Nokia in Los Angeles in October 2011. Genesis last performed *The Lamb Lies Down on Broadway* in 1975. For many who attended the original Genesis shows, the sense of the uncanny is unnerving. Not only are these the same instruments, songs, costumes, backdrops, slides, and story that were performed in 1975 at the Shrine Auditorium, but these are also the same shoulder thrusts by Gabriel, even the same banter between songs. There is Rutherford's double neck, Banks's mellotron; Hackett is customarily sitting, anathema to rock guitarist protocol; Gabriel's voice is reedy. And the band is still young! It is as if the passage of time has been conquered and the original experience returned to us. Indeed, it is as if something has "uncannily captured [Genesis] in every way."[1]

It is a concert by the Musical Box, the Genesis "clone band" known in tribute band circles as one of, if not *the* most "authentic" tribute bands performing today. It was Genesis drummer Phil Collins himself who remarked that the Musical Box had "uncannily captured us in every way." Formed in 1993, the Musical Box has far outlived the original band's roughly four-year run,[2] re-creating early Genesis tours in "painstaking detail" for thousands of spectators around the world, including *Selling England by the Pound, A Trick of the Tail,* and *The Lamb Lies Down on Broadway.* Early Genesis's complex extended song forms, concept albums, and elaborate stage shows were a model for progressive rock bands to follow. The shows of the Gabriel era were never officially recorded, however, and the Musical Box claims to fill this gap by re-creating them live for Genesis fans. As they state in their promotional materials, the Musical Box provides "the perfect illusion of a virtual time machine: to recapture the magic of those concerts and give people the impression of being at an original Genesis show. All of the song introductions and off-the-wall stories in between, every song, every movement by Gabriel, the original light impressions and all of the genuine multimedia effects are a carbon copy of the exact Genesis performance 30 years ago."[3]

This book investigates this drive to "recapture . . . every movement," to present a "carbon copy of the exact performance" of the musical past, focusing on the period from 1990 through the beginnings of the new millennium. In the history of rock, obsessive attention to "original intent" has not been the hallmark of the genre. Going back to the blues and the beginnings of recorded popular music in the United States, the musical practice that would eventually include rock, funk, pop, and soul has been characterized by the procedure of musical reworking. In the last decades of the twentieth century, however, from Civil War reenactments beginning in the 1960s to performance art at the turn of the millennium, live reenactments of past events became a popular performance practice. I will link this to live music performance, which became a particularly potent site for reenactments in this period. The jazz repertory movement began in the 1970s, and tribute bands to Count Basie, Duke Ellington, Glenn Miller, and others took hold. In the 1990s, performance artists began to reenact the past, including earlier works of performance art, as well as historical events and popular music concerts. And throughout these decades, popular cover bands morphed into tribute and clone bands as performers began to focus on a single band and re-create original shows with increasingly precise material detail.[4]

I had a front-row seat to this reenactive turn. In fact, as a female saxophonist during the 1990s' "swing revival," I found I was a glitch in the system. It was not a coincidence that four white men came together to form the Musical Box. Even if men of color or women could play their instruments or sing in a way that precisely mimicked Genesis's sound, they didn't have the authentic *look* to conjure the "correct" past. Audience members, as well as the founder of the band, informed me that to have a woman or black man in the Musical Box would make the band appear less "authentic."[5] As a working musician, I began to wonder what this prevalent practice of "authentic" live reenactment said about contemporary culture. Was this yearning for the past "as it was" bringing back social norms and circumstances that the 1960s and 1970s had started to change? And what else was going on with this desire for a "precise" re-performance of the past?

THE DING-DONG DADDY OF THE D-CAR LINE

As a graduate student in music during the 1990s and 2000s, I witnessed the popularity of "neo-swing" bands such as Big Bad Voodoo Daddy, the Cherry Poppin' Daddies, and the Brian Setzer Orchestra—a lot of white daddies dressed in suits, ties, and hats performing such songs as "Go Daddy-O," "Drunk Daddy," "Good Rockin' Daddy," and "The Ding-Dong Daddy of the D-Car Line" in a style made famous by black artists such as Cab Calloway and Louis Jordan. The swing revival fueled a growing interest in swing dancing across the country and nurtured a demand for live bands with large horn sections. In my temporary home of North Texas, I was able to earn money by performing the music of Glenn Miller, Count Basie, Duke Ellington, and other big band composers in a twenty-piece, almost all-male retro swing big band (the female exceptions being myself on tenor saxophone, an occasional substitute pianist, and the vocalist). It was apparent from the beginning that I attenuated the fantasy of a perfect return to the past. With the sequined vocalist embodying the "high femme" role, the band members, dressed in suits or tuxedos, performed the "male role" musically, including occasional vocal parts en masse from a masculine subjectivity to our female other. With my "faux tuxedo" and higher-pitched voice, I pluralized this coherent masculine subjectivity, something that was problematic representationally and professionally.[6]

While my existence in the band troubled the perfect return to the past, there was another, related hitch that I felt my body produced in the ensemble. I intuited a fundamental desire for a "selfsame," "unified" ensemble related to the expected desire to reenact these bands from the past precisely. An integrated ensemble seemed to produce undesirable signs, such as "sloppy," "iconoclastic," "motley," "unprofessional," "amateur," and perhaps containing an element of "punk." It also signaled "modernity"—our contemporary, more integrated world. It was this "modern world" that the audience hoped to escape for a few hours. I became more and more aware of how I *should* be a white male in this band in order to (re-)create this performance "accurately."

And then I heard about Yale. The women and men of Yale University were reenacting a live Glenn Miller radio broadcast in honor of the sixtieth anniversary of D-day. It was to take place at the original venue, Woolsey Hall, on the campus where Miller had been stationed during his army service. My thoughts turned to the women in the band and the necessity for them to "play (white) men" in order to accomplish this feat. It was a heightened example of what I experienced as a female jazz musician performing in retro swing bands—the problematic female horn player who was not "correct"—neither in a tuxedo nor a dress. And it struck me how these women and men of color in the band were asked to re-create specific white men in a display of national unity (the first Yale Miller reenactment took place in 1994 in the wake of the First Gulf War and its presumed overturning of America's "Vietnam Syndrome").[7] Because a university ensemble performed the reenactment, I knew the bandleader could not keep women or men of color out of the production. Therefore, this re-creation, hearkening back to a presumably "simpler" or "more unified" time, as World War II commemorations often did, would be brought to life with women and men of color dutifully taking on the identities of white men. It seemed an apt spectacle of "national unity" at a time when cars and yards were replete with "United We Stand" signs. With the affective power of music and the insidious way that reenactment inculcates the values and norms of previous eras into the present (such as, in this case, the idea of "benevolent, white, patriarchal power"), I felt compelled to investigate it all further.

In this book, I will argue that the Yale concert and the Musical Box, like the other reenactments I discuss, fetishize the live capture of the past-as-object as a way to establish ground in a world that feels unmoored. "Presence" and the original material details serve to haunthenticate the project. Such details offer the *proof* of the reality that has been captured. Regarding the 2010 retrospective of Marina Abramović's performance art career at New York's Museum of Modern Art, Amelia Jones writes,

> The live act is most often privileged as delivering an authentic and "present" body—as the 2010 retrospective *Marina Abramović: The Artist Is Present* reveals instantly in its title. The exhibition galleries were staged with the actual van she and her performance partner from the 1970s, Ulay, drove across the Australian desert, signaling the brute "presence" claimed for the performance ephemera that dominated the retrospective of this important artist from Serbia, now based in New York City. The galleries themselves, with melodramatically darkened walls, were filled with spotlighted vitrines containing objects presumably deployed in the original performances and with screenings of digital video transfers of contemporaneous film and video documentation. One entire large gallery was replete with photographs of Abramović from her birth onward and ephemera relating to her life. (Jones 2011, 17)

The "real" details of the past combine with the artist's "real" (live) presence to reach the pinnacle of the haunthentic.[8] This is the same practice deployed by performance artists re-creating David Bowie, tribute bands re-creating ABBA, or even jazz tributes conjuring masters of the past (see, for example, Teal 2014). While nostalgia is a modern phenomenon in which there is a place one imagines returning—the Old Country—many of these reenactments feel like an ever-spiraling attempt to establish ground in a world without moorings, without even a site of return. And capturing music seems to offer a particular valence to the practice. As I examined these "authentic" reenactments in different genres, I began to compile a set of characteristics that defined them. These characteristics form a performance practice that I have termed Replay.

REPLAY

As I investigated various live musical reenactments that claimed authentic and accurate portrayals of past performances, I began to discover certain characteristics that consistently appeared in descriptions and understandings of the practice. The following characteristics comprise the general parameters of what I am terming Replay:

1. *The fetishization of space, time, and material details.* Reenacting at the exact spot of the original performance, or on an anniversary, or both, is common. Original instruments are preferred over a new instrument that may sound "exactly" the same (a real mellotron rather than a sampled mellotron sound, for example). Access to the "real people"—the original costume designer, and so on—is favored.
2. *Fixing (in two senses of the term).* (a) Making permanent; (b) improving; for example, through the technological advancement of the Musical Box's better projector equipment to display the Genesis slides.
3. *Genuflection to the past as authority.* The past is to be trusted more than our own subjective decision making based on conditions in the present. For example, a performance's tempo would be based on the tempo of an original recording, not on modern-day preferences.
4. *The emphasis on the "uncanny."* Events are often marketed by stressing how the performance will uncannily bring a performance or performer "back to life."
5. *The sense of having it all.* By re-creating the past, we can now have what we thought was impossible to have: the past returned to us. The reenactment is therefore promoted as a new, innovative product that meets a need not previously satisfied by records, posters, and other objects from the past.
6. *Control.* The belief that we don't have to lose anything because we have the ability to master the passage of time. This is related to the belief that we may one day overcome old age and death.
7. *Emphasis on the painstaking work involved.* Promotional materials will emphasize the intense labor that went into uncovering every detail of the original performance and then reenacting it as precisely as possible.

8. *Desire to touch the Real.* Replay is a way to access the "Real" in a highly mediated society. It is promoted as a way to transcend mediation and provide a real experience, including giving us the "real," unmediated past.
9. *Music is understood as an event, not a text to be interpreted.* Music can be understood as moving from an "act" to a "text" to an "event" that is objectified as a "hunk of time" and reenacted.

With the exception of Jason Moran's reimagining of Thelonious Monk discussed in the conclusion, all of the reenactments examined in this book emphasize all or most of these characteristics (and Moran's performance partakes of some of them). My analysis of these performances is inspired by anthropologists Victor Turner and Clifford Geertz, who describe performance as a way for culture to show itself to itself, and from Marshall McLuhan, who argued that the medium is the message.[9] Turner and Geertz demonstrated that performance expresses important aspects and values for the community; unpacking performance aids in examining these aspects and values. McLuhan presciently noted that the medium—the way in which we consume information or entertainment—structures our world and our way of being in the world more than the content of the message. As such, I focus on the medium of Replay—the performance practice—as the message, not accepting it simply as a performance of Genesis's music, say. Psychoanalysis is also important to my study in that these cultural aspects and values are not readily transparent to the performers or consumers, but symptomatic of an underlying neurosis. I understand performance as effecting ideas and norms about culture—including ideas about race, gender, sexuality, the body, identity, the past, and other cultural expectations and norms. Stemming from a compulsion that is best recognized in the Musical Box, the other reenactments I examine in this book offer further ramifications of the practice, particularly in terms of identity norms and expectations.

That is, this book examines a variety of musical reenactments in different genres and contexts, all of which, however, either stake their claim around or against (Moran) these characteristics. I will argue that this practice is a symptom of an unexamined fear that has deleterious consequences for our world. This book is not about how such rigorously mimetic reenactments fail. Of course they fail. It is not interesting to me to point out the many ways in which we will find rupture and failure in these attempts at perfect reenactment—a source of revolutionary potential for many scholars.[10] Rather, I want to offer thoughts on the continued desire for perfect capture even in the face of knowledge that no such thing exists. I want to investigate further a definition of authenticity that equates it with the capture of a past event exactly. I consider the practice a compulsion, a symptom of something deeper to be investigated. If the modern West should know by now that we can't step into the same river twice, why do we keep trying? And what are the ramifications of doing so?

Tracing Replay

Although Rebecca Schneider reminds us that *tableaux vivants* (living stills) have a long history tracing back at least to the fifteenth century (2011, 146), it was in the late twentieth century that live reenactments developed and became commonplace. Two occurrences in the early 1960s shed light on the growth of live reenactment across art, history, and music: the advent of the modern historical battle reenactment movement and the arrival of "instant replay" on television. While rigorous live reenactments of the past make their modern appearance in 1960s historical battle reenactments, their relationship to instant replay is more oblique. Both historical battle restaging and instant replay, however, demonstrate a desire to capture, tame, know, and have dominion over the past and the flow of time and, I will argue, stoke the fantasy that the past as flowing time is an object we can now control and possess.

The birth of the modern historical reenactment movement is generally traced to the battle reenactments for the centennial celebrations of the Civil War between 1961 and 1965. Although partial battle reenactments had occurred before, it was in the early 1960s that a concerted effort was put forth on a much larger scale. From this point forward, reenactment became a serious hobby for a burgeoning reenactment community, with larger and larger groups participating in each reenactment. By the 1986 "125th Anniversary of the Battle at Manassas," more than six thousand reenactors participated in the re-creation. In 2009 it was estimated that one million Americans performed Civil War reenactments annually.[11] Thousands also reenact other battles in the United States, Europe, and Australia.

Historical reenactments are advertised as examples of "living history" in which the "experiential" allows access to a more "authentic" engagement with and, as argued by many reenactors, knowledge of history. Serious Civil War battle re-creators try to live as much as possible as a person of the 1860s would have lived, attempting to have an immersive experience (Agnew 2004). They stay in character throughout the entire event, eat seasonal and regionally appropriate food, and make sure all of their stitching is correct, right down to their undergarments.[12] According to historian Vanessa Agnew, reenactors generally believe that "information [is] gleaned and corroborated through first-hand experience. Reenactment . . . [thus] emerges as a body-based discourse in which the past is reanimated through physical and psychological experience" (2004, 330). One historical reenactor stated that the purpose of historical reenactment is to "find the real answers" (quoted in Agnew, 330). Indeed, reenactors can experience a phenomenon they call "'period rush': a state of complete absorption in the reenacted event—followed by difficulty transitioning out of the past and into the present" (330). Agnew argues that reenactors make claims of historical truth based on the embodied liveness of these reenactments as self-evident certainty. Such certainties are, in fact, highly erroneous but can have the power to persuade (2004). This tendency to believe the self-evident, real, embodied performance over the less-tangible analysis of and struggle over historical narratives has repercussions for music reenactments and their relationship to music history, as I will show particularly in regard to jazz reenactments in chapter 3.

While live reenactment was taking shape on the old battlefield sites of the Civil War, television was developing a new technology called the "instant replay." Introduced on television in 1963, but beginning in earnest with its 1967 employment for the US Skiing Championships in Vail, Colorado, "instant replay" transformed the way the television audience viewed sports.[13] Before the arrival of instant replay, television viewers missed much of what could be viewed by the game audience. Cameras were often in the wrong place at the wrong time and did not have clear access to many plays. The downtime between plays was particularly boring for television viewers, who did not have the live experience of participating at the scene with other fans. With the advent of instant replay, however, the television broadcast of sporting events changed from being attenuated versions of the live games to enhanced ones. Instant replay allowed for the exciting moments to be viewed again and again; "freeze time" enabled the viewers and commentators to stop the film at a crucial moment of the play; eventually the film could be slowed down to analyze intricate movements; and over time, more cameras were enlisted, and the viewing audience could see the same play from a variety of angles. Today the instant replay is no longer an advanced viewing device for only the home audience; most professional sports organizations now use the instant replay in order to make referee calls and to determine the precise ending of a game period.[14] Video replay of news events became equally common—for example, the continuous replay of the fall of the Twin Towers or the Rodney King beating.[15]

Instant or video replay serves a variety of overlapping functions. It replays for us moments of trauma (injury on the field, the Twin Towers collapsing); it replays moments of beauty or heroism (Olympic moments, rescues); it replays for pedagogical purposes (slowing down a player's form); it replays in order to find the "truth" (used as a tool by referees; used for exposing police brutality); and it replays in order to control: it provides a fantasy that we can tame the ephemerality and elusiveness of flowing time. While capturing injustice on video is a paramount use of video technology and its repetition can serve to galvanize a response and bring the perpetrators to justice, this is not the only way that video replay is used. And while initial video replay of a traumatic event may serve to spur a response, continual repetition can both overwhelm and dull the senses, breeding apathy. Other scholars have examined video repetition in terms of these potentialities and drawbacks.[16] My concern here is the way in which instant replay asserted in the late twentieth century that time will not be our master: we will capture time—the brute passage of events that normally would exceed our ability to *have* it—and replay it for our many uses, placing the past under the microscope of our authoritative gaze. Seen especially in the replay of sports moments, instant replay's pleasures lie in the ability to freeze, contain, and examine the flow of time. It manufactures the sense of security that we can actually "have" time: see the pivotal moment of athletic excellence again and again, control the uncontrollable, stop the unstoppable. While people may use the term "replay" now as shorthand for instant replay, Replay brings back the sense of play in the term. It is to *play* again, which highlights the theatrical, embodied aspect of the term. Performers who deploy the practices that I place under the rubric of Replay praise the unmediated quality of their work. Nonetheless, based on promotional materials routinely lauding the "return" of the original event, the desire to capture time is the same.

Replay's proximate relatives may be battle reenactments and instant replay, but its lineage is long. I place Replay within a long Western epistemology that relates to the past as a discrete object. The idea of the "original" work first arose in the eighteenth century with the advent of romantic aesthetics (Boon 2010, 48–49). Also in that century, urban memorials and museums appeared, sites where the past could be preserved, stored, contemplated, and remembered. In the nineteenth century, monuments began to be restored to their "original image" with materials characteristic of the time period in which they were built, rather than by using materials appropriate for the time of repair (Boym 2001, 15). This idea of an "original" work that should be preserved and of museums as places in which to collect and display the past demonstrates a shift from understanding the past as an integrated part of the present to something separate that would be lost if it were not saved in its original state. This view of the past was borne from an epistemological tradition that increasingly conditioned knowing on the separation of the knower and the known. That is, in order to know, there must be a subject knowing an object. Without this separation, the knowledge is considered "subjective," and as such, suspect. I address this problem throughout the book.

In her thought-provoking book *Performing Remains,* Rebecca Schneider asks: "In what ways might we use reperformance and the issues it raises . . . to help us think critically about our broader participation in neoliberal society, much as we have used object art and its discontents to help think through commodity capitalism" (137). While I do not make a sharp delineation between neoliberalism and commodity capitalism, I do argue that Replay is a stand against the fracture, flow, and dislocation of postmodernity and the developing neoliberal turn at the end of the twentieth century. I will demonstrate how Replay is symptomatic of a turn-of-the-millennium attempt to maintain security, integrity, authenticity, and rigid boundaries in what Daniel T. Rodgers calls an "age of fracture" and trace the ramifications of this in different contexts (Rodgers 2012). Scholars such as Steven Shaviro have persuasively argued that culture has moved to assimilate the circulation and fracture of neoliberalism as its modus operandi in the twenty-first century and I agree (Shaviro 2003). Replay is a set of characteristics that took hold in the late twentieth century and speaks especially to and from that time and space.

Nonetheless, the foundational beliefs that support the practices of Replay precede and exceed the turn of the twenty-first century and indicate a very long-standing problem. Characterizing the late twentieth century as an era obsessed with remembering, Andreas Huyssen describes postmodern "memory culture" as driven by the "panic of oblivion" (2003). In my view, such panic remains with us. And I believe this panic stems not so much from a postmodern compression of time and space that has upset our sense of stability in the world, as Fredric Jameson argues, but from the fact that we have never adequately come to terms with the *reality* of oblivion. The modern West has not incorporated the brute fact of impermanence (deaths of all kinds) and the nonexistence of a locatable or permanent "self" within its systems of understanding the world. In fact, the opposite—the denial of these realities over the course of Western history—has been the norm. In the era of postmodernity, this encounter with impermanence and the nullity of the subject is increasingly difficult to postpone. It is this impermanence and nullity of the subject that I connect with the term Real. The "problem" of postmodernity, then, is not that it is compressing time and space, making a relationship with history difficult to maintain, or flattening out experience into a perpetual "now,"[17] but that it is providing less and less shelter in fantasies of permanence and substantiality in which we can believe. This leaves us open to the encroachment of the Real, which Western epistemologies have attempted to keep at bay. But this Real that we fear is also "life itself," as Lacan would put it. And this we deeply crave. Replay is a product of the fanatical fear *and* the immense desire for the Real that characterize contemporary Western culture.

THE FEAR OF AND DESIRE FOR THE REAL

Replay is a particular performance practice that manifests out of this desire and fear, seen especially around the turn of the millennium. I understand Replay as a "last-ditch attempt" to preserve the declining liberal subject or a "bulwark against postmodern emptiness and inauthenticity," as Steven Shaviro argues in regard to nostalgia for film noir (Shaviro, 146). Or as Marcus Boon suggests in his book on copying, Replay could be an attempt to ameliorate the threatening instability of life itself (89–90). Boon argues that a certain urge to copy is an attempt to master impermanence: "an aggressive attempt to fix this impermanent flux through imitating it in an apparently controlled way" (96). What is interesting about Replay, however, is that it attempts to be a "bulwark" against impermanence, instability, and "emptiness" (which I will connect to the Real) all while claiming it is capturing the very Real that we fear and desire.

The Real is primarily a psychoanalytic term; however, I do not limit it to this specific usage. I use it to indicate the impermanence of life, the unlocatability (or void) of the subject, and the basic complexity and mystery of life that is intersubjective and interdependent. While the rise of the Enlightenment initiated the decline in Western religious solace regarding eternal life, it offered the consolation prize of the self-standing individual. It is with postmodernity that this last fortification against the Real has precipitously dissolved. Societally, we are faced with this final truth: "The world, unfortunately, is real" (Jorge Luis Borges, quoted in Weinberger 1999, 332). While we have certainly deferred this engagement with the Real, it is also, as Borges says, "the world." So while we may fear this final truth, we have also longed for it. Steven Shaviro gives a précis on the predicament we have found ourselves in since at least the 1970s: "We get uneasy, and suspicious, when we learn that so many things are simulations. Disney's California Adventure™ is a simulation of the State of California, but isn't California itself already a simulation of the American Dream, which in turn is itself a simulation? We want to know what is behind all the virtual reality displays that we seem to be living in" (Shaviro 2003, 88). We've created a hypersymbolic world that retreats upon retreats from the Real.

Replay becomes a type of embodied "instant replay" that attempts to capture the Real. Thus, while instant video replay can be compared to records, CDs, films, and other mediated representations of the past, Replay claims to bring the past back in the flesh. Its "liveness" and materiality are promoted and marketed as an encounter with an increasingly scarce Real in a hypermediated culture. It speaks to a desire to experience the materiality of the world in a way that is often considered lost in postmodernity. Capturing both "liveness" and music offers a double dose of the fantasy of locating and containing the Real. Not surprisingly (from a psychoanalytic standpoint) the fantasy to capture the Real functions perfectly to further distance us from it. To the extent that music has been associated with the Real, it is unsurprising that Replay has found such a secure home in live *musical* performance. In reenacting music, we both attempt to satisfy our craving for the Real while simultaneously controlling and containing it, keeping it at a distance.[18]

Music and the Real

Music has had a fraught relationship with the West's intellectual and philosophical traditions that emphasize a split between mind and body, and a consequent privileging of "Reason." Music's effect on the body, its appeal to the emotions, and its sensuous (im)materiality in sound have long associated it with Reason's enemies: the feminine, the racial other, the body, and sexuality.[19] This association holds true whether the philosopher is "pro-Reason" or not. To give a salient example, in his 1961 book, *Music and the Ineffable* (translated into English by Carolyn Abbate in 2003), Vladimir Jankélévitch argues for music's power by equating it with Reason's others: women, children, the exotic, magic, and the body. Jankélévitch writes:

> Something that wants to persuade us with singing, rather than convince us with reason, implements an art of pleasing that addresses the passions, that is, one that subjugates in suggesting and that enslaves the listener through the fraudulent and charlatan power of melody, weakens him through harmonic

> glamour or the fascinations of rhythm. To accomplish this, the process does not tap the logistical or governing aspects of the mind but rather engages the mind's entire psychosomatic element. If mathematical discourse is thinking that wishes to make itself comprehensible to other thought by becoming transparent to it, a harmonic modulation is an act that expects to influence a being; and by "influence" one must also understand a clandestine causality, just as in astrology or sorcery: illegal maneuvers, black arts. Solon the lawmaker is a sage, but Orpheus the enchanter is a magician. A vocalization is not an excuse and a perfume is not an argument.
>
> Thus, when a human being reaches the age of reason, he struggles against this unseemly and illegal seizure of his person, not wanting to give in to enchantment, that is, to go where the songs are leading. The magical induction becomes a seduction and thus trickery, and an adult refuses to be captivated, resisting the beliefs suggested to him by the auletic. A woman who persuades solely by means of her presence and its perfumes, that is, by the magical exhalations of her being, the night that envelops us, music, which secures our allegiance solely through the Charm engendered by a trill or an arpeggio, will therefore be the object of a deep suspicion. Being bewitched is not worthy of a rational person. Just as a masculine Will insists that its decisions are made on concrete grounds—and will never admit a preference founded in emotion—so masculine Reason will never admit itself prone to seduction. What is science for if not to sustain us against the intoxications of night and the temptations exercised by the enchantress' appearance? (2)

Jankélévitch encapsulates this "otherness" of music, here related to women and the "black arts." Whether Jankélévitch is buying into this equation (and siding with the "dark side") or merely restating the connection and the fear, he has pointed to the "trouble" of music.[20] He connects music to what Kaja Silverman describes as "the feminine as Real," the "dark continent" that threatens the Symbolic (Silverman 1983, 187). Silverman highlights the connection of the feminine with the dark continent, the also-feared "African," who equally resides on the body side of the dualism. Jankélévitch goes on to outline the Western fear of music found in Plato's railing against the "Carian muse" (2003, 6), Nietzsche's "grudge against the musical eternal-feminine" (7), and Tolstoy's "melophobia" (stemming, Jankélévitch argues, from a hidden melomania) (7–9). This is music's long association with the dangerous seduction of the feminine, the "dark continent," madness, and sexuality within Western understanding.[21]

In its nonlocatability, evanescence, and ability to skirt away from the Symbolic, music, like women and racial others, is associated with the Real that threatens Reason. Although she does not use this terminology, Carolyn Abbate's article "Music: Drastic or Gnostic?" places music within the realm of the Real—that which cannot be mastered by, and which threatens the sovereignty of, the Symbolic. Abbate argues, via Jankélévitch, that music exists in only the present as a performed art: the actual experience of music is "drastic" rather than "gnostic," ephemeral rather than remembered, and immediately encountered, not retrospectively intellectualized (Abbate 2004). According to Abbate, in the moment that the listener perceives music, the powers of analysis and abstraction are suspended in favor of the experience. Music can be "devastating, brutal, etc., resistant to the Gnostic," that is, "the hermeneutic order of knowledge" (Jankélévitch, quoted in Abbate 2004, 505).[22] Like the Real, Abbate is describing the immediate experience of music as drastic, brutal, and impervious to interpretation and critical distance. Further, Jankélévitch writes, "Music, like movement or duration, is a continuous miracle that with every step accomplishes the impossible" (Jankélévitch 2003, 18). Here we see the link between music, "like movement or duration," the Real, and the impossible: the Real may not be captured via the Symbolic, and yet, it is accomplished. The Real *is:* it is the (symbolically) impossible (accomplished). The Real is as impossible as our own death, as our own past, as the perpetual flow of time. It is accomplished, and yet it remains impossible to grasp through the Symbolic.[23]

I locate the root of all of these anxieties over the body, the feminine, woman, the racial other, sexuality, and music in the fear of the Real. The feminine, the body, sexuality, the exotic, and music all take shape in various cultural "figures" and "grounds" in relation to each other in the continual dance to skirt the encounter with the Real. Music is feared because it is like the feminine; the feminine is feared because it is associated with the body, which is associated with exotic racial otherness, and so on. But all are feared because they are associated with the Real, the dissolution of Reason's boundaries.[24] The desire to objectify music is the desire to locate music within the Symbolic field, rather than dwell within the space of the accomplished and yet impossible: the uncapturable—the impermanence of life itself, the emptiness and nonlocatability of the subject. The world in its nature is interdependent and impermanent, and live musical performance can especially highlight this fact.

The Western art music tradition has "tamed" music's purported unlocatability and ephemerality in several distinct ways. During the nineteenth century, classical musical performance began to be reified into the preservable, bounded "work," concomitant with the growth of art museums and the rise in stature of the individual artist.[25] As Richard Taruskin has written, the advent of the "work concept" and growing commitment to "work fidelity" made music "solid and durable like the museum masters" (Taruskin 1995, 14).[26] Indeed, the "sonic museum" had appeared in the eighteenth century in the form of the concert hall (simultaneously with art and history museums) (Kivy 1995, 94–101), and now "works" of music would be performed (or is it displayed?) there. Lydia Goehr completes the metaphor with her outlining of the "imaginary museum of musical works," which float around awaiting performance by dutiful musicians (Goehr 1992). In music's further move from an "act" to a "text,"[27] the mid-nineteenth century introduced "the collected edition, something which strove both for epic completeness and—so far as the science of musical editing had developed—fidelity to the 'original'" (Butt 2008, 134). In his article linking the rise of the work concept in the nineteenth century to changes in judicial practice, Desmond Manderson writes, "Perhaps it is not entirely fanciful to suggest that the two great inventions of the nineteenth century that helped enforce this new division of labour [between the composer/law and the performer/citizen] were the metronome (1815) and the policeman (1829)" (2010, 6). The work concept was thus, in part, a practice of turning music as a collective, unruly art form into something that could be secured, bounded, and maintained.

Concert decorum was a further method of containing the intercorporeality of music into a display that emphasized the distance between subject (audience member) and object (music). As public concerts of Western classical music became prominent in the nineteenth century, musicians became increasingly distanced from their listeners, performing on a raised stage and adopting a uniformity of dress. The various rituals that have formed around classical music further serve to distance the audience from the orchestra: audience movement is to be kept to a minimum; spontaneous clapping is forbidden; and of course, no one is allowed to hum or sing along. By the 1950s the tradition of silence between movements was firmly established. The increasingly strict decorum established around the classical music concert enforced boundaries between the listeners and the music and contained the threatening intercorporeality of sound, preventing the audience from interacting bodily with the music and each other. Suzanne Cusick links these distancing procedures directly to the connection between music and sex. Interrogating music's "power to ravish," its ability to make us "open," its power relations begging us to consider "who is on top," Cusick asks, doesn't the "kinkiness of these questions account for the extremely rigid social codes surrounding concert decorum for all concerned?" (Cusick 1994, 79). The fear of sex is the fear of the loss of reason, of self, of will. This is the same fear of the Real presented by the body, time, death, and it would seem, music.

REPLAYING THE PAST THROUGH SIGHT AND SOUND: MY CASE STUDIES

Musical Replay, then, is a late-twentieth-century development of the ways that music has been desired and tamed in the West for centuries. But it speaks to a time and place when security became a paramount concern. It was a world that both felt and was repeatedly described as fragmented, destabilized, and heading toward an uncertain new millennium. International relations scholar David Campbell described this time as an era of "writing security," when US political leaders increasingly portrayed the world as a dangerous threat that needed containment through various means of establishing a secure "identity" for the nation-state. I outline this in chapter 1, "Performing Security: Replay as the Performance of the 'Perfectly Known,'" linking this political narrative to the rise of musical reenactments in the 1990s. Within that context, musical reenactments performed a type of zero contingency in which everything was bounded and accounted for, including time and space. In a "culture of fear," performances of precisely contained reenactments of popular music served as a type of "comfort entertainment" for a populace fed a daily diet of contingency and threat.

The chapter begins with an examination of the paragon of Replay: the Genesis tribute band, the Musical Box (TMB). TMB has all the characteristics of Replay described previously and offers an exemplary introduction to the practice. The band strives to capture every detail of the original band, fixing Genesis in time, yet guaranteeing a more technologically reliable performance because of advanced video and audio equipment. With the exception of these seemingly nondiegetic details, the past is taken as the authority, and a type of "musical originalism" is deployed in every performance decision. As such, TMB makes clear that there is "no interpretation" and they are uncannily enacting the actual Genesis concerts. It is such a containment of identity as to be the mathematical definition: 1 = 1 with no remainder and no other. It is a fantasy of perfect border control that I also link with an invisible and omnipotent whiteness. I contextualize TMB's project within Western ideologies found in classical music discourse that, in part, fuel a desire to connect with the Real in a world of interpretation.

Like all examples of musical Replay, TMB performs their 1 = 1 identity primarily through visual, not sonic, precision. Replay is principally a *visual* practice. Part of musical Replay's allure as a superlative capturer and tamer of the Real is the way in which it places sound in its "sight." Replay is embodied, but it is the *look* of the bodies, not their sound, that is most important. Similarly, it is seeing the "real" mellotron, not hearing a sound that is just like it (through a sampler), which makes the performance "authentic." (This is also why updated audio technology such as concert speakers and the unseen technology of the video projector do not count as things to be authentically redeployed.) In this, musical Replay relates to Richard Leppert's work on Western music in the nineteenth century. Leppert argues that music's "semantic ambiguity" was channeled toward "acceptable meanings" through its visual representation in paintings and instrument decoration (Leppert 1993, 7). Replay is another example of channeling music's semiotic instability through the fetishization of musical performance's material and visual components. This "sight of sound" plays out in a variety of ways in the case studies I examine.

For example, the many tributes to the band ABBA, which I also take up in chapter 1, claim a certain vision that sanctions their authenticity. Having broken up in 1982, ABBA is nonetheless one of the top-selling bands of all time, rivaled only by the Beatles and Elvis.[28] This status was achieved through ABBA's long afterlife in tributes and revivals in the 1990s and 2000s. The two earnest reenactments of ABBA that I examine (Arrival from Sweden and ABBA the Concert) have been touring for over two decades, performing for tens of thousands of spectators each year. True to the practices of Replay, they highlight their ability to bring back the original experience, promoting the performance as just like going to a "real ABBA show." The original ABBA stressed their "neat," "clean," "wholesome," and heterosexually coupled status in their image, all while focusing on presenting the band as universal. Indeed, they were described by some as "too perfect," something I highlight in their embrace of the perfectly contained and bounded palindrome, which became their signature. After their breakup, however, gay men were the main group of ABBA aficionados who kept the music alive. I argue that these two large-scale ABBA tribute groups authenticate their performances as "real" through their implicit contrast with drag performances. While claiming they are uncannily precise and the closest thing to the "real ABBA" that any of us will experience, these tributes do not, in fact, fetishize every possible material detail in the manner of the Musical Box. What these tributes take as real is the white, heterosexual, middle-class family associated with the original ABBA, all while claiming its universality. Any campy or queer elements one could read in the original are taken as "interpretation" and neutralized by the emphasis on a non-campy, fun-for-the-whole-family, "real" ABBA show.

In chapter 2, I delve more deeply into the desire for the Real in a hypermediated modern world. I describe a mid-century move away from interpretation in order to come closer to the Real. In 1966, Susan Sontag famously argued against the interpretation of art. Art without interpretation encourages us to experience "the luminousness of the thing in itself, of things being what they are" (2001 [1966], 13). Interpretation, however, leads us away from the (real) world: "To interpret is to impoverish, to deplete the world—in order to set up a shadow world of 'meanings.' It is to turn *the* world into *this* world" (7). One can already understand how TMB partakes of this broad worldview, where their uncanny noninterpretation brings them closer to the thing in itself. While chapter 1 established connections between Replay and Western classical music, in chapter 2 I demonstrate how Replay relates to conceptions of Western art, in particular performance art. An analysis of the film *Synecdoche, New York* illuminates the desire to capture the Real through live reenactment in the figure of MacArthur-winning theater director Caden Cotard (played by Philip Seymour Hoffman). I discuss this film because it so beautifully elucidates the turn-of-the-millennium desire for and fear of the Real and the pursuit of this Real through live reenactment. My analysis of the film illuminates my conceptions of the Real and of Replay as the fantasy project that claims to capture the Real all the while ensuring it is never (intentionally) encountered. I go on to investigate the reenactment of David Bowie's final performance of his character Ziggy Stardust by the performance art duo Forsyth and Pollard. I argue that through reenacting David Bowie under the auspices of performance art, fragmentation of the figure of Bowie in the 1970s is contained and tamed as a readymade in the 1990s. This turn away from interpretation and toward "being" represents a deep fear of the messy subjective and a preference for the object as authority. It also displays a cultural resistance to accepting the reality of loss, something I investigate further in the following chapter on jazz.

With its foundation in improvisation, jazz music would seem to be the antithesis of Replay. Yet jazz was one of the first musical genres to be reenacted in the concert hall. The objectification of jazz goes back to Paul Whiteman's famous 1924 Aeolian Hall concert, an "Experiment in Modern Music," in which the bandleader traced the evolution of jazz much as one would learn the "evolution of man" through pictorial charts in grade school at the time.[29] Indeed, jazz fell into commodity fetish treatment early, with white "experts" examining it as a scientific object of study: taming and naming it from a position of presumed authority, rather than as devoted students attempting to learn something they did not know.[30] A cogent image for this model of jazz knowledge based on power rather than respectful apprenticeship is found in Madonna's music video "Express Yourself" (directed by Fincher 1989), where the malevolent, exploitative factory owner also has an inanimate jazz trio that, with a switch, performs for him on command. Here, black male jazz artists are explicitly objectified for the owner's enjoyment, fully contained, tamed, named, and we are to infer, understood. Any mystery (for example, the owner's ignorance of how to perform such music himself) is rendered moot in his ability to capture, display, and order their performance on command.

Madonna's video came out just as trumpeter and composer Wynton Marsalis was moving toward institutionalizing jazz at Lincoln Center. In chapter 3, "If I Should Lose You: Keeping Jazz Alive," I examine the repercussions of remembering jazz through a model of Replay. I begin by contrasting different conceptions of the past, in particular, the conception found in a Western epistemology which has led to Replay and that found in a West African drumming tradition. Replay objectifies the past in order to locate and, ostensibly, preserve it. Other epistemologies, such as those found in West African, Buddhist, and some African-American practices, do not separate the past in this way, and as such, it is not considered lost, but contained in the present. As I show, Wynton Marsalis and Jazz at Lincoln Center adhere much closer to the line of Replay than the counterepistemologies to be found in much jazz practice. By the late 1980s, Marsalis began the process that eventually led to the founding of Jazz at Lincoln Center in New York City in 1991, now known as the preeminent site of jazz's institutionalization. The resident Jazz at Lincoln Center Orchestra is known for its "stylistic authenticity" and is dedicated to performing works from the Count Basie, Duke Ellington, Chick Webb, and Benny Goodman songbooks in the "original" style, much to the dismay of many critics and jazz performers. I examine Marsalis's efforts to preserve jazz in light of conceptions of the past and of feelings of loss. I argue that while Marsalis has attempted to address the "naming and taming" of jazz by white and male "authorities," he has done so in a way that quite fully accepts the "master's tools" (Lorde 1984). In an examination of his reenactment of Louis Armstrong's *Hot Five* and *Hot Seven* recordings, I also demonstrate how the participation of Lil Hardin Armstrong as performer, composer, and arranger of many of these works is elided through Marsalis's "strict" and "precise" reenactment that performs this music as a fully male endeavor.

A second case study in chapter 3 takes up the Glenn Miller reenactment at Yale University. If Marsalis is concerned with remembering jazz and its cultural importance, Yale's reenactment demonstrates how musical Replay can be deployed more directly to offer images of the American nation. Yale University Band's first Glenn Miller reenactment occurred in 1994, in the midst of the swing revival, the rise of the tribute band, and the aftermath of the First Gulf War. As I detail, Yale's commemoration was not only popular cultural memory, but a part of the sanctioned national memory of World War II. Fiftieth anniversary commemorations of World War II closely followed the First Gulf War and its supposed triumph over America's "Vietnam Syndrome." Such remembrances served to supplant dissenting, plural, cacophonous 1960s wartime images with those of a "popular" World War II, and Yale's reenactment clearly participated in this widespread tendency. Yale's production also revealed important strategies for enacting and maintaining boundaries that speak to both political and musical gatekeeping. Contemporary Yale women and men of color would not have been welcome in Miller's original orchestra; and yet in their reenactment, two men of color (trumpet and piano) and four white women (two cornets, trumpet, and tenor saxophone), along with their white male bandmates, took on the identity of a particular white man, wore his uniform, and spoke his words, in a spectacle of national consonance.[31] I argue the reenactment attempts to "patch up" feelings of loss characteristic of the late twentieth century while simultaneously presenting images of the American nation with secure borders, benevolent patriarchal control, and the eradication of difference.[32] The image of Glenn Miller as idealized white masculinity leading a unified band is mobilized as a synonym for American nation, offering audiences the performance of unity and identity. The women and people of color engage in something I call in-passing, a form of liminal identity that does not disrupt unified identity, but rather "fashions unity" through its particular signifying practice. In the Yale reenactment, women and men of color perform a type of obedient transvestism in a display of national unity.

Chapter 4, "The Importance of White Women Being Earnest: Lez Zeppelin and the Performance of Cock Rock," further pursues the question of obedient or disobedient transvestism. In a book that examines rigorously mimetic reenactments, a reader may wonder how an all-woman tribute to an all-male band would qualify. The women of Lez Zeppelin, however, do not claim to be performing Led with a difference, but in earnest. They perform Led Zeppelin not as ironic, not as in-passers, but "for real," by claiming "androgyny" as a portal. Following the 1 = 1 identity of the clone band, Lez Zeppelin mimics precise details of the original, including instruments, equipment, clothing, and gestures. They re-create specific, treasured concerts in their entirety and have recorded a painstaking recreation of Led's first album in an analog studio ("to remain true to the vinyl version"), using the original instruments and effects. Parlaying Led's "androgyny," gender ambiguity, and pansexuality through an algebraic twist where xy = yx (androgyny = gynandrous), they claim to perform this music with bodies that are *the same* as Led's. According to fans, "These ladies are not trying to mess with a perfect recipe," and "You blur your eyes from far enough away, and you think you're seeing the real thing." Thus, while some may tout the band's "gender bending," in fact, in performing Led in earnest, they unveil the phantasmagorical quality of gender and the uncanny emptiness of identity itself.

The uncanny pervades this book and culminates in chapter 4, when I elaborate the full import of this sensation. In Lez's strict doubling, they open up the conundrum of gender—its uncanny emptiness, which is also the emptiness of identity itself. Cutting into various narratives and counternarratives of identity—its presumed "realities," changes, options, sameness, difference—the feeling of the uncanny is that brush with the inherent emptiness of identity. But this absence of identity must not be confused with a type of invisibility and universality that is the hallmark of whiteness. Invisibility as a tactic of whiteness is pretending there is not an origin while secretly solidifying originary naturalness around whiteness. This is ignorance—ignoring. In my conclusion, I argue for the opposite of ignorance: a clear-seeing acceptance of emptiness. All of the attempts at the perfect double described in this book ultimately lead to this glitch in the system: the eruption of the uncanny emptiness and the voiding of Symbolic attempts to tame and contain this emptiness. Rigorous reenactments promote their uncanny performances because the uncanny gives us a charge. The uncanny is that moment when our intellectual certainty about ourselves as subjects is revealed to be deeply uncertain. Eliciting the uncanny is a way to flirt with this knowledge that we both desire and fear.

If we understand identity as fantasy, we can comprehend how flipping the script does not have much purchase. For decades women will break stereotypes and yet each time still be described as groundbreakers. It would seem that the ground always encroaches around them to be broken again, as if for the first time. The stereotypes continually resurface because the Western epistemology that sets boundaries between self and other serves precisely to keep whiteness and maleness in privileged positions. I demonstrate this in my discussion of Janis Joplin as an influence on Robert Plant in chapter 4. Even as Plant was routinely described as the "male Janis Joplin" early in his career, the origin story that must find one beginning and one genius innovator eventually settled around his white male body as he became known as the originator of heavy metal vocals.

James Baldwin wrote that "not everything that is faced can be changed. But nothing can be changed until it is faced" (quoted in Peck 2017). In the conclusion, I call for the necessity of facing, culturally, what we have not faced: the Real. The Real is, indeed, "just what Western philosophy has mostly been designed to ward off" (Morton 2015, 228). This "warding off" has produced the nefarious consequences that stem from a basic misapprehension of the world: that things and selves exist apart from other things and selves. Thus, in my final chapter, "A Different Lean: On Intimacy and Emptiness," I suggest ways to accept the Real and argue that its acceptance is much more powerful than attempting to fight the master with his tools: counternarratives and identity claims that stem from the Symbolic.

While we fear the Real, we also deeply crave it, for it is life and connection itself. It is intimacy with experience in its fleetingness. I use the Buddhist term and concept, "emptiness," to help further describe this Real. Emptiness acknowledges that we cannot find a permanent, unitary, independent anything. Neither a self nor an object. When we examine the world closely, we find that everything is impermanent, multiple, and interdependent. In this sense, self and other (all objects) are empty of inherent existence. They exist; yet this existence is not inherent, but contingent: impermanent, multiple, and dependent on conditions. Accepting this truth is accepting the Real: the impermanent, interconnected qualities of self and phenomena. If the term "emptiness" sounds cold, a warmer synonym could be "relationship."[33] Everything is in relationship. Apropos of the discussion on repetition in chapter 3, many traditions accept this basic premise of the world.

I build upon these traditions of thought to help steer contemporary Western ways of thinking more toward an acknowledgment of the messiness and blur of selves and others. Scholars such as Timothy Morton and Marcus Boon on Buddhist philosophy and the Western condition, Avery Gordon on "haunting and the sociological imagination" (2008 [1997]), in which haunting is not corralled into "haunthenticity," and Nathaniel Mackey (2005) and James Baldwin (1998 [1949]) on African-American counterepistemologies, have offered insights into ways of thought that are deeply necessary in our modern world. While attempting to uncover and address hegemonic and nefarious ways of thinking and being in culture, most current critical and cultural theory continues to have difficulty with all things "subjective" or interior, preferring clear objects and names.[34] But scholars such as Morton, Boon, Gordon, and others are pushing back, calling for an acknowledgment of the real complexity of life as subjective, blurred, connected, impermanent, and unlocatable.[35] This is an acknowledgment of the Real, a way to take all that normally "escapes [us] . . . this, here, now, alive, active" as a basis, rather than ignore and malign it as opaque, unknowable "personal" or "subjective" experience (Raymond Williams (128), quoted in Gordon, 199). This is radically important. For again, to quote Baldwin: "It is only this void, our unknown selves, demanding, forever, a new act of creation, which can save us" (16–17). Baldwin is calling for an acceptance of life rather than a "rejection of life, the human being, the denial of his beauty, dread, power, in [an] insistence that it is his categorization alone which is real and which cannot be transcended" (18). In this quote, Baldwin is speaking specifically of the categories allotted to black Americans, but it is part of the author's larger argument that this erroneous worldview yokes us all. The cage is not recognizing the humanity of the human being, preferring an abstract Humanity. "But," he writes, "our humanity is our burden, our life; we need not battle for it; we need only to do what is infinitely more difficult—that is, accept it" (18).

For my final case study, I examine Jason Moran's "In My Mind: Monk at Town Hall, 1959," a multimedia "restaging" of Thelonious Monk's famous concert in New York. Moran's reenactment was precipitated by the forces that perpetuate Replay. He was approached in 2007 by the San Francisco Jazz Festival to do a note-for-note reenactment of Monk's famous concert for its "Monk-at-90" tribute. Moran demurred on such a strict restaging. Yet he was also intrigued and secured a co-commission from Duke University, the San Francisco Jazz Festival, Chicago Symphony Hall, and the Washington Performance Arts Society to create a "making of" combined with a "historical recreation." In my reading, Moran responded to this obsessive remembering with a commentary on the past in jazz. In a direct counter to the error of Replay, Moran staged an interaction with Monk that blurred past and present, self and other, performer and listener, demonstrating the unlocatability of self and other and the connection of the past and the present. Moran's performance offers a way to conceive of the past and the present as blurred, connected, and intimate. This worldview has been available in African-American traditions of music and writing, but it must be recognized and practiced. In support of this broad worldview, I conclude by offering my own theoretical model of the subject that I believe is more helpful than the dominant Hegelian model now found in cultural theory. I argue for a new lean toward the Giving Subject rather than the Subject that must be Recognized. If modern cultural and critical theory acknowledges the contingency—interdependence, impermanence, and multiplicity—of the subject, then it is already tipping into the well of emptiness. I argue that if self and other are both empty (as already acknowledged by cultural theory), it will be more helpful to have a model of being that recognizes the phantasmagorical self that can nonetheless give to an other (thus leaning in that direction, toward a self who gives), rather than a phantasmagorical other that nonetheless must recognize (thus contingently stabilizing this powerful other who can give or take based on its power to recognize). We make a deep mistake when we both claim the emptiness of the subject (its constructedness and contingency) and unconsciously and firmly stabilize it in the form of an other who must recognize. A model that leans toward an (empty) self who nonetheless can give offers a way to conceptualize identity as a foundation for positive and creative action.

ONE

Performing Security

Replay as the Performance of the "Perfectly Known"

This music will never die, even though you will.

Tribute band reviewer

"I have seen the future of classic rock, and it is the tribute band."

Reviewing a 2012 Musical Box performance, the writer continues, "More so than most popular music genres, a key component to so-called classic rock is live performance on analog instruments. As bands that began in the sixties suffer the loss or aging of [their] members, the best of [their] music demands to live on somehow" (Morgenstern 2012). And "somehow" seems to be through live, precisely copied re-performance of the original bands. Evidently sheet music, photographs, sound recordings, film, video, and "covering" are not enough. Even with all of these technologies, the fear of the past fading into oblivion endures. The reviewer esteems the "liveness" and "analog instruments" of classic rock in support of his claim that a precise re-performance is the only way the music can "live on." And he hints at the underlying compulsion that drives us toward this future: "I can only see more expertly put-together tribute bands rising from the ashes of classic rock legends on the horizon in order to keep the music alive. This music will never die, even though you will." And thus, the real issue at hand: one day we each will die. What should we do about this? By giving the answer of modernity—save the material, objectified remnants of the past through the latest fetish (previously photographs and sound recordings, now live reenactment)—the reviewer continues the soothing, yet ultimately ineffective fantasy that the future will contain us if we can only preserve and solidify everything around us, including now, impossibly, the original event itself.

While there is important scholarship on the neoliberal subject's assimilation into fragmentation and continual flow (Shaviro 2003), it would be erroneous to believe that the long fetch of a Western worldview which establishes the individual and other forms of border control as the bulwark against all threats has transformed into a completely new epistemology. The fact that this review was written in 2012 belies the notion that we now easily accept fragmented identities and improvisatory corporate-led flow without pining for old (imagined) senses of security. However, the current ubiquity of the Internet, in particular, has affected how we think about ourselves, as well as the ways we work and consume in the twenty-first century. Other forms of popular music, such as EDM, are perhaps more apt exemplars of these forces in our current moment.[1] The performance practices of Replay found in the rigorous reenactments of the 1990s, however, are particularly indicative of the types of fears and desires that were on the rise then. In many ways, they can be understood as a last-ditch attempt to cling to old models of the coherent, freestanding individual. Historian Daniel T. Rodgers characterizes the last quarter of the twentieth century as an "age of fracture," while David Campbell argues the United States shored up its identity in this era through "writing security" against the loss of earlier moors of stability. I contend that Replay grew in popularity at that time as a type of "comfort entertainment" in response to the cultural atmosphere of fracture and insecurity.

In this chapter, then, I examine Genesis and ABBA tribute bands as particular responses to these crises of late-twentieth-century postmodernity. These bands, which continue today, exemplify the characteristics of Replay outlined in the introduction. The Musical Box, in particular, is a paragon of Replay and a textbook case of the symptoms of an illness I associate with the Western epistemology. In examining the Musical Box and Genesis in the context of progressive rock narratives, I situate Replay as an outgrowth of this epistemology by way of the classical music tradition. It is a concept of knowing that creates separation through its obsession with objectivity. Such object fetishization propels a desire for connection and the Real, which is also feared because it stands outside of objectivity. This creates problems for the establishment and maintenance of identity, which also stem from this way of knowing. Tracing this epistemology via musical performance and using a psychoanalytic lens, I demonstrate how the Musical Box's

Replay performs a fundamental fantasy of a real, coherent identity in an age of fracture—a type of embodied Werktreue that attempts to paste over a sense of loss. Unfortunately, this fundamental fantasy has nefarious consequences. I will argue that the Musical Box is symptomatic of a neurosis that must be examined if we want to root out psychic structures that support whiteness as "true" and universal through a need for a coherent, safe, immortal identity.

I further this analysis of whiteness and identity through an examination of the band ABBA. ABBA has been a particularly popular band to reenact and revive, so much so that revivals have pushed the band into the highest echelons of record sales. I focus primarily on the qualities of the original band that led to its fetishization through revival and reenactment in the 1990s. While Genesis may be a prime candidate for reenactment as an extension of a Werktreue fetish, the band ABBA has a different, but related, appeal. I argue that reenacting ABBA offered a fantasy of imagined safety, security, and control that was based on the original band's visual, sonic, and emotional performance of a universal, "tidy," perfect identity (qua white, heterosexual, middle-class normativity). Through the performance of mainstream ABBA tribute bands claiming to give audiences a "real" ABBA show, any camp or queer aspect of the band is eliminated, and the heteronormative and conventional nuclear family features are foregrounded.

Finally, I address the glitch in this system of rigorous reenactment, one that sends the whole charade into an encounter with what is both feared and desired. In attempting to be a perfect double, the clone band rubs up against the uncanny, which erupts in unexpected ways with the return of a particular repressed within the postmodern psyche. I return to this throughout the book. For indeed, it is by means of the uncanny that we encounter what we both desire and fear—a brush with the Real. And as such, a brush with a necessary truth.

THE MUSICAL BOX

The Rise of the Tribute Band

One of the most popular and widespread examples of musical reenactment in late modernity is the tribute band. Some "earnest" tributes re-create classic tours or specific individual shows using the original instruments and set designs, and market themselves as uncanny conjurers of the past. These extremely earnest re-creators are often termed "clone bands." "Ironic" tributes give their reenactments a twist. Examples include the all-male Madonna tribute band, Mandonna, or the band Gabba, who perform ABBA songs in the style of the Ramones. The tribute phenomenon in music can be traced back to the production of Beatlemania, the live tribute to the Beatles, and to Elvis impersonators, both of which appeared in the 1970s as exemplars of late-modern "memory culture."[2] A modification of the "cover band" that performs the music of a variety of bands, tribute bands began to overtake the live music scene in the 1990s with their live re-creations of one well-known band or even of a single performance or tour. Tributes may be to a band that broke up decades ago or a band currently touring. Thus, tribute bands offer audiences who may not have regular access to the original artists (because the original band is no longer together, or because of geographic distance or prohibitive ticket prices) a chance to hear the "band" live. The practice has grown steadily since the 1990s, and tribute bands are booked as often as original bands (or more so) at many live music venues. Some tour internationally and play for audiences in the thousands with fifty-dollar ticket prices. These tend to be the earnest re-creations, such as the Musical Box. Ironic tribute bands often have a smaller, though often just as devoted, following.[3]

Certain performers and bands have lent themselves to tributes more than others. Elvis and the Beatles had tribute acts in the 1970s, well before tributing and live musical reenactment hit its stride.[4] The incredible pop culture status of these artists made them ripe for fetishization, and they served as early examples of the ways contemporary culture would go on to preserve and memorialize popular music. Since the 1990s, there are a few bands that have joined the ranks of highly popular tributees through the efforts of long-term, internationally touring tribute bands. Genesis, Pink Floyd, and ABBA all have several highly devoted earnest tribute bands that perform for audiences in the thousands or sometimes tens of thousands.

Reenacting Genesis and Progressive Rock

We don't change anything, we don't interpret anything,
we don't modify anything, we don't improvise anything.
We never invent anything. That's the whole point.

Sébastien Lamothe, The Musical Box

The Genesis tribute band the Musical Box has the reputation of being *the* tribute band most committed to the precision of their live recreation. The original Genesis members have given the Musical Box access to their master tapes, slides, stage blueprints, and certain instruments; attended and introduced concerts; and "sat in" with the band.[5] Genesis members have praised the tribute band, and the Musical Box uses these quotes in their promotional materials, marketing themselves as "licensed by Peter Gabriel and Genesis."[6] Because the Musical Box has been granted the license and lent original equipment by Genesis, they feel a special responsibility to faithfully portray Genesis's original shows. As bassist and band cofounder Sébastien Lamothe says, "It is just us that will be able to have access to this information. So if it's not us, it's nobody. It became a mission."

According to interviews and promotional materials, the Musical Box's goal is to re-create an original Genesis performance as precisely as possible, right down to Gabriel's original body movements and stage banter gleaned from bootleg videos. As their website stated:

> Many Genesis enthusiasts (old and new) have never seen these legendary shows. But the real pity after all is they never had the chance to experience the young Peter Gabriel. The Musical Box makes this dream come true. The result is the perfect illusion of a virtual time machine—to recapture the magic of those concerts and give people the impression of being at an original Genesis show. All of the song introductions and off-the-wall stories in between, every song, every movement by Gabriel, the original light impressions and all of the genuine multimedia effects are a carbon copy of the exact Genesis performance 30 years ago. (www.themusicalbox.net, accessed May 23, 2018)

This statement situates the Musical Box's performance as a direct antidote to loss, to the pity of not experiencing the young Gabriel, to not being there. It is a performance of what was thought to be impossible, an answer to our dream: a "carbon copy" of the "exact" past returned to us. They will "recapture" the original Genesis—in the beginning, we can be there.

This project is redolent of the desire to capture something else known for its evanescence—music itself. As described in the introduction, the West has a long history of fearing and desiring the intersubjectivity and unlocatability of music. The past and music are both messy and blurry in this way—they are not objects in themselves. The Musical Box's attempts to locate, contain, and preserve the "original Genesis show" are related to the desire to preserve music in the tradition of Werktreue. I therefore find it apt that Genesis would be vigorously cloned through an exacting approach when understood within the context of the genre of music the band helped to establish: progressive rock. Progressive rock bands, audiences, and critics lauded the style's connection to the Western classical music tradition and its values, which were often presented as an antidote to the excesses of (African-)American rock and blues. I ultimately hope to show how the desire for the security of the object in the long Western tradition has ramifications for those "others" necessarily constructed as boundaries of a needed coherent self.

Progressive rock refers to a style of music developed by 1970s British bands, including Yes; Genesis; Emerson, Lake, and Palmer; Pink Floyd; King Crimson; Gentle Giant; and Jethro Tull (Macan 1992, 101). These bands became hugely popular in the United States; however, their distinct "prog rock" style was not often copied by American bands (Holm-Hudson 2002, 4). The era is considered to have its earliest roots in 1967 (the Beatles' *Sergeant Pepper's Lonely Hearts Club Band* and Procol Harum's *Whiter Shade of Pale* of that year are considered important precursors) and to have "gone horribly wrong" by 1977 (Holm-Hudson, 8). The peak years of classic progressive rock are considered to be roughly 1973 to 1975, the years when most of the bands listed previously were at their height of popularity. Yes and Genesis achieved even greater popularity later, however, when they were no longer producing classic progressive rock, but had, according to many, "gone commercial."[7]

Music critics and scholars have typically defined progressive rock as the music of educated, middle- to upper-class white musicians who merged Western classical music and art with popular music (Macan 1992, Spicer 2000, Covach 1997). Musicologist Edward Macan writes that "English progressive rock has been known above all for its emphasis on instrumental virtuosity, its use of timbral resources and large-scale structures drawn from European symphonic and church music and its fascination with surrealistic visual imagery and a type of epic subject-matter (often dependent on science fiction or fantasy literature) that suggests the influence of late nineteenth and early twentieth-century programmatic models" (Macan, 101). Macan has been an influential advocate for establishing the connections between progressive rock and classical music (Macan 1997). John Sheinbaum creates a table of these characteristics from Macan, which, in addition to those noted previously, include: "reaching 'beyond' conventional rock instrumentation; less reliance on 4/4 time signature; less reliance on 'three-chord' songs, and the simplest chords; surrealism and modernism [in lyric and visual material]; longer songs; concept albums; less focus on singer; virtuoso playing; unconventional [song] forms; toward the mind, less focus on the (dancing) body; white, educated, upper middle class (slight differences in the United States); primarily male musicians, primarily male audience" (Sheinbaum 2002, 26). Macan's highly influential scholarship on progressive rock (which has found its way to Sheinbaum, as well as Mark S. Spicer, John Covach, and others) has both described and often inscribed the cultural meanings that place progressive rock on the "serious" side of the "serious vs. vernacular music" debate, with all of the concomitant values associated with this dualism, including mind/body, educated/natural, art/entertainment, male/female, and white/black.

Indeed, Macan has argued specifically for the connection between progressive rock and the twentieth-century English styles of Holst and Vaughn Williams. Describing progressive rock as "a late twentieth-century extension of [the composers'] 'English' musical language," Macan argues that this affinity "appears to result from the parallel influence of three common sources: English folk-song, Anglican Church music, and the music of early twentieth-century nationalist composers such as Bartok and Stravinsky" (Macan 1992, 101). I will not detail Macan's analysis; however, his overall argument is that progressive rock should be viewed within a matrix of English nationalism. Such nationalism is most often couched in terms that hint at an African-American invasion in the form of American popular music. Battling the earthy and dominating music coming from the United States, English popular music stands its ground, according to Macan, and produces its own unique form of creativity. He writes,

> English music of the twentieth century is almost unique in its single-minded development of a specific musical language that appeared near the beginning of the century; it is also unique—in the context of twentieth-century music, at least—for the way in which its "art" styles and "popular" styles have largely shared a common musical language. The tenacity of this musical language is such that, when the rhythmic sensibilities of twentieth-century Afro-American popular music, with its omnipresent rhythm section, were fused with the pre-existing modal framework by English popular musicians of the 1960s, a new, distinct idiom of popular music resulted—one of the few truly important stylistic contributions to twentieth-century popular music to originate from outside the United States. (Macan 1992, 123–24)

For Macan, progressive rock was important, original, and bred in England.

Value-laden terminology clearly pervades all of these descriptions of progressive rock. The style is described through its implicit comparison with pop music: it is "reaching 'beyond'"; it has "less reliance" on convention, on "the simplest chords"; it is represented by the "virtuoso" and is "unconventional." After the list of stylistic features, the class, race, and gender characteristics are then explicitly described: it is "toward the mind, less focus on the (dancing) body"; it is "white, educated, upper middle class" and "primarily male musicians, primarily male audience." The influence it does take from African-American popular music is from that form's "omnipresent rhythm section," a phrase that does not suggest complexity, unconventionality, or "reaching beyond."

Ultimately, Macan credits English progressive rock musicians for being able to do what Holst and Vaughn Williams were unable to—spread the "English style" throughout much of the "industrialized world" (124). He cites most bands' *lack* of overt nationalism (compared to Holst and Vaughn Williams) for this success; however, he does find five bands (including Genesis) that present a more overt form of nationalism in their pronounced use of English literary sources, such as myth, and medieval and Renaissance imagery (124).

Of all the progressive rock bands, Genesis hews closest to the definition provided by Macan and others. When scholars deconstruct academic discourse on progressive rock, Genesis is usually the exception that conforms to the "rule." For example, in critiquing Macan's analysis, Durrell S. Bowman writes that, "With a few notable exceptions (the members of Genesis, for example) most progressive rock musicians came from the same small town and working-class British origins where hard rock and heavy metal originated" (Bowman 2002, 185). Genesis is also singled out for their particularly overt "literariness," including their inspirations in Ovid (Holms-Hudson 2002, 14), Philostratus, and Keats (Nicholls 2004, 131) and comparisons of their work to Eliot, Pound (Weinstein 2002, 108 n. 26), and the great operas of the Western art music tradition (Nicholls 2004, 136). Their large-scale compositions and elaborate stage shows are considered to be the prototype for other progressive rock bands.

Thus, true to classic progressive rock biography, four students of the exclusive British "public school" Charterhouse formed Genesis in 1967. Bassist Mike Rutherford, keyboardist Tony Banks, original guitarist Anthony Phillips, and lyricist/singer/flautist Peter Gabriel met manager Jonathan King, "scion of U.K. Records and . . . a public school lad himself," who soon signed them with British Decca (Ross 1975). After two albums (*From Genesis to Revelation* and *Trespass*) and a change of manager, Phil Collins joined as the drummer and Steve Hackett replaced Phillips on guitar to create the lineup that would last though 1975, when Gabriel left the band. This incarnation produced three seminal progressive rock albums, which were promoted through highly theatrical tours: *Foxtrot* (1972), *Selling England by the Pound* (1973), and *The Lamb Lies Down on Broadway* (1974).[8] This 1972–1975 era is considered Genesis's classic progressive rock phase and is the era primarily re-created by the Musical Box.[9]

A propos of the growing narrative on progressive rock, positive reviews of the band tended to emphasize the band's "seriousness" and culture compared with "typical" pop music, which was assumed to be either simplistic, superficial, and "wimpy," or too macho ("phallic") when based in African-American styles. A review by Ron Ross exemplifies this narrative: "In a musical world dominated by dueling banjos, pop boys, wimpoid artists and Soul Train, is there a place for a British group that writes epics on such trivial matters as death, money, government, sex, freedom, nature, war, and power?" Ross hinges the difference between Genesis and popular rock at the juncture of the guitar, the symbol of rock's overmasculine excess, writing, "Steve Hackett . . . is helping to define what the electric guitar will sound like in the seventies, no longer an overbearingly phallic solo instrument, but [just] one more versatile and piercing voice in the arrangement." Ross emphasizes Hackett's more classical-music-inspired embodiment (Hackett would usually sit onstage), averring that "so careful is Hackett to give the impression of a craftsman rather than a pop star, that his standing on one number seemed a concession." Ross further makes the explicit connection between Genesis and opera: "Because songs like 'Get 'Em Out' so completely blend mime, costuming, music and lyrics into a perfectly reasonable synthesis, Genesis come [*sic*] closer to a real form of rock opera than anything yet. Opera is the sum of all the performing arts into a whole greater than its parts, which is exactly the way Genesis work [*sic*] collectively." Genesis is then prized over "B. B. King's endlessly permutated macho ravings," and we are given "the bottom line . . . that Peter Gabriel looks roughly ten times better in a jumpsuit than Mick Jagger and doesn't have to foam at the mouth to impress his audiences" (Ross 1973). Ross's positive appraisal of Genesis is based almost entirely on distancing the band from superficial white pop ("pop boys" and "wimpoids") and blackness qua excessive masculinity (Soul Train, B. B. King, phallic guitars, and Mick Jagger's Delta Blues–inspired music) and aligning it with Western classical music.

The Musical Box: The Return of the Work

Québécois musicians Denis Gagné, Serge Morissette, and Sébastien Lamothe formed the Genesis tribute band the Musical Box in 1993, just as the tribute band phenomenon was gathering steam.[10] Their initial project was to re-create Genesis's 1973 international *Selling England by the Pound* tour for its twentieth anniversary. Taking their name from a Genesis song on the 1970 *Trespass* album, flautist, percussionist, and lead vocalist Gagné (as Gabriel), artistic director Morissette, and

Lamothe on bass, guitar, and vocals (as Mike Rutherford) brought on François Gagnon on acoustic and electric guitars (Steve Hackett), David Myers/Michel Cloutier on keyboards, twelve-string guitar, and vocals (Tony Banks), and Martin Levac/Marc Laflamme on drums, percussion, and vocals (Phil Collins). Over the twenty-five years since their inception, the Musical Box has become stunningly popular, adding the shows *Foxtrot, The Lamb Lies Down on Broadway,* and eventually *A Trick of the Tail* to their repertoire and performing regularly in Europe and North America for audiences often of a thousand or more.[11]

The Musical Box goes far above and beyond re-performing all of the songs in the exact order of the original concert. Working from bootleg videos, they mimic the exact movements of Gabriel, reenact the words he spoke in between songs, and use the original instruments and effects boxes—such as a decrepit Mellotron and aging Echoplex—rather than a sampler that could perfectly mimic the sounds. They employ the original costume maker to create the costumes and the original projector operator to flash the original 1120 slides given to them by Genesis. They have studied stage blueprints, lighting rig schematics, and even the original master tapes in order to re-create the precise arrangements and textures of the original. According to Lamothe:

> We go beyond just playing the music part of it. It's beyond just playing some notes. We're trying to understand . . . the arrangements, the sounds, the equipment of the time. And then this kind of approach is being applied to all the visual aspects, as well, and the presentation of the show, the stories between the sets, all the props, the projections, everything that has to do with the live experience in the end that will affect us. We're really trying to go as far as that.[12]

Much like the historical reenactors described in the introduction, the Musical Box rejects "interpretive thinking for the sake of fact-gathering," to cite Adorno's withering critique of music in the twentieth century (Adorno 2006 [1991], 16). And this is taken as "truth." As fan photos and film of the original concerts continue to come to their attention, they fill in more details. Lamothe compared their project to musicologists who go back to uncover the original manuscripts in classical music, but now the source is the event itself with all of the unique idiosyncrasies of its particular moment (Lamothe 2011).[13] And their most ambitious re-creation was Genesis's prog rock magnum opus, *The Lamb Lies Down on Broadway.*

In 2011–2012 the Musical Box performed their third tour of Genesis's *The Lamb Lies Down on Broadway,* a double concept album originally released in

1974 and toured from November 1974 to May 1975. *The Lamb* was Genesis's last album of their progressive phase and their most ambitious work, musically as well as theatrically. It was also Peter Gabriel's last album and tour with the band. Not considered particularly coherent as a narrative by most reviewers, David Nicholls cheekily summarizes the "plot" of the story:

> This double album tells the story of Rael ("not even a pure-bred Puerto Rican") who is mysteriously transported from New York City's Broadway to an under- or other-world of strange experiences. Among other things, he is wrapped in a cocoon, trapped in a cage and led to a tunnel by a blind female guide; he meets death, is ravished by three snake-like women, becomes hideously disfigured and is later castrated; finally, he descends a ravine, swims in rapids, saves his brother from drowning and as a consequence achieves some kind of ultimate transmogrification. (131)

As such, the plot provides a loose skeleton over which to lay sound and spectacle rather more than a particularly compelling storyline.

Unlike previous tours, the original Genesis tour of *The Lamb* was never professionally recorded. Genesis felt they had never mastered the visual elements of the performance, including the complex array of slides projected above the stage, Gabriel's various elaborate costumes, and the pyrotechnics that occurred three-quarters of the way through the show. Of the approximately one hundred performances Genesis gave, very few (if any) went off without a technical problem. The Musical Box, then, considers their project a curative that provides an incarnation of a live show that would otherwise be lost to the ages and one that actually outperforms the original in mastering the visual elements. The Musical Box tour visited over fifty cities in the United States, Canada, and Europe. Their final performance of the tour was before an audience of four thousand at the Bell Center in Montreal. Throughout the tour, the Musical Box received reviews that described their performance as "near perfection" and an "uncanny replica" of the original band (Leventhal 2011). As one reviewer put it, "The greatest thing about the Musical Box performing the *Lamb* live were the moments that the musicians made themselves seem invisible as they re-created this legendary work, and art transcended the artifice on stage" (Morgenstern 2012). Indeed, the Musical Box tries to create the illusion that they *are* Genesis. Singer Denis Gagné states, "The whole point of the show is to give the audience the illusion they are watching Genesis in '74" (quoted in Morgenstern 2012).

All of these intense efforts to bring Genesis back to life take place under the aegis of a type of "authenticity" that is within a tradition of the Werktreue concept, as musicologist Richard Taruskin has argued in regard to the Early Music movement (Taruskin 1984). Unlike the romantic, Rousseauian idea of authenticity as a type of "truth to oneself" that characterized the rock era of the original band, the Werktreue concept is that of "fidelity to the work," as described in the introduction. The concept of the musical work crystallized around 1800 and then defined the norms, expectations, and behavior patterns that have come to characterize classical music practice. During this time, musical performance began to be reified into the preservable, bounded "work" and collected, with an eye toward "epic completeness" and "fidelity to the 'original'" (Butt 2008, 134). This tradition has continued in the work of rock music collectors, and it is within it that the Musical Box undertakes their project to preserve Genesis.

In fact, the Musical Box suggests they are able to go beyond even the musicologists or classical performers in their fidelity to the work. I asked Lamothe if he thought they were taking a "classical music" approach, trying to perform a Beethoven or Brahms and attempting to get the work right. He responded,

> Absolutely, that's actually been said for a long time. That is absolutely the approach. Not to sound snobby . . . We go beyond just playing, for example, the music part of it. It's beyond just playing some notes. We're trying to understand who wrote the piece, how the structure was made, how they were experimenting on new instruments, and so on . . . the arrangements, the sounds, the equipment of the time. And then this kind of approach is being applied to all the visual aspects, as well, and the presentation of the show, the stories between the sets, all the props, the projections . . . And the difference between us and people who are trying to do the same kind of effort with classical music is that this piece of art is much more contemporary, so we have access to much more information because of the technology [audio and video recordings]. I mean, at the time [of Beethoven or Brahms] a lot of references are really about musicology itself—the charts, the original notes of the composer, and stuff like that. In the context of a rock band that existed forty years ago, the information is very different. It's much more complex. (Lamothe 2011)

Lamothe suggests that the project is even more difficult than what musicologists who study Beethoven encounter because there is so much more information available to accurately capture and re-create. Not confined to notes on scores, recent popular music is preserved in recordings and bootleg films, which provide evidence of the band's intent. The original technology is still around, and so that must also be maintained, mastered, and used. Finally, even the band members' movements and words between sets are included as important information to preserve.

The clone band is thus the return to the "work" concept, but instead of imagining the work has a meaning to be uncovered, the work becomes so inert and solid and "true" that to interpret it is tantamount to degrading it to the form of the "text." The Musical Box pushes the Werktreue tradition found in classical music to its near-absurd limit. The work moves from something in the composer's mind that is *represented* in the score (so terrifyingly close to a *text* now in postmodernity) to the actual "chunk of time" of the performance itself. They are no longer representing Genesis, they *are* Genesis, becoming invisible as "art transcends artifice." In a highly mediated world, they become *im*mediate. The return to the work concept I am describing here, then, is not a return to interpretation and critical distance, to follow Jameson's conception of the work (2003 [1991]), but rather it is a return to the solidity and "realness" of the object in the face of the object's vacuity as it turns into a "text."

Put in structuralist terms, the Musical Box attempts to take Genesis as a signifier—language that represents—and turn it into a signified—the thing itself, or the Real. Their presentation of the material perfection of Genesis attempts to "give body" to the lack inherent in its status as signifier, language that can only point to other signifiers and not to anything "real." Kaja Silverman illuminates this modern desire to turn alienating signification back into a real relationship with the world through a scene from Werner Herzog's 1974 film *The Enigma of Kaspar Hauser.* Herzog's film is based on the chronicle of a nineteenth-century man who was apparently locked in a dungeon for his entire life and then released for unknown reasons as an adult onto the streets of Nuremburg, barely able to speak or walk. As the man becomes "civilized," he resists the acts of civilizing him. In one scene he enjoys looking at his name, Kaspar, which he had planted in seeds that eventually grew into grass. As Silverman points out, he turns his symbolic marker—his name—into a real thing—grass, effectively turning the symbolic world into the real world (Silverman 1983).

Like Kaspar Hauser, the Musical Box demonstrates this longing for the signified, the "real world," in a modern, increasingly mediated world. The signifier will no longer always point away to other signifiers, as Saussure argued about language; it is made Real and brought to life. As such, the clone band vigorously rejects the play of texts. It attempts to counteract the intertextuality of the cover band—the idea that part of our enjoyment and understanding depends on all the inflections of the other various interpretations and readings of the performance. The Musical Box does not want to interpret anything. Indeed, "interpretation" is the practice that led to the world of "texts" in the first place. The belief in multiple meanings is the road that led to no "real" meaning.[14]

The Real is all that cannot be contained through meaning. Therefore, while it is the "unmediated world," it is also sickness, death, and impermanence. In reenacting music, the members of the Musical Box attempt to satisfy their craving for the Real while simultaneously controlling and containing it, keeping it at a distance. They perfectly avoid what they seek in their painstaking work seeking it. That is, in obsessing on the material details of the past, they paste over the "lack" of the past with a fetish. The fetishizing character of TMB is perhaps most revealed in their focus on the painstaking work that goes into their performances.

At the performance of their final show in Montreal to end their 2011–2012 North American tour, the Musical Box presented a thirty-minute documentary outlining the making of the original "Lamb" and the difficulties involved in their precise reenactment of it. The original guitar maker described making Mike Rutherford's double-neck guitar; the visual coordinator outlined the technical challenges of the slides; the set designer elaborated the various problems with the complex sets. The Musical Box then detailed the difficulties they had and the efforts they went through to create the show that evening. Examples of original bootleg films were revealed to be exceedingly blurry, and the sound seemed as if it were filtered through a gurgling brook. The incredible complexities of the original music, instruments, sets, and costumes themselves were highlighted, as well as the additional complexity of trying to unearth all of these original elements and bring them back to life.

This relationship to the past can be conceived of in terms of the past's "needs." Through such painstaking work, we can see that the needs of the past are great. But these needs are eminently straightforward—a matter of material detail. Rather than undecidability and the eruption of "unexpected desires," the clone band contains the unexpected desires of the past by objectifying the past into a coherent and bounded event that needs only the straightforward performance of its precise material details. It is through this obsession that we can imagine we are meeting the past's needs, but only in a way in which the past never threatens to undo our fantasy of ourselves as solid, durable, and in control. The complexity of interpretation or any type of "give and take" with the past is ruled out. But it also serves to convince the band and others that they are meeting the past's needs precisely and that, therefore, they are in control. Reminiscent of Nathanael in E. T. A. Hoffmann's famous story "The Sandman," the Musical Box dotes on the past like the wooden automaton, Olimpia. "Oh! What a profound soul you have! My whole being is mirrored in it!" The automaton allows the "suitor" to meet her needs perfectly.[15] Hence the persistent promotion of these reenactments as the product of "painstaking" labor. Through their particular construction of the past's needs, the Musical Box is able to create the "perfect other without desire"—perpetuating the perfect endless fantasy that defers an encounter with the Real. The past is simplified. It does not haunt us, as Avery Gordon argues (2008 [1997]). We maintain control over it, not vice versa.

And as with Nathanael, those who enjoy the Musical Box demonstrate a willful desire to sustain the fantasy. One fan posted on an online Musical Box forum that, "I enjoyed *The Lamb* tremendously, even more than *Selling*. Always had seats in the back rows so I got more of an overall impression. That's actually a good thing in my book, because . . . the musicians resemble their Genesis counterparts better from a distance." This fan prefers to create the belief that he is seeing and hearing a live Genesis concert by avoiding the dissonance of seeing the musicians up close. Other tribute bands have commented on this phenomenon. Roy Hitchen, of the Beatles' tribute band Cavern Beatles, commented that meeting fans after a concert can be an awkward experience. The swept-up fan comes close and only then disappointingly realizes that Hitchens does not resemble the original member (Inglis 2006). These fans encourage the fantasy to take hold, like Nathanael feeling Olimpia warm to his touch.[16]

We want to believe so we help the story along. As the previously mentioned reviewer wrote, "Denis Gagné not only hit all the notes in Gabriel's dynamic range, but also captured the nuances in his voice and nailed his poses and gestures" (Morgenstern 2012). To say that Gagné "nailed" Gabriel's poses and gestures strikes me as odd. When musicologist Lisa Barg attended the Montreal performance with me, she noted the highly awkward movements of Gagné as he attempted to mimic Gabriel's every move. I noticed this myself in the videos I watched and also in the first live performance I witnessed. But as I continued to watch, I "got used to" the awkwardness. I eventually learned to look past it as I focused on other things. It was only after my attendance with Barg that I remembered how the performance struck me the first few times I saw it. Thus, much like Nathanael's experience with Olimpia—what was a little weird at first eventually melted away as I began to account for or assimilate into the "woodenness." I think for much of the audience craving to see Genesis again, there is a willful attempt to see the object come to life.

By focusing on a "perfect other without desire" over an engagement with the Real (Nathanael's first real-life love, Klara, or the past—both of which present us with infinite and uncontainable complexity), we avoid confronting our not knowing. We avoid understanding that we cannot know Klara, the past, or ourselves in the way we want (by pinning this information down). And we relatedly evade a certain knowledge that we do vaguely sense: the knowledge of the void of our own subjectivity. In creating an automaton out of the past, we create a fetish to paste over the *lack* inherent in the past. We delimit a past chunk of time in an object into which we can continually put our energy, continually finding detail after detail to mimic precisely in an asymptotic project. We give body to the lack and imagine this hunk of time to be a "real" other. In continually having to meet the past's needs, we avoid the confrontation with our own abyss. Thus, this project pastes over the lack of the past that acts as a stand-in for the lack at the heart of our own subjectivity.

While we attempt to paste over this sense with ceaseless activity, the type of ceaseless activity we engage in reveals our sense of personal impotence. That is, we place the locus of knowledge in the object and shun the idea of subjective decision making. Replay demonstrates a desire to find the truth in objective fact and a distinct fear of subjective decision making in the act of interpretation. It is a type of "pseudo-activity" (Adorno 2006 [1991], 26) that imagines the answers are anywhere but in our own decision-making capacity in the here and now. Thus, much of the pleasure of reenactors derives from "being done" by history: reenactors relinquish responsibility for knowledge themselves and defer authority to their chosen "Subject Who Knows"—sometime in the past, generally fetishized into the objects themselves: the double-neck guitar or the intricacies of an elaborate costume. In Replay, the live past itself as an automaton—a hunk of time—becomes the "Subject Who Knows" whom we must obey.

The irony is that while a sense of loss is generated in regard to the past, the past, in fact, is very much with us. The Western epistemology continually generates a feeling of loss, alienation, and separation. Thus one must go back to try to capture the past. One can imagine the Musical Box agreeing with James Baldwin when he writes, "History, as nearly no one seems to know, is not merely something to be read." TMB attempts to redress this fallacy through their work. Baldwin goes on, however: "It does not refer merely, or even principally, to the past. On the contrary, the great force of history comes from the fact that we carry it within us, are unconsciously controlled by it in many ways, and history is literally present in all that we do" (quoted in Rodgers 2011, 112–13). Thus, imagining the past is over and then controlling how it is "remembered" serves to elide the ways that the past remains with us in the form of habits of society: white privilege, capitalism, patriarchy. This different understanding of the past is something I take up further in chapter 3.

Performing Security

Summarizing Fredric Jameson, David Harvey, and others' work on the era of late capitalism and postmodernity, historian Daniel T. Rodgers (2011) writes that the last quarter of the twentieth century is a time when "selves became more flexible and less unitary, time horizons shrank, artistic forms that had been radically separate in space and time collapsed into each other, [and] attention moved from structures to surfaces" (9). Rodgers characterizes this time as "an era of disaggregation, a great age of fracture" (3) when "identities became fluid and elective" (5). He writes that "conceptions of human nature that in the post–World War II era had been thick with context, social circumstance, institutions, and history gave way to conceptions of human nature that stressed choice, agency, performance, and desire"(3). The individual was torn from ideas of the social and more than ever left to stand on her or his own, no longer embedded, but fragmented and separated.

Similarly, international relations scholar David Campbell describes the late twentieth century as an era of "contingency [and] the erasure of the markers of certainty" (1998, 17).[17] According to Campbell, "The problem of securing identity was posed in terms of how to handle contingency and difference in a world without God" (46). Thus, while Campbell situates his study of international relations within the specificities of the Cold War, its end, and the rise of terrorism, he ultimately argues that the need to define the identity of the United States stems from the condition of late modernity for the West—the absence of previous moors of stability. He argues that the creation of international relations was a specific way to establish identity through the construction of difference—the idea of the state. With the creation of these now locatable states, there is nonetheless the continued threat of "ambiguity." Borders are created in order to establish identity. They then need to be defended in order to maintain this now naturalized sense of identity.

Inculcating fear is how one secures the support for solid borders from the populace. If there were no identity or difference, there would be nothing to fear. As Campbell puts it, "Were there no borders, there would be no danger" (81). But "given that difference is a requisite for identity, danger is inherent to that relationship" (81). A "culture of fear" creates the need to enforce boundaries, to fend off this disorder and contingency, both without and within. Campbell argues that the United States needed to establish danger in order to maintain its sense of identity. This stoking of fear far preceded the events of 9/11. In 1987 Oliver North famously stated that, "It is very important for the American people to know that this is a dangerous world; that we live at risk and that this nation is at risk in a dangerous world" (quoted in Campbell, 33). The famous 1950 policy paper NSC-68, which established the basic trajectory of US foreign policy during the Cold War, declared that "'even if there were no Soviet threat' the United States would still pursue a policy designed to cope with the 'increasingly intolerable absence of order'" (31).

As the late twentieth century offered up these various threats to identity and old senses of order and control, Campbell's book argues that "the theory of international relations is one instance of the pervasive cultural practices that serve to discipline ambiguity" (17). I believe the cultural practice of musical performance, in particular, strict musical reenactment, is another.

The Musical Box hyperdisciplines the ambiguity of identity, and they use performance explicitly to do so. Because the Genesis tours were so overtly and elaborately theatrical, they offer the ambitious re-creator much to bite into. The theatricality of the Musical Box, however, is of a particular kind. Phil Collins states in an interview,

> They have taken a period and are faithfully reproducing it in the same way that someone would do a theatrical production. You know. . . you can take Shakespeare to a new place where no one has ever done it, or you can do it [as a period piece] . . . I'm giving you an analogy here, it's probably a bad analogy, but that's what they do. I [asked them], "Do you come off stage at the end of the *Lamb*," and they said "[W]ell no, you didn't. You stayed on stage and then played *The Musical Box*." So, that's what they do. (Collins 2005)[18]

The Musical Box's performance understands past popular music concerts as important "events" along the lines of battles or other historical moments, not as scripts to be interpreted. When re-creating the *Selling England by the Pound* tour for its thirtieth anniversary, the Musical Box's promotional material stated that the original was "the first ever multimedia performance in rock music" and that now "the huge worldwide Genesis fanbase finally gets a chance to see a precise reconstruction of the historic event."[19] As such, the performance of popular music becomes synonymous with US Civil War reenactors re-creating their battles at the original site for their various anniversaries.

The Musical Box is not creating theater in the sense of "twice-behaved behavior," as described by performance studies scholar Richard Schechner (2006). What marks the twice-behaved behavior of theater is the distance between the actor and the role. And while Schechner believes that all behavior is twice-behaved, theater highlights this "restoration" of behavior. The Musical Box does not present itself as interpreting Genesis, but as performing Genesis without distance or difference—in some sense, *being* Genesis, or at least creating the illusion of the *once-behaved,* the classic mathematical definition of identity, 1 = 1. To perpetuate this illusion, they have removed information about themselves on their website. In honoring Genesis, they do everything they can to disappear and give audiences the experience of being at a "real Genesis show."

The Lamb, however, offers an interesting encounter with "difference." It was not the strictly white and English production so characteristic of earlier Genesis tours; the main character was the distinctly "brown" Rael. Yet the self-sameness of the clone does not truck in the complexities of interpretation, and when Denis Gagné puts on brown makeup to play Rael in the Musical Box's flat re-creation, interpreting the layers of Gagné playing Gabriel playing Rael seems moot. Eclipsed by the star power of Gabriel, Rael was never a full-bodied character anyway. Nonetheless, Rael caused anxiety for some Genesis fans and reviewers concerned that the band might be turning to the dark side. Ron Ross trots out the prog rock tropes that delimit the style against "disco queens" and "soul, funk, and agro" as he addresses the issue with his readers,

> So what's a fly dude of Spanish extraction got to do with five well-bred, highly educated and frequently esoteric young Englishmen, with a penchant for moody myths and subtle self-satire? . . . Could it be that having flirted with seductive naiads and ancient hermaphrodites, Genesis are attempting to be trendy and up-to-the-minute by creating a contemporary Third World character? After all, with Bowie now a disco-dancin' cha cha queen at a time when all the world seems unlimitedly in love with Barry White, who could blame this quaint quintet of scholarly surrealists for hoppin' onto the soul train? [Who

> could blame them] if they chose to funk up their music (slightly) and allow Peter Gabriel's image some room to wax agro. (Ross 1975)

Ross goes on to aver that Genesis is not simply pandering as other bands do by introducing a little hip dark skin ("a contemporary Third World character") into their project. He writes that "The Lamb" is not an "exposé on the psychology of race by a band on the make . . . Rael serves as a psychologically and morally alienated adolescent with whom Genesis's audience can identify" (Ross 1975). Here the assumption seems to be: a white audience.

True to scholarly progressive rock definitions, Rael seems to be used in the manner of traditional Western opera, partially as a figure of earthy, passionate authenticity (something that America also signifies for the English band) and partially as a nonbeing. Peter Gabriel says, "The New York setting is a device for making the character more real, more extroverted and violent. . . . But this guy is slotless; his name is supposed to be raceless. . . . The point of Rael being accessible, earthy and aggressive is that he provides an earthy response to these fantasy situations" (quoted in Ross 1975). Thus, Rael is a character for white consumption, not a disloyal "change" in Genesis's project or target audience. Ross writes, "Rael's purpose [is] not so much to attract a larger integrated following by virtue of his ethnicity, but to lure Genesis's existing audience more totally into the illusion and mood all five of the band have worked so carefully to project throughout their career. . . . So, while *The Lamb* and Rael appear to be a major departure from Genesis's past, . . . the band's motivation and method have remained inherently the same" (Ross 1975). Ross clearly defines Rael as part of the project of Western Orientalism and not a move toward "integration" of the music or of the audience. Gabriel's crossing of racial boundaries is of the kind seen in Russian-born Yul Brynner's Siamese king in the *The King and I* (1956). This crossing over racial boundaries can be productively compared to the work of Anna Deavere-Smith or to the theater troupe Culture Clash.[20] Much like the Musical Box, Deavere-Smith embodies her characters from the outside in. She takes on their accents, physical gestures, and stances rather than some type of "inner" essence. The difference here is in the acknowledgment of theater and the "twice-behaved" behavior. In playing these characters, Deavere-Smith reveals the constructedness and mutability of identities as well as the structures of power that inform, produce, and manage them. By performing identity as "once-behaved," the Musical Box performs hegemonic, immutable identity as natural. And this identity is that of Gabriel, Genesis, and progressive rock, an identity that plays at being Rael without ever touching anything close to the possibility or alterity of a "real" existence for Rael.

The precision and exactness of progressive rock stem from the same tradition that undergirds obsessive reenactment, one which we can find in the tradition of Werktreue in classical music. In choosing Genesis, the values associated with progressive rock are brought forward. These values could be described, in part, as Whiteness and its properties. Ron Ross had to make the strong case that Genesis wasn't bringing in an "exposé on the psychology of race." This is what brown skin, marked by race, may signify. White skin is raceless—and universal.[21] The story was about an "alienated teenager" with whom "Genesis's audience" could "identify"—"raceless" white males, predominantly. For Gabriel to describe Rael as "raceless" and "slotless" reveals the ignorance of the white perspective that does not recognize its own privilege and universality. This whiteness as universal norm, as invisible power and privilege is then re-performed by the Musical Box. In refraining from "interpreting" Genesis, the Musical Box performs Genesis without distance or difference—they attempt to *be* Genesis, or at least to create the illusion of the *once-behaved.* They want to give the impression that there is no band that is "behaving" Genesis again, that is, performing a "twice" of the band, that there are no performers taking on the roles of Genesis. The illusion they want to create is that there is no actor, no time, no change: only the original brought forward again. In this sense, they perform whiteness as Real, the Signified, the one without an other (a signifier defined by other signifiers). But this can take place only with four white males reenacting the band. This fantasy of perfect identity and its association with whiteness is even more strongly put forward in my next example.

THE CASE OF ABBA

> Ipseity: the circular return of the self to itself . . .
> sovereignty is round; it is a rounding off.
> *Jacques Derrida,* Rogues: Two Eassys on Reason

In 2018 the group ABBA is firmly among those bands that have sold the most records worldwide, with an astronomical 380 million units (and counting) sold. This is in large part because of tributes to the band. Indeed, ABBA experienced a type of rebirth through the revivalism and tribute mentality that characterized popular music consumption in the 1990s. While the Beatles and Elvis are generally credited with selling the most records worldwide, because of continued revivalist efforts, ABBA is "one of the few contenders to third place" (Palm 2002, 1). Thus, while not attaining the astronomical presence and sales of Elvis and the Beatles during their heyday, ABBA has enjoyed a long and steady afterlife through tributes and revivals—enough to propel the group into the top echelon of worldwide consumption.

A decade after their last album as a group, ABBA mania began to resurface with the response to their greatest hits albums, ABBA *Gold* (1992) and *More* ABBA *Gold* (1993), and the four-disc box set *Thank You for the Music* (1994). The band's music figured prominently in the films *Muriel's Wedding* and *The Adventures of Priscilla, Queen of the Desert* in 1994, and bands and artists including Erasure, Sinead O'Connor, Evan Dando, and Dionne Warwick recorded covers of ABBA songs. Two ABBA tribute albums appeared later in the decade with bands such as Go West, Culture Club, and Madness contributing. The musical *Mamma Mia!*, with its plot built around ABBA hits, premiered in London in 1999 and has since been seen by over 42 million people and grossed over $2 billion worldwide, helping to propel the ABBA revival into the twenty-first century. The film version came out in 2008 with the soundtrack going to number one on the US Billboard charts.[22] Finally, popular ABBA tribute bands were formed in the late 1980s and 1990s: Björn Again in 1988, Arrival from Sweden in 1995, and ABBA the Concert in 1996. All of these bands are still going strong, regularly touring internationally past their twentieth anniversaries (like the Musical Box, far outliving the original band's tenure). What is it about ABBA that makes them so tribute-friendly? Certainly other bands of the 1970s, such as the Bee Gees, would appear to be valid candidates. But it is ABBA that has become a tributed group extraordinaire. Contextualizing ABBA and its tributes within late-twentieth-century fears and desires brings forward several characteristics that make ABBA particularly enticing to reenact.

During their ten years together (1972–1982) the Swedish band became one of the reigning pop groups in the world. Agnetha Fältskog, Benny Andersson, Björn Ulvaeus, and Anni-Frid Lyngstad had their big break when they won the annual Eurovision contest in 1974 with "Waterloo." They followed with a string of hits that topped the charts in the Americas, Europe, Asia, and Australia. Their most famous song, 1976's "Dancing Queen," "reached number one almost everywhere in the world where charts were compiled." According to Carl Magnus Palm, "It seemed it never fared worse than the Top Five anywhere" (2002, 297).

From the earliest stages of their career, the band and their manager, Stig

Anderson, eyed an international audience; and specific decisions were made to situate the band within a world market. They chose the name ABBA because it had no specific connection to any one language or culture. It was "a name that sounds right in as many languages as possible" (quoted in Palm 2002, 210).[23] They also crafted their music to sound universal and relatable. On thinking of a song title that would become "Waterloo," Stig Anderson (who often contributed lyrics early in ABBA's career) said, "I was looking for a word that wouldn't need a translation, something that everybody would be familiar with. . . . I needed a three-syllable word that would fit the melody" (quoted in Palm 2002, 220). With the exception of certain "ethnic sounds" intentionally deployed to capture a wider market (for example, the Latin-influenced "Fernando" ostensibly to appeal to a broad Latin audience), the group sought to avoid what they considered the "particular." "The group's image was based on accessibility," as Palm puts it. "Their credo was to entertain and make everyone feel welcome and included: 'we aim to please' was the motto" (270).

Part of this aiming to please was satisfying the needs of an international public reacting to the tumult of the late 1960s. In this effort, ABBA was ahead of its time in its turn to being behind the times. An important aesthetic model for ABBA was the "wall of sound" production technique pioneered by Phil Spector's work with the early 1960s "girl groups." ABBA's powerful female unison vocals are highly reminiscent of "Da Doo Run Run" by the Crystals (1963) and "Be My Baby" by the Ronettes (1963), both produced by Spector. According to Palm, this stylistic return to an early-1960s sound seemed to suggest that psychedelic, hard-rocking, political, late-1960s music never happened: "In many ways," he writes, "Abba created music that suggested that the past ten years hadn't happened: genres such as psychedelia, progressive rock and heavy metal were virtually untraceable in their output. Instead the group's music recalled some of the innocence of early Sixties pop, adorned with a framework of modern production techniques. It was a form of displacement that was both effective and unexpected in the popular music landscape at the time" (Palm 2002, 261).

The allure of ABBA's "clean," wholesome image, abetted by its presentation of normative heterosexuality, also appealed to many fans. As Palm (2002) puts it, "Not only was the group perceived as 'nice and clean' compared to other more rowdy acts at the time, but their two couples image portrayed them as symbols for healthy family values" (273). One Australian reporter wrote, "To adults, it's a pleasure to be able to enjoy watching a group their youngsters like, a group without unpleasant gimmicks like pop star Alice Cooper's killing chickens. With Abba, adults can feel reassured because their young are watching two nice clean-cut heterosexual couples" (quoted in Palm 2002, 273). Fans interviewed in the film, ABBA: *The Movie,* repeatedly used the word "clean" to describe the band, opposing this to other bands of the time, without mentioning any specific bands.[24] The overwhelming majority of acts at the top of the charts in 1977 could be described as clean. The Bee Gees, Barry Manilow, Stevie Wonder, Electric Light Orchestra—popular acts of the late 1970s were predominantly flashy, organized, glitzy affairs. "Shock rock" was not on the rise at that time (Cooper's chicken incident happened in 1969). What was certainly not clean at the time of ABBA's rise was punk music, which was making the headlines in Europe if not topping the charts or gaining radio play. This music with its dirty performers and audiences was connected with the grimy working class and threatened to influence young listeners. In contrast, ABBA offered a band that was middle-class, "wholesome," nonthreatening, and ultimately, clean.

ABBA was also ahead of its time in the use of music video (then film). By 1974 they were making short music films in order to market themselves in distant countries where they were reluctant to tour, such as Australia. These films were played on music television shows such as *Countdown* in Australia, and fans began to fervently call in requesting them again and again. In the televised films, fans could see the band up close on-screen, deeply identifying with and cathecting on the images, which fueled the desire to see them live. This was part of the hypervisibility the band was striving for. Ulvaeus stated, "We wanted to do videos where [the fans] could actually see us. There were many videos that were very, very obscure and artistic but you couldn't actually see the group at all" (Bjorn, quoted in Palm 2002, 244). ABBA focused on a film image that was bright, highly visible, and straightforward. "The clips were one hundred percent in accordance with the group's philosophy that they should be clearly visible," Palm writes. "The Abba members were not facing sideways or posing with an attitude, they were looking straight into the camera, their eyes interlocking with the viewers. Both the music and the visuals were invitingly bright—it was as if Abba were made for colour television" (270). Such an approach led to a veritable fan frenzy in Australia in 1975.[25]

Of course, ABBA had its detractors from the beginning. At the time, many critiqued ABBA for their universalism qua vacuity. In a representative example, one critic wrote:

> In an artificial world of neon, Abba appeared onstage and disappeared in the same way. Afterwards these four people seemed just as unreal and elusive as the smoke that stayed behind at the stage. . . . A perfect show with well-directed spontaneous laughter and musicianship. Nothing personal that could disturb Stig Anderson's consummate hit products. . . . The songs are built on simple harmonies and multinational repetition . . . "I love you," Abba sing and point towards the audience. But it's a lie. Abba don't love us. They love the 20 kronor they can steal from us when we've been swept away by the Abbamania and lose our grip on reality for an hour. (quoted in Palm 2002, 268)

Most critiques followed the basic logic that the group was "inauthentic"—a glitzy commodity ready for easy consumption. Another critic stated that "Abba's music seems much too calculated, it doesn't feel spontaneous. Their music doesn't express any feelings, and a sort of product thinking shines through. The music becomes a cold and unemotional, targeted product that is commercially marketed" (quoted in Palm 2002, 307). This view was typical in Sweden where the band was ruthlessly derided during its international heyday (Palm, see especially 277).

But apart from most Swedes at the time and the withering critiques from many international music critics, general audiences worldwide clamored for the tidiness, the hypervisibility, the cool superficiality, and the straightforward unisons and harmonies. Because it was so visible, perfect, delineated, and vacuous, Palm suggests "the audience could spin their own fantasies around Abba's slightly unreal, almost too perfect appearance" (272).

A part of ABBA's "almost too perfect" appearance was the band's seemingly inevitable gravitation toward the palindrome in their visual presentation. The band came up with the name ABBA in 1972, a palindrome consisting of the first letter of each member's name (Agnetha, Björn, Benny, and Anni-Frid). In 1976, on their album *Dancing Queen,* the first "B" was turned around to create the iconic visual palindrome we know today. "This famous trademark symbol . . . was based on the group's foundation as two couples," Palm writes. It was their heterosexually coupled status that "made it natural to turn each 'B' towards each 'A'" (297). The palindrome aspect of the band was reinforced with costumes, choreography, and promotional photographs that incorporated mirror-image designs, moves, and poses. The song title "SOS" is a palindrome, and its accompanying video accentuated the play of symmetry by turning images of the members and other shots into palindromes. Other videos also highlighted the "perfect symmetry" of the band by turning images into palindromes, as does ABBA: *The Movie* during many music sequences.[26]

As Derrida notes, sovereignty is round, it is a rounding off. Ipseity—or selfhood, individual identity—is the return of self to self. The palindrome is a structure that goes into reverse halfway "as if to negate itself or to deny a forward progression of time."[27] It is considered to have a type of absolute symmetry: a model of perfection, completion, and changelessness. The theoretical astrophysicist and author Mario Livio defines symmetry as "an immunity to change." Livio states, "Namely you do a certain operation and something does not change, you call that a symmetry" (quoted in Than 2005).[28] The palindrome is an example of a perfect symmetry, with no remainder, residue, or remnant. It "denies the forward progression of time" by turning back and retracing where it has been before. As such, it can represent the image of the perfectly known because it has no movement unaccounted for, no edge that opens into the unknown. Dressed in their usual sparkling white outfits, their relentless performance of the visual palindrome proffers a contained, accounted-for image with no remainders, no loose ends, no dirt, no confusion—just pure, bright, perfect symmetry. Cut down the middle, they all perfectly reflect themselves. Like 1 = 1. Or like "I." They are an identity that is completely contained, perfect, and immune to change.

In the introduction, I discussed the containment of music through the establishment of the work concept and through concert decorum, citing scholars who do not use the term "Real," but who nonetheless draw out related points of music's ambiguity and threats to coherency that I connect with the Real. What have been less discussed are the ways in which the look of the ensemble itself serves to discipline musical sound. I argue elsewhere for the ways in which the ensemble personnel create signs—for example, how the "integrated" band-body of punk that especially brought in female instrumentalists was another way for punk to present its abjection (McMullen 2007). Or my female body, which pluralized the otherwise all-male retro swing ensemble and produced undesirable signs, such as modernity or a lack of unity. Thus, in addition to the other ways musical performances, and in particular reenactments, serve to contain and discipline ambiguity that I discuss in this book, the look of the band also performs such disciplining. One allure of reenacting ABBA in the age of fracture, then, is their staging of the ostensibly perfectly bounded, complete being. The band is a disciplined body that performs the containment of contingency. If ABBA offered a comforting image by corralling themselves into a perfect, neat, tidy, bounded palindrome made of natural, white, middle-class, married heterosexuals—reenacting ABBA brings time into the containment.

ABBA-*Mania All Over Again*

That audiences could "spin their own fantasies around Abba's slightly unreal, almost too perfect appearance" helped ABBA live on in the 1990s and beyond. Disbanding in 1982, Björn Ulvaeus assumed that their era had passed. But ABBA-mania resurfaced in the 1990s and with a vengeance, something Ulvaeus attributed, in large part, to the gay community.[29] Gay clubs and drag queens kept the music alive during the 1980s, according to Ulvaeus. The international appeal that led to hundreds of millions of records sold over the next decades was not based on a love of camp, however. The tributes that would eventually garner audiences in the thousands presented ABBA much as the band was initially marketed: family fun that was "universal." That is, safe, white, middle-class, and heterosexual.

ABBA was a favorite in the gay community, continuing in popularity in dance clubs even after the band's breakup. The band's 1976 international hit "Dancing Queen" tops the list of most "gay song" collections proffered by Internet aficionados. Lyrics declaring "you are the dancing queen" and you "come to look for a king," and melodramatic music underscoring "you're in the mood for a dance," are campy, cheesy fun and were also direct signifiers gay men and lesbians embraced as their own in the 1970s and 1980s. That the music was derided by rock critics as inauthentic, superficial, and commercial could only raise its status in the gay community. Such attributes were always associated with femininity as opposed to the authentic masculine (hetero) man. Self-appointed "dean of American rock critics" Robert Christgau was representative in his evaluation in 1979: "We have met the enemy and they are them" (Christgau 1979).[30] And he was correct if he meant the enemy of white, straight men who established themselves as the arbiters of cultural taste for everyone. But gay men in particular embraced the "cheerful artificiality" as their own (Shewey 2001, 62). Writing in 2015, and referencing the divorces undergone by the two couples before the band broke up, Barry Walters reflects on his own youthful embrace of ABBA: "Gay people particularly respect entertainers who cloak suffering behind carefully constructed artifice because it's a skill most of us are still forced to learn" (Walters 2015).

In addition to filling DJs' rotations, ABBA spawned live drag performances and campy, gay-friendly covers of their music. The English synth-pop duo Erasure released *Abba-esque* in 1992, a video EP that covered four ABBA songs by way of synth-heavy, techno dance beats. Online commentators perhaps best sum up the gay dance club sound signaled by the music: "Every time you listen to this, a little homophobe dies. So listen again." And: "This is gay as hell and I love it so much."[31] The 1994 Australian film *Priscilla, Queen of the Desert* follows three drag queens through the outback and culminates with a drag performance of the song "Mamma Mia." The scene could have been inspired by performances at the Unicorn Hotel in Sydney, a center of the gay scene and host of ABBA nights that began in 1987 ("Björn Thanks Gay Fans" 2011). In the 1970s and 1980s, ABBA, with their cheesy outfits, luminescent stage shows, and Europop/disco dance music, was embraced as sparklingly queer and adored accordingly.

Rigorous tribute bands that played, and continue to play, internationally to tens of thousands of spectators did not highlight the queer elements of ABBA, however; they followed the dictates of Replay. Like the musical *Mamma Mia!*, which opened in 1999, these were live, mainstream performances that did not queer their material. Don Shewey, a reviewer for the *Advocate,* wrote about *Mamma Mia!* in 2001, asking why a gay audience would be interested in it, even though it has no "gay content to speak of." Describing it as a "big, schlocky, fun-for-the-whole-family, Broadway musical," Shewey writes, "Maybe the dirty little secret [*Mamma Mia!* reveals] is that gay taste isn't so different from the mainstream's anymore. [*Mamma Mia!* is not] a cartoonishly trashy campfest. . . . A couple of decades of pop culture have smoothed the sting of camp into the more acceptable flavor of kitsch" (Shewey 2001). Perhaps it is unsurprising that those ABBA revivals that toured internationally, whether as *Mamma Mia!* or the rigorous tribute bands that also began in the 1990s, were not "trashy campfests" but "fun-for-the-whole-family." But in their huge appeal, they also represented a return to a "universalism" that implicitly declared itself in opposition to queer performance.

Two of the top internationally touring ABBA tribute bands, ABBA the Concert and Arrival from Sweden, promote themselves as the closest you will get to experiencing the "real ABBA." Faithful to the dictates of Replay, ABBA the Concert and Arrival from Sweden promote their authenticity in terms of their ability to look and sound just like ABBA and their connection with and sanctioning by the original band. ABBA the Concert has performed for audiences in the tens of thousands at venues such as the Hollywood Bowl in Los Angeles and Highland Park in Chicago.[32] They promote themselves as "the closest performance to Abba that you will ever experience."[33] Arrival from Sweden has visited twenty-plus countries, and they sell up to twenty thousand tickets a night. They claim to bring ABBA "back to life" with "their upbeat, fun and uncanny replication of a real ABBA show, complete with stitch-for-stitch copies of the original stage outfits. . . . With uncannily authentic sound and stage presence, [. . .] identical arrangements, costumes and choreography, [. . .] Arrival from Sweden is virtually a 70's ABBA concert."[34] Both bands have "original" instrumentalists from ABBA. ABBA the Concert asserts that on every tour "the show has always consisted of two ORIGINAL MEMBERS of the original ABBA rhythm section." Arrival from Sweden, in fact, boasts the same musicians who tour with ABBA the Concert.[35] In 2013, Arrival from Sweden claimed to be "the only group who [received] an unreleased ABBA song directly from ABBA (the song was released worldwide in 2009)" and to have "the exclusive right to copy ABBA's original outfits [and that] has the exclusive permission and trademark ABBA in their production name ABBASOLUTELY—permitted by Universal."[36] While these claims have since been removed from their website, their emphasis on their connection to the original ABBA via the original musicians and their assertion that "it's hard to believe that it's not the real ABBA on stage" remain the same.[37]

These bands prize the same types of fetishizing detail observed in the Musical Box, wearing the same outfits and attempting to look as much as possible as the original. They bring in as many of the original ancillary people as possible, including costume designers and backup musicians. Arrival from Sweden has the blessing of the original band, receiving special gifts and licensing. And the bands highlight the uncanniness of their performance, telling the audience it will be "just like seeing a real ABBA show." The allure of the show is not only the performance of ABBA's music, but also the precision with which the past is brought to life. While gay fans may prize the surface and inauthenticity that is opposed to hetero-male hierarchies, ABBA reenactments perform the haunthenticity of Replay by focusing on this surface in terms of the material details of the band. It is a type of surface authenticity that is not queer at all.

That is to say that when Arrival from Sweden perform, they re-perform the same, dull nonchoreography of the original. While Agnetha and Anni-Frid were certainly lively during concerts, running across the stage high kicking, and Agnetha inevitably turning around to display her famous derriere, these movements can barely, if at all, rise to the term "choreography." The background singers had very basic choreography, which Arrival reenacts, but otherwise, there is not much to latch onto. Without the power of the original group, the tribute band singers mostly sway awkwardly from side to side. They hew to this detail, rather than update the performance to be more in line with contemporary progeny of

ABBA's glitzy, showbizzy camp—acts such as Lady Gaga, Katy Perry, and almost every other stylized pop megastar of today. Arrival does not offer any campiness, any knowing wink, but only an earnest tribute band trying to sing those harmonies in tune and bobbing like middle-school teenagers at their first dance. And while the band claims that it will be "just like seeing a real Abba show," they can't come close to capturing a complete show like the Musical Box. ABBA shows were *more* complex than those of Genesis, including mini-orchestras, two drummers, backup singers, a pop horn section, and other characters. For example, the song "I'm Just a Marionette," as part of the mini-rock-opera-within-a-concert, "The Girl with the Golden Hair," could be described as progressive rock with its characters in costume and its grand use of orchestration and inspiration from classical music. But re-creating ABBA precisely is not about such details as re-creating the orchestra or the harlequin who introduces "I'm Just a Marionette." Fans of ABBA aren't looking for authenticity in the same place as Genesis fans. It is more the wholesome, clean, family fun of the two heterosexual couples that seems to be the "real" ABBA.

Thus, in a compilation video of performances of "Dancing Queen" during an international tour taking Arrival from Sweden throughout Europe and the United States, children and an occasional adult are brought onstage to dance with the band, without a drag queen in sight. Gay ABBA fans of the 1990s, 2000s, and today might want to attend one of these grand events, but they will be "part of it" only to the extent that they embrace the "universal," middle-class family ethos. Still studying the question, a 2014 article asks "Why Are Abba So Popular?" The author suggests an answer: "If rock 'n' roll is about escape and outsiderdom then Abba's pop songs excavate the dreams and disappointments of those who never wanted to rebel" (Harrison 2014). It is the music of the center. Which makes me want to return to that "dirty little secret." Is it true that "gay taste" isn't so different from the mainstream's anymore? That a couple of decades have "smoothed the sting" into something "more acceptable"?

Can (should) "queer" go mainstream? Tick, the gay father in *Priscilla,* tried to wear khakis briefly, in an attempt to be what he thought was a "normal" dad. But it was his eight-year-old son, Benjamin, who unquestioningly understood queer as tantamount to dad. If the storyline expressed hope for a more enlightened generation in the years to come, it was not fully realized. Mainstream acceptance of gay men and women has been less embracing of difference than Benjamin's. Gay rights have made tremendous strides in the twenty-first century, but many have questioned and critiqued the turn away from an emphasis on queer difference and toward a focus on "just like you" that has characterized gay activism since the 1990s. Verta Taylor and Leila J. Rupp write that "the shift to a rhetoric of 'marriage equality,' rather than 'same-sex' or 'gay' marriage, indicates a desire to take the messiness of sex out of the picture, to remove the specter of homosex from the hominess of marriage. Just as the main pro-gay-marriage organization has the bland name 'Human Rights Campaign,' effectively nullifying the specificity of queerness in the very title, so too does 'marriage equality' implicitly de-queer our inclusion in that institution, making heterosexual unions the default point of comparison" (Taylor and Rupp 2014). "Equality" is forged under the aegis of heteropatriarchy. We are all the same in our reproduction of patriarchy, monogamy, the nuclear family, and consumerism.

And in our allegiance to whiteness as universal. The whiteness of ABBA hardly needs mentioning. Robert Christgau averred in 1976 that ABBA's "disinclination to sing like Negroes" probably "reassures the Europopuli" (Christgau 1976). And reflecting on the band years later, Barry Walters describes the music as "some of the brightest whiteness pop has ever known." I make a distinction between constructions of race (for which I use the terms "whiteness" and "blackness") and traditions. That ABBA's music is primarily influenced by European forms such as Schlager or Europop demonstrates the traditions of music from which they draw. For me, the "whiteness" is in the claim of, and desire for, universality that makes this tradition and their white skin "unmarked" or "invisible." As Maureen T. Reddy writes, "Whiteness is constructed in a way that makes it possible to think that there is *no such thing* as 'white people'" (Reddy 1998, 60, emphasis in original). The white person, and in particular, the white male, becomes the universal, unmarked subject, invisible and pure: "whiteness defined as *absence*, as purity" (61).

Through their ostensibly "accurate" reenactments that perform the "real" ABBA without any "campy" difference, the earnest ABBA tributes perform, then, what is given truth status in mainstream culture. The heterosexuality of the band is taken as the real performance, now brought forward without any "signifying" in the form of camp or drag. The campy aspects of the original band are taken as an excess of meaning, and the heterosexual aspect is taken as the "real" meaning. The reenactments perform the original band's stated objective of hypervisibility, their straightforward surface that "aims to please." And this hypervisibility hides (again) in plain sight what is invisible: white, middle-class, heteronormativity as the center by which all others are measured and must obey if they want to receive any benefits. As two white, heterosexual couples who were "good" and "clean," ABBA performed the hypervisible norm. Tracing race and sex norms from the nineteenth century, Reddy writes that the "notion of 'dirt' figured largely in the vocabulary of sex, with some heterosexual sex—marital, reproductive, between whites—seen as 'clean' and other heterosexual sex (along with all homosexual sex) cast as 'dirty.' This rather quaint notion of 'clean' sex is as foundational to even contemporary constructions of heterosexuality as is the fantasy of the 'purity' of whiteness to constructions of race" (60). The class aspect of this clean/dirty binary must also be foregrounded. Even if you were white and heterosexual, if you were poor, you were unclean. Nadine Hubbs describes the "media's hunger for images of white working people as rednecks and 'trash'—replete with dirty kids, clothes on the line, and cars up on blocks" (2014, 62).

The fetish certainly pastes over the lack of talent of the tribute bands. Unable to reach the heights of the original band, whether the astounding intonation of ABBA's vocalists or the simple *je ne sais quoi* of a band that rose to international fame, it is exceptionally rare for a tribute band or tribute band member to reach that height.[38] Thus, fetishizing costumes and body movements "gives body" to this lack. But the preponderance of and immense popularity of such clone bands belies this as the only lack. These bands were also responding to an audience need.

Beginning from playing the music they loved, musicians moved into activities that exceeded their desire to play a band's music. They began to focus on the uncanny capturing of every detail of the performance. They began to perform "perfection," containment, and control. They were "performing security"—performances of the perfectly known with zero contingency. A propos of the clone according to Baudrillard, they "monstrously" parodied the mirror stage (2006 [1994], 97). The monstrosity was in the literalness of the project. In trying to actually *become* the image in cloning, one transforms desire from a structure of identity to something one actually fulfills. Especially in the Musical Box, we see a representation (wanting to) become Genesis itself—what is in the mirror and what is outside the mirror are the same. They are one. There is no difference. The signifier becomes the signified. It is an Oedipal scenario where rather than overthrowing or somehow assimilating or even identifying with the father, now one (after garnering his permission) literally *becomes* him. And this unleashes the uncanny, with unexpected consequences.

THE GLITCH IN THE FANTASY

The Uncanny of the Double

Human existence is uncanny and still without meaning.

Nietzsche, Thus Spoke Zarathustra: First Part

It may be only a coincidence that just as earnest tribute bands were exploding on the live music scene, biological cloning was a hot-button issue. As scientists attempted to clone animals, the prospect of reproductive cloning consumed much of the nightly news in the mid-1990s.[39] A considerable part of the debate centered on the ethical issues of creating life that was not the "natural" product of a "father" and a "mother" and how this cloned material would be used. These debates often took the form of "science" versus "family values," including concerns that cloning would "eliminate the need for fathers" and the traditional heterosexual, monogamous union consecrated in matrimony. Even without the predictions of the redundancy of men, however, discussion of the ethics of using living human material for therapeutic purposes, as in the case of stem cell research, consumed the airwaves.

As the epigraph at the beginning of this chapter shows, clone bands also elicited comments on life, death, and mortality. And while science may have other motives and uses for cloning cells, in the tribute band we have the pure, unadulterated fantasy of re-creating the identical, both as an end in itself (to overcome the introduction of difference) and as a way to triumph over the passage of time. The clone band does not avoid the philosophical conundrum raised by the clone, however: the problem of the double. While the clone strives to be one again and wants to avoid the issue of two, it is perpetually confronted by its twiceness, its status as double. And the double calls into question our very belief about ourselves. As Sigmund Freud puts it, "A person may identify himself with another and so become unsure of his true self; or he may substitute the other's self for his own" (Freud 2003 [1919], 142). The presumed coherency of one's self, therefore, becomes deeply uncertain. Further, the double presents the "uncanny harbinger" of our own death; we see in the double the *objectness* of ourselves: "other" and separate, not all and immortal. This is why Freud, Otto Rank, and Ernst Jentsch all place the uncanny in the realm of that which evokes fear and dread and cite the double—"the appearance of persons who have to be regarded as identical because they look alike"—as eliciting the strongest sense of the uncanny (11).

If the double appears to us as the uncanny harbinger of our own death and if we take the practice of the rigorous tribute band as the creation of the uncanny double, why do we seem so especially interested in reminding ourselves of our own death at the turn of the millennium? With the loss of the aura of the artwork that Benjamin describes, why is it that this loss was "filled in" with the different magic of the uncanny found in these rigorously mimetic reenactments? In proposing an answer, I revisit the theory of the uncanny as initially theorized by Freud.

Much of Freud's essay on the uncanny is taken up with a thorough dissection of the word *unheimlich* (which we translate into English as "uncanny"). He begins with the root word, *heimlich* ("familiar" in English), which is deeply inflected with connotations of the comforts of domesticity and home. He presents a barrage of synonyms and sample phrases that suggest the ease and security of a safe, secure, established home life: "tame, domesticated, friendly, cozily homely, quiet contentment, secure protection, comfortable repose, pleasant homeliness, very comfortable and familiar, true ease, at ease in the house, dreamy and restful as a lullaby, wonderfully restful." The synonyms suggest a safe and comfortable space, indeed, even a nest of protection, ease, and rest. The second definition of heimlich, however, is something "concealed, kept hidden, behind someone's back." In a sense then, unheimlich can be understood as the opposite of both the familiar and of something concealed—as the unfamiliar revealed. But because heimlich can mean both familiar and hidden, Freud ultimately argues that unheimlich is that which is taken as familiar made unfamiliar. The familiar, the perfectly safe, cozy, protected, and assumed becomes terrifyingly unfamiliar.

I find the strong emphasis on homeyness in the root word, *heimlich*, important. As many scholars have noted, the pursuit of nostalgia is often the search for ground and home in an unpredictable world (for example, Butt 2008 and Boym 2001). Home is also identity. What is more familiar than our own self? We take this self for granted. And we take others' selves for granted in the same way. But what happens when this home, this identity, this familiarity that we think we know so well and can depend on is suddenly rendered terrifyingly unfamiliar? What happens when what we took for a certainty turns out, in fact, to be entirely uncertain?

I want to turn to a personal experience I had with the uncanny to highlight this particular breach. During a postdoctoral fellowship in Ontario, Canada, my schoolteacher housemate asked me one afternoon if I would help her carry some material from her car. Upon later reflection, it was true she had a glint in her eye, but I was utterly unprepared for what I encountered in the passenger seat of her car. Seated there was a man, and as I approached him, I let out a scream as I discovered this gentleman in his dark suit and hat was a life-size man made of papier mâché. We dragged him in, and for months he sat in the front living room. For at least four or five days when I would come down the stairs and see the legs and especially the shoes that were of the 1940s leather variety, I would let out a small yelp before I could help myself. I found myself staring at those shoes, with the profound sense of the uncanny still reverberating in my being. Clearly, I had had the experience of the uncanny described by Ernst Jentsch of taking something that was inanimate for animate. While it took many days for me not to startle every time I saw the man sitting in the living room, eventually the sense of the uncanny diminished. What lasted the longest, however, was the sight of his shoes. The shoes were absolutely the strongest elicitors of my feelings of the uncanny. For a long time, just looking at them gave me the feeling that there was a person there. Of all items of clothing, shoes remain the most "themselves" whether occupied or not. Clothes do not animate themselves; hats will rest on a table or hook; but shoes remain in the functional state, on the floor. If one sees only shoes poking out from underneath a curtain or from a doorway, one does not know whether there is a person attached to them or not. In looking at empty shoes, one sees the absence of the wearer and may have the fleeting thought that the person may never return to fill them again, vanishing from the earth through their death. In my experience with the papier mâché man, I could feel how I imputed significance to those shoes, how I constructed a living being who inhabited them. The uncanny then was the realization that what I had taken to be real was a construction of my own mind. The uncanny is that feeling of the rug being completely pulled out—this "person" was merely my own projection.

This sense of the uncanny suggests a different valence on Freud's discussion of the "omnipotence of thoughts"—the belief that through our thoughts we can make inanimate objects come alive. Freud recounts his work with a woman who disclosed that until she was quite old she believed that if she concentrated hard enough she would be able to bring her dolls to life. I would argue that our relationship to the world is one where we regularly believe in the omnipotence of thoughts without realizing the extent to which we are bringing our world to life. We imagine the people in our world. Certainly these people exist; but they do not, in fact, exist in the ways we think. We fill them out. My sensation of the uncanny was the momentary shattering of this fantasy, of realizing the extent to which I manufacture this identity. Because this point is so important to my argument, I want to give one other example, this time from Freud himself.

In a footnote to his essay on the "Uncanny," Freud recounts an experience he had while sitting alone in his sleeping compartment in a train. Just as the train made an unexpected lurch, the door of an adjacent toilet opened and an "elderly gentleman in a dressing gown and travelling cap" entered Freud's quarters. Freud's immediate reaction to this man was to deem him "thoroughly unpleasant." As he jumped from his seat to put the man "right," he realized that he was looking at his own image in the mirror bolted to the door that had swung open when the train pitched forward. In the brief moment of the uncanny, when Freud realized that the man he had instantly had opinions about was in fact himself, there was the millisecond sensation of "intellectual uncertainty"[40]—the moment when the unquestioned assumptions he had instantaneously made about this man were revealed to not be based in reality (who the man was) but in Freud's own projection of who this man was. The man, as it turned out, was Freud himself and therefore not the "other" about which a host of information had sprung into Freud's mind upon his initial sighting (enough for him to deem the man "thoroughly unpleasant"). I want to emphasize a definition of the uncanny as that sense which arises when we realize that we have in fact imputed a being, and then we glimpse the power of this conjuring: what we were taking as reality (our perception of an other) is revealed as fantasy (the workings of our mind). The uncanny is the realization about our entire world order that all of our assumptions about reality are in fact imputations, not the solid facts we take them to be.

If we understand the uncanny as the realization of how we "impute significance" rather than "perceive reality," we can see that the uncanny is that moment when our intellectual certainty about ourselves as subjects is revealed to be deeply uncertain. In glimpsing our imputation, the "void which is the subject" comes to light. The familiar subject (ourselves) is revealed as deeply unfamiliar, indeed, as an unknowable emptiness that has been pasted over by our fantasy.

In my view, the fascination with the double at the turn of the millennium is precisely this titillation that brings us closer to the familiar/unfamiliar knowledge that we both deeply crave, yet intensely fear. These strict reenactments attempt to provide the comforts of the perfectly familiar where identity is known, decided, safe, and comfortable. But in creating this double, they inevitably call forth the uncanny, and it is through the uncanny of the double that we glimpse the terrifying absence of identity and the subject to which we have only imputed presence and solidity. For indeed, don't the perpetual life-and-death rumors about celebrities reveal our understanding of the uncanny of identity, the sense in which its familiarity is not quite as familiar as we would like it? Living celebrities are perpetually rumored to be dead: Paul McCartney, Justin Bieber, Miley Cyrus. Dead celebrities are rumored to be alive: Elvis Presley, Tupac Shakur, Michael Jackson. Iconic identities are representatives of what is true for all of us: that there is the inability to pin down identity/being and that we can disappear at any time. And our hypervisible world of Facebook and videologs only makes our lives and deaths more uncanny and difficult to differentiate. Human existence is uncanny in that the self cannot really be found and ensured—it appears familiar, and yet it is deeply unknown and ungraspable, uncontainable through meaning yet interacting with others via meaning (culture and language). Eliciting the uncanny is a way to flirt with this knowledge. It is titillating to brush up against this emptiness, this truth that we both want and fear. Tribute bands promote their uncanny performances because the uncanny gives us this charge. As I will argue in chapter 4, this emptiness that is revealed through the uncanny is a way toward accepting the void that is the subject. The ways in which the uncanny inevitably erupts through rigorous reenactment offer a chance to recognize and come to terms with the Real. A full recognition of this Real would dissolve our root anxieties that produce the construction of otherness and its concomitant prejudice.

LONGING FOR THE REAL

> What we are really interested in is re-creating
> the experience as real as it could be.
>
> *Sébastien Lamothe, The Musical Box*

These clone bands would appear to be classic embodiments and symptoms of the postmodern—depthless simulacra that allow for no interpretation and therefore, to follow Jameson, lack a real sense of historicity. The radically rigorous mimesis of these reenactments, however, is better understood as an attempt to answer the crises of postmodernity at the turn of the millennium, rather than as an example of the depthlessness and lack of historicity of postmodernity itself. The Musical Box performs a return to a romantic idea of the work that is so Real it is outside of interpretation; Arrival from Sweden and ABBA the Concert create a fantasy of a "return" to a (white, heterosexual) world without difference. Especially in regard to the Musical Box, these tributes are not producing simulacra (copies with no original), but striving to be that original. TMB attempts to return a type of depth to a world that has become only "texts." This "depth" does not elicit interpretation. Rather than a world that, as Fredric Jameson describes, feels "too close in," clone bands perceive a world of too much distance, which impels their retreat from interpretation. That is, even with photographs, sound recordings, film, and video, it seems we still can't get "close enough." The world continues to elude our grasp. TMB attempts to take their representation of Genesis and make it Genesis, just as Kaspar Hauser attempted to turn his symbolic representation (his name) into grass—representation made Real, signifier made signified. As will be argued in the next chapter, these rigorous reenactments do not in fact want to encounter this Realness that they proclaim to seek, however. Fear keeps them from ever (intentionally) encountering this Real.

In chapter 2, I discuss in more detail this search for, and deep fear of, the Real. In attempting to cohere a fixed, locatable, and permanent identity, we end up pushing "the Real" farther away. In looking at the film *Synecdoche, New York* and the reenactment of Ziggy Stardust by the performance art duo Forsyth and Pollard, I demonstrate how capturing the Real through Replay serves to perfectly keep us from ever encountering it. The perfect performative, the once-behaved behavior, and identity without difference are all patent fantasies.[41] But as I will demonstrate, the subject is much more comfortable with fantasy than it is with reality.

TWO

Capturing the Real

Ziggy's Strain and Old Hells

So I turned myself to face me
but I've never caught a glimpse.
I watch the ripples change their size
but never leave the stream
of warm impermanence.
Turn and face the strain
Changes.
David Bowie

[The] first performances in the early seventies were not even documented because most of us believed that any documentation—by video or photos—could not be a substitute for the real experience: seeing it live. Later on, though, our attitude changed. We felt the need to leave some trace of the events for a larger audience.
Abramović 2007, 9

Tom Wolfe famously described the 1970s as the "Me Decade" when "Me" became a site of active exploration and invention. As Wolfe wrote in his now famous 1976 essay in *New York Magazine*, "The new alchemical dream is: changing one's personality—remaking, remodeling, elevating, and polishing one's very *self* . . . and observing, studying, and doting on it. (Me!)" (Wolfe 1976; italic in original). The social and political work of the 1960s had met a violent pause, if not end, and the culture moved from collective concerns to individual ones. The project now was one's self: finding it; adorning it; freeing it. For some, this represented immense liberation. The feminist and gay rights movements grew from the Civil Rights struggles of the 1950s and 1960s and incorporated the identity-esteeming proclivities of the 1970s. The personal was political, and expression of one's "true self" had societal implications. For others, this represented a more frightening fracture of former "knowns." Now even the self was up for grabs.

This chapter examines the live capture of such self-exploration in the performance art duo Forsyth and Pollard's reenactment of David Bowie's 1973 live performance of "A Rock 'n' Roll Suicide." In the previous chapter, I described tribute bands' performances of the perfectly known and 1 = 1 identity in an age of insecurity and fracture. I described them as "comfort performances" of zero contingency that also perpetuated values, such as white, heterosexual, middle-class subjects as the universal norm. In the 1970s, David Bowie was an important expediter of the age of fracture. His performance of multiple selves, including his sexual and gender ambiguity, unmoored pillars of identity taken for granted in earlier decades. Described as a "conceptual art project who had become a rock 'n' roll star" (Doggett 2012, 173), Bowie advocated an embrace of fragmentation in the loss of society's "gods." During the same period, another offspring of conceptual art, performance art, radically contested the "work" and "great artist" concepts in art that traced back to the romantic period. The 1990s brought anxiety over the loss of 1970s performance art, however, and a move to preserve such ephemeral works with reenactments. With its turn toward preservative reenactment, discussions about performance art exemplified a return to a romantic ideology by taking nineteenth-century classical music as its model, particularly as articulated by performance artist Marina Abramović.

The previous chapter also touched on the fear of loss and the yearning to connect with the Real, which I will develop in this chapter. Performance art has often been described by artists and critics in terms of the Real. While tribute bands may long to have a certain past again, performance art reenactments often stress the project of capturing the Real in itself. In order to elucidate more fully what I mean by the pursuit of the Real through reenactment, I closely examine a film, though one that traces the efforts of a theater director's live reenactment: Charlie Kaufman's *Synecdoche, New York.* I link such capturing of the Real through performance to a turn away from "meaning" and toward "being" in art, looking especially at Susan Sontag's famous essay "Against Interpretation," which I contextualize within a mid-century longing for the Real. I proceed to a discussion of performance art, in particular its radical beginnings and its professed focus on loss and disappearance, before examining performance art's turn to reenactment in the 1990s and early 2000s. In looking at David Bowie's artistic practice in the 1970s and comparing it to the 1998 reenactment of him under the auspices of performance art, I demonstrate how a certain artistic radicalism of the 1970s changed into a conservatism and border-control mentality characteristic of the 1990s. To embrace the Real demands accepting loss, *really.* As this chapter shows, such loss is still deemed too high a price to pay. Abramović's assertions, in particular, demonstrate a turn away from the radicalism of ephemerality and nonlocatability back to the "work" and the "great artist." This move is part of a larger discomfort with the subjective and a need to have an object in order to know.

THE REAL ON OUR TERMS

On the one hand, the "reality" of life is something we find irritating and would like to avoid, particularly the reality of most other beings and their desires. The modern Western world is increasingly sanitized of "unnecessary" human interaction. We shop online (for products and people to date), mail packages from our home, and receive groceries there. As other human beings seem to increasingly stand in the way of our desires, we may continually "postpone" actually encountering an other. TV, movies, and fiction dominate our lives, as modern characters going back to Madame Bovary (in regard to romance novels) to Frank Cross in *Scrooged* (memories of "his" childhood all come from TV shows) attest. Online sites such as Second Life give us unprecedented control over "our" identity, allowing us to choose our race, sex, sexuality, and economic status and thus how we imagine we are understood by others. We curate our life for others on Facebook and Instagram. Indeed, we can have myriad online interactions and identities that will never lead to actual physical meetings. Even online dating can turn into a perpetual quest where the endpoint of actually meeting a partner is endlessly deferred in the fantasy that maybe the next person will be "the one." The fantasy of whom this person might be can far outweigh the actual encounter with the person and all of his or her mundane imperfections. If we never fully engage with the real, messy person, we can continue to believe that perfect joy and romance do indeed exist. This way of being, where the "real point will never be reached" has been described by Adorno, Žižek, and many others. As K. W. Jeter writes in his novel *Noir,* "always at the brink of satisfaction but somehow [they] never get there. Because if they did, the game would be over and everybody would go home" (quoted in Shaviro 2003, 250).

These examples display a basic aversion for encountering the unexpected, unmediated, and uncontrolled contingencies of being alive among other human beings in a modern world that increasingly eliminates these contingencies. Our biggest aversion, of course, is to the Real of death. In fact, whether we think we are encountering the Real or not, the Real will indeed *encounter us* at the time of our death. At that moment, in the midst of our fantasies about ourselves and others, death will interrupt us. The Real, far from being impossible, will assure us of its existence irrespective of our symbolic attempts to master it. As Borges reminded us, "The world, unfortunately, is real." Death is real. And so is life (though we may be distracting ourselves from its reality). While we want the connection of "real life," we don't want its difficulty. Our fear of death, of the uncanny absence of our very self, and of all the contingencies of being alive, propels our fantasies of containment and control. But our fantasies leave us alienated and impoverished because they disconnect us from the here and now. This impoverishment in turn propels a desire for the Real, despite our fears of it. Therefore, I want to make clear that I agree with Borges that the world is real, with the best example being the fact that death will cut into our life. I also believe that we can more directly experience this "realness" of the world, as explained more in the conclusion. But "the Real" is also an idea—a construction built on our anxiety regarding the realness of the world. Perhaps the best way to describe this is that when the Real is an idea—something we fear or desire—it is a construction. The brute facts of life: not only impermanence, sickness, and death (which we see because we generally don't like these things and cannot control them), but also the quiddity, the facticity of life—what we tend to take for granted—I am also calling the Real. I maintain this terminology primarily because I do not want to perpetuate the ideology that we encounter only a symbolic world.

So to return to the other hand: we desire the Real and set out to capture it. We attempt to capture life as it slips away—to fend off the impermanent nature of life. In the late nineteenth and early twentieth centuries, photographs were described as ways to "halt the passing of time in its tracks" (McClintock 1995, 124) and audio technology as a way to hear the voices of the dead (Sterne, 2003). As such, they were marketed as devices able to capture the Real—the endless flow of time, impermanence—and to fend off the finality of the most dreaded instance of the Real, death. With the rise of the Internet in the 1990s, this desire to capture the Real took on an ever more frantic pace. In order to verify our life to ourselves, to ensure that we did not, indeed, miss it, we must capture it. And yet, we still always feel as if life is moving very fast and we are, in fact, missing it.[1] Although we no longer have to wait for our photos to be developed or engage with the irritating materiality of buying and filling a scrapbook, we still are not able to capture our life fast enough to feel as if we are not missing it. Therefore, we try harder to capture it. Because indeed, the world around us, unreported, unrecorded, but privately experienced, certainly *that* could not be the life that is passing us by.

The reenactments I describe in this chapter continue the fantasy of the photograph and the recording. I argue that they exemplify the quixotic wish that if we can now, this time, capture our past in its *realness,* in its *liveness,* in its ostensible brute thingness as an *im*mediate "hunk of time," we will now (finally!) connect with the Real and heal our sense of separation. The tendency is to dismiss the liveness of the real encounter in favor of "liveness" as an object with some distance and separation, controlled, and pointed to by an artist. This desire stems from a way of conceiving the past described by W. G. Sebald in his novel *Austerlitz,* when the narrator states: "Even now, when I try to remember . . . , the darkness does not lift but becomes heavier as I think how little we can hold in mind, how everything is constantly lapsing into oblivion with every extinguished life, how the world is, as it were, draining itself, in that the history of countless places and objects which themselves have no power of memory is never heard, never described or passed on" (Sebald 2011 [2001], 24). Avery Gordon offers a different perspective in her book *Ghostly Matters,* in which she describes the haunting of the past—stories that will not go away because they have not been examined, healed, and worked through. The irony here is that the "loss" Sebald describes is based on a majoritarian construction of the world that, in fact, avoids much of the past. I argue that the strict reenactment of Forsyth and Pollard does not recognize or certainly does not underline how "performance remains," as Rebecca Schneider puts it, but rather is a type of hypervisibility that continues to construct the past as uncannily gone. As such, despite the "liveness" found in live reenactment, in attempting this capture we succeed only in pushing what we're after further into the distance. Charlie Kaufman's 2008 film, *Synecdoche, New York,* offers a brilliant elucidation of this phenomenon, illustrating the relationship between identity, fantasy, live reenactment, and the Real that has characterized turn-of-the-millennium postmodernity.

Capturing the Real: Kaufman's Synecdoche, New York

In Kaufman's film, theater director Caden Cotard wants to put his "real self" into something, and he pursues that venture in a particularly postmodern manner.

Unlike the patently nonmodern Kaspar Hauser discussed in chapter 1, who attempted to turn the Signifier/Meaning/the Symbolic into the Signified/Being/the Real by planting his name in grass, Cotard attempts to locate and secure the Real through its (Symbolic) capture: the precise live reenactment of life as a theater piece. In his increasingly desperate attempts to capture the "brutal truth," Cotard reenacts his own life as it continues to slip by.

The film traces the decades-long obsessions of Cotard (played by Philip Seymour Hoffman), offering us a protagonist who both intensely fears the Real and desperately longs for it. The film is described as a "comedy," and it is funny in the Kaufmanesque way of *Being John Malkovich* and *The Eternal Sunshine of the Spotless Mind*; but it is also dark and ultimately, profoundly moving. I divide the film into three sections, with the first section offering a meditation on Cotard's fear of the sudden encroachment of the Real. In the beginning of the film, where we witness Cotard in primarily domestic situations with his painter wife and five-year-old daughter, death or serious illness lurk everywhere: in the color of one's stool, the dilation of one's pupils, and the terrifyingly upbeat pharmaceutical commercials directed toward cancer patients. Cotard is presented as a hypochondriac, obsessed with death, but he is also beset with a series of "real" symptoms. His gums begin to disintegrate, pustules break out on his face, he loses his ability to generate saliva and tears, his urine turns the color of Pepsi. These outbreaks of the Real are contrasted with his work as an artist. He tells his therapist, "I think [my wife] is right when she says I'm not doing anything real." After the therapist asks him, "What would be real?," he answers, "I think I'm going to die." In the face of this Real, he wants to do something important with his life.

Shortly thereafter, he receives a MacArthur grant; and the film moves into its second phase, where Cotard's concerns with the Real turn to preoccupations with fantasy (despite his claims to the contrary). The MacArthur grant is the screenwriter's device to allow Cotard freedom from the limits of money and time (not that Charlie Kaufman treasures realism in his screenplays, and indeed, even a MacArthur grant wouldn't fund Cotard's massive, decades-long project). And what does Cotard want to do with his freedom? Again speaking with his therapist, he tells her that this definitive masterwork will be a "theater piece—something big and true and tough. Finally put my real self into something." "What is your real self, do you think?" she asks. "I don't know, yet." At the first meeting with the actors, he tells them the brute fact of life: "I will be dying and so will you." It is this realness, this everythingness "that . . . I want to explore." Thus, there is no script for this play; it is an attempt to capture actual "real life." The actors will enact the reality of New York, the set of which is being erected in a giant warehouse.

As the work progresses, Cotard is driven on by the pursuit of the Real, which he is never quite able to capture. By year seventeen of the project (which has yet to be staged for an audience), Cotard tells the ever-growing cast that he "won't settle for anything less than the brutal truth. Brutal. Brutal." The latest tactic he introduces is handing out notes for the actors that will set the stage for that day—"Today I felt a lump in my breast," "Today my wife had a miscarriage," "I keep biting my lip"—events that highlight the vulnerable materiality of the body. And from that day forward, Cotard himself will not be exempt from this brutal truth. He will hire an actor to play him, someone who is to re-create his life on the set, which is slowly growing into a "life-size replica of Manhattan." With this, we enter the third and final section of the film. After Cotard brings himself into the piece, the staging of the Real as a reenactment of (his) life begins.

In the attempt to move closer to what he imagines as the Real, Cotard begins to stage his own past, traipsing behind it. He eventually adds another actor to play himself directing himself. Yet with all of this effort, Cotard is still not catching what he is after. The horizon of the Real beckons, but forever eludes him. He moves further and further from the action as he is left watching a character playing himself directing a character playing himself. This vertiginous representation within the representation takes place as another warehouse is built in the warehouse and then another and then another, all seen on a map that includes another minimap, which contains another minimap. In the effort to capture "real life," the representations move us farther away from the epicenter rather than closer in.

Within all of this chasing of the Real, however, it is the Real itself that keeps breaking into the fantasy. Over the course of the "rehearsals," which go on for decades without an audience,[2] the Real consistently breaks into the pursuit of capturing it. The character who is playing Caden falls in love with the "real" Hazel, not the "character Hazel," and at one point becomes heartbroken and really jumps to his death—despite the fact that Caden was pulled away from the ledge when his heart was broken by Hazel and he stood at the precipice. Sickness, old age, and death make their mark on the cast. Caden's father, famous (now ex-)wife, mother, daughter, and lover all die during the course of the rehearsals. And at the end of the film, the Real literally invades the warehouse when a war that had been raging outside of its walls breaks in and destroys much of the set and kills most of the actors. The final scenes are of Caden touring the warehouse filled with *really* dead actors. At this point, the elderly Caden has relinquished his role as director and is playing the part of Ellen, a cleaning lady whom he had indeed impersonated in "real life" to clean and therefore snoop in the apartment of his ex-wife. As he ambles and later drives a motorized cart through the ruins of the ravaged warehouse, the new director (Ellen, the cleaning lady, playing "Cotard") speaks into an earpiece, feeding him his thoughts and telling him what to do and say.

> What was once before you, an exciting and mysterious future is now behind you, lived, understood, disappointing. You realize you are not special. You have struggled into existence and are now slipping silently out of it. This is everyone's experience. Every single one. The specifics hardly matter. Everyone is everyone. So you are Adele, Hazel, Claire, Olive. You are Ellen. All her meager sadnesses are yours. All her loneliness. The gray, straw-like hair. Her red, raw hands. It's yours. It is time for you to understand this. Walk. As the people who adore you stop adoring you, as they die, as they move on, as you shed them, as you shed your beauty, your youth, as the world forgets you, as you recognize your transience, as you begin to lose your characteristics one by one, as you learn there is no one watching you, as there never was, you think only about driving. Not coming from anyplace, not arriving anyplace, just driving, counting off time. Now you are here. It's 7:43. Now you are here. It's 7:44. Now you are gone.

He encounters a fellow survivor, a woman who had played Ellen's mother in a dream. He sits down next to her, and she listens to and comforts him. As he listens to "his" thoughts provided by the director and speaks the words he is told, he has a sudden inspiration again as to what he wants to do with his theater piece. The scene is slowly fading to white; he gets a small burst of energy as he begins to tell "his" mother of this new insight; as the scene fades further into white, we hear the director's voice gently and brutally instruct him: "die." The scene has become completely white, and the film ends with Jon Brion's gentle song "Little Person," all that remains. Still fully in the midst of his own fantasy, Cotard is interrupted suddenly, gently, brutally by his own death.[3]

As the Buddhists say, "Death is real and comes without warning." When Cotard was interrupted by his death, he was just ratcheting up his ideas about the piece as he had countless times through the decades. All of the loves, the struggles, and the successes and failures are, in the moment of death, revealed to be nothing more than a dream. The events of his life continually disappeared, and he could not capture them. His identity—that which he had cherished, invested in, and taken so seriously throughout the years—slowly disintegrated. As he approached his death, he was both the character Ellen and (the character?) Cotard. She ("Cotard") tells him ("Ellen") that everybody is everybody, echoing an earlier character who had divined that "everything is everything." Everyone's experience is essentially the same. We all have our desires and our fears, our obsessions, our compulsion to prove ourselves, but in the end our characteristics and obsessions begin to dissolve into the Real that we have both longed for and been afraid to confront. Not that we have longed for death, but death is a manifestation of the impermanence that characterizes the Real.

The shadow of the Real hangs over every event of this film. We can never get lost completely in the desires and fantasies of the characters; we can never take their aspirations and struggles as the "real" content of the film. At first, Cotard is in constant fear of the Real as he obsesses over death and illness. When he later has the chance to be consumed with fantasy, the work is cast in the shadow of his statement that "someday I will die" and therefore must do something important with his life. And while his fantasy takes on the project of chasing the Real, it actually serves to keep his distance from it. Cotard's fantasy could be characterized as the pursuit, following Huyssen, of "total recall." Cotard remains "always at the brink of satisfaction but somehow never [gets] there. Because if [he] did, the game would be over and everybody would go home." In his misguided attempts to create something "real" and find his "real" self, Cotard establishes a fantasy that will never end. For indeed, in its Adornian pseudoactivity, there is no end to the quest for total recall. Cotard will never be able to capture all of Manhattan, all of the lives in it, all of his life. But this is what he construes as the Real—the Real cannot simply be lived, for that is too ephemeral, unlocatable, and most important, unsymbolizable. For Cotard, the Real must be found, captured, stabilized, and staged. The film is then, in part, a meditation on our deep discomfort with impermanence, our confusion about how to access the Real, and our commitment to separating ourselves from our life in order to report it back to ourselves as some proof of our existence and experience. The film suggests that our understanding of ourselves as distinct and unique, as a person who is watched by some giant somebody out there who is signing off on our projects and individuality—that this is all, in fact, only a fantasy.[4]

PERFORMANCE ART, LOSS, AND THE REAL

It is not surprising that Kaufman's meditation on loss and the Real takes place via the workings of a theater director. Performance art and contemporary theater have been, and remain, enamored with their presumed connection to the Real, especially in terms of the Real as rare, shocking, and brutal in a "media-saturated age." In an interview in the *New York Times* about art's concern with "shock value," playwright and director Adam Rapp suggests that the focus on the sensational aspects of many art and theater performances "fail[s] to appreciate," as the interviewer put it, "the deeper shock of seeing life as it really is. Especially in a media-saturated age" (Schuessler 2012). Sounding like Caden Cotard in his attempts to perform the "big and true and tough" reality of life, Rapp states, "It can be incredibly powerful to see something real, to have things feel like they are really happening." Rosalee Goldberg speaks in similar terms when she describes the experience of engaging with the reenactments of famous performance art works at the Performa 05 Biennial. She states that "through eye contact, the shock of the 'live' would stand out in a sea of mediated images" (Goldberg 2007, 16). According to Rapp and Goldberg, theater and performance art shock us into witnessing the Real. They break us out of our perpetually mediated world to give us something that is "really happening," "life as it really is."

Cotard's project begins by attempting to enact the Real through live performance, and then in order to get closer to this brutal truth, he begins to reenact his life. Moving away from creating scenarios for the actors, as "real" as they were ("I felt a lump in my breast"), he started to reenact the actuality of his life as it happened. This turn from creating a scenario (which could then elicit interpretation) to displaying the Real as a past event mirrors a move in mid-twentieth-century art: a move away from "meaning" and toward "being." Heeding the call to bring "real life" into art, much performance art, often described as "performance—by artists," turned the "Real" into a readymade. While much of performance art can be described as attempting to engage with the Real, turning the Real into a readymade can be especially accomplished when the Real is conceived of as a hunk of "completed" time, chosen by the artist. The artist thereby curates and points to the Real for the audience.

Longing for the Real: The Turn from Meaning to Being

In 1966, Susan Sontag famously argues against the interpretation of art. Sontag asserts that modern society is glutted with meaning in ways that diminish our capacities for sense experience. What is needed from art in the modern era, she believes, is "pure, untranslatable, sensuous immediacy" (Sontag 2001, 9). As such, critics should allow art to be "just what it is," without interpreting it to reveal presumed complicated meanings and hidden significance. She writes that "once upon a time (say, for Dante), it must have been a revolutionary and creative move to design works of art so that they might be experienced on several levels." In a society already replete with information and narrative, however, less (meaning) in art is most certainly more. Art without meaning encourages us to experience "the luminousness of the thing in itself, of things being what they are" (13). Interpretation, on the other hand, leads us away from the (real) world: "To interpret is to impoverish, to deplete the world—in order to set up a shadow world of 'meanings.' It is to turn *the* world into *this* world" (7).

Sontag's essay is exemplary of a turn away from "meaning" and toward "being" in mid-century art. While these terms are synonymous with how I'm using the Symbolic and the Real, they are more appropriate to mid-century terminology and may offer another valence in understanding these ideas. "Meaning," in terms of Sontag's essay, designates language and narrative, interpretation and explanation. "Being" signifies what she describes as "sensuous immediacy" or "*the* (as opposed to *this*) world" or the "thing-in-itself"—a world that exists apart from meanings (interpretations) that Sontag, among others, believes we can access (or perhaps at least partially access). The belief that *being* can be accessed at all apart from *meaning* is far from a universal belief, and in this philosophical era dominated by constructivism, more likely a distinctly minoritarian view. Nonetheless, many artists and others felt that one could move at least more toward the realm of what I am designating by the term "being" by reducing the emphasis on *meaning*.

Composer John Cage's mid-century work was enormously influential for this turn toward being. Influenced both by Dada (especially Marcel Duchamp) and Zen (as well as Thoreau, who himself was influenced by Eastern thought), Cage's work was structured on the belief Sontag articulated: "To interpret is to impoverish, to deplete the world—in order to set up a shadow world of 'meanings.' It is to turn *the* world into *this* world." Cage stated this basic idea almost two decades earlier and throughout the rest of his life with such pithy phrases as "No purposes, sounds" and "I have nothing to say, and I'm saying it." Cage disdained narrative, symbolism, and "intention," anything that attempted "communication" through the arts.[5] He believed that one should not search for meaning in the sound, but enjoy the sound itself. His 1952 "silent piece," *4′33″*—by Cage's and most others' accounts, his most important work—cast away meaning and representation, and presented in its place being. Based, in part, on his realization in an anechoic chamber that there was no silence, the piece was structured in three movements, delineated by pianist David Tudor opening and closing the piano lid. Each movement entailed Tudor resting his hands on his lap in silence for the noted duration as the audience sat listening to and observing the piece and the performance. Attempting to sidestep narrative, symbolism, and communication, Cage asked the audience to attend to the sounds of "silence," which then became the sounds of the room itself. Thus, *4′33″* moved away from meaning, interpretation, "purposes," and narratives in order to come closer to the thing in itself—in this case: sound, time, space. Being. This is perhaps the first example of what Cage's New School student Allan Kaprow would call the bringing of "real life" into art itself.[6] Deeply influenced by Cage, Kaprow further moved art into the realm of being with his staging of "happenings."

Kaprow's seminal 1959 "Eighteen Happenings in Six Parts" is considered the first "happening"—a structured event that involved temporary sculpture, avant-garde set design, seemingly random or nonrelated events, ambiguous beginnings and endings, and an audience often walking amid, or seated in the midst of, the activity. Kaprow conceived of happenings as moving art into the realm of being and everyday life: the Real would now be the material of art. Regarding happenings, he stated that "it was only a matter of time before everything else foreign to paint and canvas would be allowed to get into the creative act, including real space" (quoted in Schechner 2006, 163). Also influenced by Harold Rosenberg's article on "American Action Painters," Kaprow began to conceive of art as an "act" or an "event." Calling happenings "lifelike" art rather than "artlike" art, he wrote that "despite formalist and idealist interpretations of art, lifelike art makers' principal dialogue is not with art but with everything else. . . . Indeed, it's never certain if an artist who creates avant-garde lifelike art is an artist" (quoted in Schechner 2002, 32). Thus Kaprow, like Cage, wanted to break down the separation between art and life, artist and everyday person.

While we may be able to read Dadaism in the context of "being" now, it was in only the mid-century that being as the "actual," as "the world," became sought-after in art.[7] By the 1960s performance artists sought "the 'pure' or the 'raw' or the 'actual' or the 'natural' act *untainted* by theatricality, untainted by 'imitation,' untainted by reproducibility" (Schneider 2011, 129; italic in original).[8] Performance art was *live* art: alive and "real." Performance art is not a live art in the same way as "performing arts" (dance, music, theater) are live arts. In the performance art world, performance art is *art* art—brought to life. With this in mind, we can now recognize that Sontag's 1966 essay was exhorting critics to take up what was the compelling move for many artists of that era. She writes,

"The aim of all commentary on art now should be to make works of art—and, by analogy, our own experience—more, rather than less, real to us. The function of criticism should be to show how it is what it is, even that it is what it is, rather than to show what it means" (14).[9] While at other times art may have had a different function, *now* it was needed to turn us back toward our own experience, to make the world "more real" to us.[10]

Performance artists were doing just this. And one of the key elements prized in performance's connection to the Real was its "ephemerality." In the 1960s and 1970s, many artists believed so firmly in the importance of performance's ephemerality that they intentionally did not record their performances. Internationally acclaimed performance artist Marina Abramović has become a principal spokesperson for this view and the ways in which it has changed over the decades. She attests that the early performances were not documented because the artists thought "any documentation—by video or photos—could not be a substitute for the real experience: seeing it live. . . . [We decided] we wouldn't make any documentation of our work. It would only exist afterward by word of mouth" (Abramović 2007, 9). The radical conceptual artist Lee Lozano went so far as to leave the art scene as an act of art, as well as live her "real life" as her art, including such activities as "thought, conversation or marijuana smoking."[11] As the decades wore on, however, artists changed their mind about documentation. As Abramović puts it, their "attitude changed. We felt the need to leave some trace of the events for a larger audience" (Abramović 2007, 9).

Maybe We Don't Want to Embrace Loss after All: Reenactments of Performance Art

What changed? How did artists go from embracing the radical disappearance of performance art to wanting to preserve it? Surely they knew at the time that to disappear means to, um, disappear. One obvious answer is that the artists grew older and more concerned with their legacy. Their eventual literal corporeal disappearance became more of a reality than the distant abstraction we imagine our demise to be in our youth. Indeed, after remaining true to her abandonment of the art scene for decades, on receiving a terminal cancer diagnosis, Lozano agreed to three retrospectives of her work, which took place in the year preceding her death in 1999.[12] No longer throwing caution to the wind, the eventuality of her disappearance became a more palpable reality, and the prospect of her complete and real absence loomed. But this move toward preservation and remembrance was also part of a broader cultural understanding of identity and truth.

The beginnings of performance art coincided with the radicalism of the sixties and seventies. This radicalism, however, did not succeed in altering the primary way of conceiving of identity and truth in the Western tradition—through the separation of a subject and an object, a pointer and a pointed-at. Further, the dislocation and identity crises of the 1970s led to the consolidation and shoring up of boundaries in the 1980s and beyond. Performance art was caught up in this larger shift. It would seem the embrace of disappearance was ephemeral.

Eventually, the real ramifications of disappearance would not be tolerated. Performance's radical vanishing was vanishing it from the canon of art history. In writing about the Performa Biennial, *New York Times* art critic Roberta Smith reiterates the view that "[performance art] is a disappearing art form, even in these days of video and virtual reality. Once it is over, it is gone, and as a result, it tends to be omitted from history" (Smith 2005). And while many events in the past have not been omitted from history, for Smith, performance tends to be omitted from art history because it is not an object that can, in a sense, speak for itself through its continued existence as an object. Performance's nonobject status was bringing up fears of loss. The initial readiness to confront and accept loss was being reevaluated. The question became, how do we preserve what we claim is unpreservable? In my view, it became a question of how can we eat our cake and have it, too? That is, how can we allow for "disappearance" without actually having anything disappear?

The primary answer in performance art has been live reenactment as a way to maintain the "realness" (aka "liveness") but not lose the art (which are now unabashedly considered "artworks"). From performances by Vito Acconci to Carolee Schneeman, efforts have been made to re-perform what are deemed "important" works from the 1960s and 1970s and thereby establish a canon.[13] The launch of the Performa Biennial in 2005 under the direction of historian and curator RosaLee Goldberg has been the most significant of these preservationist efforts. Goldberg founded Performa in order to establish a central space for performance art, both new works and re-performances of old works. The 2005 Biennial included new works and "remixes"/restagings of classic works, including Marina Abramović's *Seven Easy Pieces:* Abramović reenacting six performance works from the 1960s and 1970s and adding a new one of her own.[14]

Thus, since the turn of the millennium, many early performance artists, and Abramović in particular, shifted from an initial emphasis on ephemerality to a concern with locating, re-creating, and preserving texts. Sounding much like Sébastien Lamothe of the Musical Box, Abramović states that:

> It is a very big problem that when certain performance works were made, the artists never left a set of instructions or clues, because they didn't think it necessary at the time. I think that there is huge work to be done—it is almost archaeological. Sometimes we can go backwards and find out information, even if the artist is dead, and see if we can come up with a set of instructions. It's better to have instructions than not, because people will re-perform the work anyway. (2007, 21)

Abramović seeks to acknowledge the primacy of the artist/creator. She states, "Today, there are so many young performance artists who repeat different performances from the seventies without giving credit to the original source" (Abramović 2007, 10). In order to rectify this repetition out of control, Abramović wants to make clear that the performance is correct (deciphered through archaeology), that the works will therefore be re-performed "accurately," and that the "original" artist is credited.[15]

This desire to preserve what has been hailed as uniquely ephemeral and to establish the primacy of the "original" artist (as opposed to Kaprow's suggestion that we let go of ideas of the "artist") has led Abramović to the Western classical music tradition. Art, now no longer an object, turns to the model of Western classical music, where the master artist leaves a score for the music's devoted reproduction in perpetuity by performers uniquely skilled in this endeavor. She writes, "I feel the need not just to personally re-experience some performances from the past, but also to think about how they can be re-performed today in front of a public that never saw them. In this manner, I can open a discussion about whether we can approach performance art in the same way as a music composition. Can we treat the instructions of the performance like a musical score—something that anyone who is properly trained can re-play?" (Abramović 2007, 10).[16] Abramović stresses the need for "skilled performers" who can interpret the works, stating: "It's different if Maria Callas or Renata Tebaldi sings. It's the same way with performance" (23). Thus, in a move from its radical ephemerality, Abramović's conception of performance art seems to unproblematically accept the tradition of Western classical music, a tradition itself under scrutiny for its objectification and reification of the ephemeral art of music and critiqued for a conception of authenticity rooted in textual "accuracy" and the genius of the composer. Works of performance art can now join the "imaginary museum" of great works, as Goehr writes of classical music. Rebuffing the rejection of art as an object in a museum that was performance art's raison d'être in the 1970s, "performance—by artists" is now returned to its museum; and an initially radical practice finds itself the bedfellow of nineteenth-century Western art music values.

Despite this, however, performance art's ephemerality and nonreproducibility are still proclaimed, even while the art is archived and treated like an object. The attempt to establish the truth of these performances based on the author's intention shows the very limited moment of radicalism in the trajectory of performance art. At least in terms of Lozano, Abramavić, and the historicizing of Goldberg, it would seem that after a relatively brief moment of radical bravery, the truth came to the fore: really losing (or being lost) is too radical. Real disappearance, in the end, is not entertained as a genuine option. While some performance artists have resisted this turn to rigorous documentation and the privileging of truth and the author,[17] Abramović has been a central narrator of performance art for at least two decades, and most contemporary curators of performance art reflect her view.

Reenactments as Performance Art

Reenactments are not staged only as preservative practices *of* performance art, but various events from the past are reenacted *as* new works of performance art. Performance art reenactments participate in the legacy of performance art as brute experience, beyond interpretation, but they relatedly avail themselves of the idea that live reenactment brings the past back to us—a brute hunk of time that is not lost but that we are able to experience again. As with the Musical Box, the past is not something to be interpreted, but to be brought forward "exactly." In the case of performance art, this bringing forward of the past is understood in the tradition of the ready-made, with the "live past" now the *thing* that is displayed as art. Performance art reenactments generally make more overt claims about the thingness and brute realness of their reenactments than tribute bands. Indeed, the presentation of the Real is often considered more important than the actual content of the reenactment—the actual content certainly being less important than, say, Genesis is for the Musical Box. But indeed, the content can be more unconsciously delivered as values that are taken for granted, as I will argue.

Reenactments *as* performance art began mostly at the turn of the millennium, about the same time as reenactments *of* performance art and about a decade after the explosion of the tribute band scene.[18] Based on artist comments, promotional materials, audience reactions, reviews, and the performances themselves, the great majority of the reenactments that I have encountered display the characteristics I associate with Replay. They fetishize and objectify space and time by reenacting in the original space on an important anniversary; they are promoted and reviewed in terms of touching the Real; they emphasize the uncanny; they present the flow of time as an object and thus participate in the Western preoccupation with controlling boundaries and fluidity; and they claim to offer us what we've never had before—the very past itself, objectified. Characteristics of Replay abound in Forsyth and Pollard's reenactment of Ziggy Stardust. While David Bowie embraced fragmentation, variability, and impermanence, Iain Forsyth and Jane Pollard demonstrate how containment, capture, the known, I = I identity, and a continued desire for the Real were the preoccupations at the turn of the millennium.

"A ROCK 'N' ROLL SUICIDE"

One of the earliest examples of the use of reenactment in performance art was the work of the performance art duo Iain Forsyth and Jane Pollard. Their first such work was a 1996 performance by the Smiths' tribute band the Still Ills, followed the next year by "The Smiths Is Dead," billed as the last-ever performance of a Smiths' tribute band (the Still Ills) on the tenth anniversary of the original band's breakup. In 1998 they staged what became their most famous reenactment, "A Rock 'n' Roll Suicide," at the Institute of Contemporary Arts in London over two nights in July, "exactly 25 years to the day since David Bowie's legendary 'farewell' performance as Ziggy Stardust" ("A Rock 'n' Roll Suicide" 1998). As with Genesis and ABBA, it is important to first examine David Bowie in order to consider why this particular artist and performance became fodder for such strict reenactment.

David Bowie

> David Bowie is at any given moment
> in time a given moment in time.[19]

In all of their promotional materials, Forsyth and Pollard say little about the importance of Bowie himself and why they chose to reenact the concert in which he intentionally "killed off" one of his several personae, Ziggy Stardust. But David Bowie's work was almost singularly concerned with questions of identity in the face of a new era: postmodernity generally and the 1970s in particular. During the "Me Decade," the search for meaning in a contingent world without God was on. For many, this world unmoored from previous value systems offered a welcome dose of freedom and the opportunity for identity exploration. The feminist and gay rights movements began to dismantle the straight male privilege pervading the Left. The heteronormative "authenticity" of the counterculture, typified by a bearded, jeans-wearing, liberal, yet still patriarchal masculinity, was beginning to be uncovered as the mask it was.[20] In an era characterized by dislocation and fragmentation, identity was now a question, not a given.

David Bowie became an iconic artist of this identity exploration, using the tropes of popular music as his palette. As the artist himself relates, "Realism, honesty and all these things that came out of the late 60s had got really boring to many jaded people going into the early 70s" (quoted in Doggett 2012, 164).[21] He delineated the era as a loss of the old moorings that, while frightening, may open up new possibilities:

> It is the inheritance of the sixties, not only with the breakdown of the American dream and the conflicts of the period, and the emerging pluralistic attitude towards society, but also a spiritual loss. A realization that absolutes weren't law, weren't the thing that one could abide by. There's no absolute religion, no absolute political system, no absolute art form, no absolute this and no absolute that. Things weren't black and white like we'd been told (especially during the great stiff fifties). (quoted in Stevenson 2006, 120)

Indeed, for Bowie, the era of the "Overman" (Homo Superior) was upon us. In his 1971 song "Oh! You Pretty Things," he declared, "We've finished our news / Homo Sapiens have outgrown their use. . . . Let me make it plain / You gotta make way for the Homo Superior."

As Zarathustra declared, "Man is something that shall be overcome": *Homo sapiens* needs to evolve into *Homo superior.*[22] "Dead are all gods," says Zarathustra, "now we want the Overman to live" (Nietzsche 1977, 191). In the new modern era described by Nietzsche, Homo sapiens must awaken to the realization that "god whom I created was man-made and madness, like all gods!" (141). It was as if Bowie were saying, close to one hundred years after Nietzsche's significant works, that 1970s Americans and Europeans, crashing from the faith in or antagonism against 1960s social movements, needed to awaken to something less locatable. Faced with the knowledge of emptiness that was once filled by projections of

God and all the other persons, things, and activities we made into gods, Bowie points a way forward as these gods dissolve.

That is, God is an invention, but so is the self. As Nick Stevenson has written, "Bowie's music aims to demonstrate the extent to which culture and the self is an invention" (2006, 42). In his song "Quicksand," Bowie writes, "I'm not a prophet or a stone age man / Just a mortal with potential of a superman / . . . / Don't believe in yourself." Nietzsche suggested that ideas about the self's agency are specious. But from Zarathustra, Bowie took the idea that one could at least strive to become Homo superior and invent one's self. As an artist concerned with these ideas, Bowie employed strategies that were particularly apt for the decade.

One was fragmentation. The artist applied cut-up techniques to his language and employed noise as a way to augment or replace melody (Doggett 2012, 4). He took the same approach to his identities and images, creating different personae by combining aspects of other popular characters or phenomena. Ziggy Stardust, the Thin White Duke, and Aladdin Sane—Bowie's main characters in the seventies—were all conglomerations of symbols taken from phenomena that fascinated the artist, including space travel, Hollywood glamour, and pop art. Indeed, the character of Ziggy Stardust is a composite of many famous identities. According to Doggett, Ziggy Stardust was born from "Judy Garland, the Rolling Stones, the Velvet Underground, the Stooges, the Beatles, Elvis Presley, [and] Little Richard. Strands of Pop Art were also visible in Ziggy's disguise, from Richard Hamilton's assimilation of science fact and science fiction to Andy Warhol's obsession with surface and the borrowed sheen of stardom" (2012, 4–5). Fragmentation of music and "self" demonstrated a type of play and freedom in answer to the identity crises of the decade.

Relatedly, Bowie emphasized the undecidability and variability of identity. "I'm continually aware that I'm an actor portraying stories and that's the way I wish to take my performance." He could confess that impersonating Ziggy had imposed a bizarre sense of dissociation from his "real" self: "'It's a continual fantasy. . . . I'm very rarely David Jones anymore. I think I've forgotten who David Jones is'" (Doggett 2012, 173). And he did have concerns with mental illness in his family history. But at this stage at least, Bowie did not seem overly concerned with finding his true voice or being his true self.

Such undecidability could be observed especially in his gender play. Doggett notes that in 1971, "Bowie began to erase gender distinctions in his songs. 'Lady Stardust' moved painlessly back and forth from 'he' to 'she' like the hero(ine) of Virginia Woolf's novel *Orlando*" (2012, 120). Nick Stevenson writes that in

Bowie's performances "questions of sexuality and gender were open to question" (2006, 2). During the 1970s, Bowie preferred to leave the gender and sexuality status of his characters and himself open to speculation.[23]

Bowie's use of fragmentation and undecidability was a part of his general fascination with impermanence. Like other identities he would temporarily take on, Ziggy was the guise he had chosen to adopt "for a couple of months." His 1971 song "Changes," performed on the original *Ziggy and the Spiders from Mars* tour and reenacted by Forsyth and Pollard, offers insight into Bowie's thoughts on time, change, loss, and identity.

In one reading, "Changes" addresses the political and social transformations that occurred in the 1960s and were continuing in the early 1970s. The protagonist addresses the older generation, stating that the younger generation is breaking away, "immune to your consultations" as "they try to change their worlds." It is the members of the younger generation who are aware "of what they're going through / Changes." Bowie is asking the older generation, or anyone who cannot acknowledge change, to "turn and face the strain"; that is, to have the courage to live in awareness of the changes, rather than resisting and imagining that change is not occurring. The protagonist tells the old guard, "Don't tell them to grow up and out of it," a hope that as these youth age they will not grow more conservative and deny the changes in favor of a specious stability.

But the song is also full of references to time more generally and to the protagonist's relationship to its continual movement. The protagonist wonders, "I still don't know what I was waiting for / and my time was running wild." Every avenue seemed to lead nowhere: "A million dead-end streets / every time I thought I'd got it made / it seemed the taste was not so sweet." It is as if the protagonist were trying to get somewhere and yet never able to greet what he is waiting for or trying to taste. In an attempt to answer this question of what he is trying to find, he turns "myself to face me / but I've never caught a glimpse / of how the others must see the faker / I'm much too fast to take that test." So he tries to turn to face himself, but he can't catch even a glimpse of who this being is, this "faker" whom others see.

I would argue that he is a "faker" as we all are "fakers"—the identity that others are seeing, and in fact imputing, as described in the previous chapter in relation to the uncanny, is not who we "really" are. As Nietzsche has said, "Human life is uncanny and still without meaning." We cannot capture who we *really* are, and our identity is certainly not it. In fact, the protagonist can't see his being because it is too fast to be captured. His being is much too fast to be able to catch a glimpse of itself. It cannot be symbolically located. Caden Cotard wasn't "fast" enough, that is, smart enough, to realize that he would fail that test. Or perhaps he was just more adamant in his belief in his fantasy. Nonetheless, when Cotard attempted to turn and face himself, he was also not able to catch a glimpse. Being is too fast to be caught. Unlike Cotard, the protagonist of "Changes" seems to recognize the impossibility of seeing and locating one's self.

Further, the protagonist intimates that it is not so much us who measure time, but time that measures us. The lyrics state, "Time may change me / but I can't trace time." Time is beyond our ability to affect it. It marks our bodies and ties us to our mortality. We can "watch the ripples change their size," but we can "never leave the stream of warm impermanence." So we watch the changes, but we can't step out of the stream. They continue to ripple, immune to our consultations and machinations. And Bowie sees the consequences for his generation, full of their social capital as "youth." "Look out you rock 'n' rollers," Ziggy says, "pretty soon now you're gonna get older." This youthful power, this belief, this radicalism will turn into middle, and then old, age. Will you still be able to face the strain when it is you who is now without the cachet of youth? When you age and become so much more aware of your own certain disappearance? "Changes" acknowledges how time measures us and how we cannot "trace time," or step out of the stream of impermanence that we are in. As with the Nietzschean Overman, the answer was to "face the strain," to become the "creator" in the face of a world unmoored from all "gods."

In embracing this world of no "absolutes," David Bowie performs his fantasies *as* fantasy. "Changes" recognizes the impossibility of seeing and locating one's "true" self. It acknowledges the self that others see as a "faker." David Bowie, Ziggy, and the protagonist of the song all perform fantasy as fantasy, creating a world within it, without trying to establish a permanent, locatable self. One fantasy identity will be replaced by another and by another and so on. They operate in a world recognized as constructed, provisional, and impermanent. Indeed, at the end of the 1973 performance, Ziggy meets his demise.

But how long did Bowie's "pleasure of mutation" thrill society as a whole, if it did much at all (assuming other aspects of his music were more culturally compelling)?[24] To what extent did this embrace of fragmentation, mutation, and personal courage in "facing the strain" take hold in society? As the swinging seventies turned into the return-to-conservatism eighties, the answer seemed clear: fragmentation was not a pleasure. As discussed in the previous chapter, borders and security became much more appealing. Not ready to embrace our

Nietzschean Overman, culture fell back into looking for "gods" to shield us from the unknown. The past became one of our primary "gods" in this era: the "One Who Knows."

"Fantasy Is Reality in the World Today":[25] *Forsyth and Pollard's "A Rock 'n' Roll Suicide"*

David Bowie may have advised taking a Nietzschean approach to the collapse of "absolutes," but unsurprisingly, this difficult process did not take hold in the wider society. Even Bowie wrote in his lyrics, "I'm not a prophet or a stone age man / just a mortal with potential of a superman" ("Quicksand") and expressed difficulty in letting go of his "idols": "I'm tethered to the logic of Homo Sapiens / Can't take my eyes from the great salvation / of bullshit faith" ("Quicksand"). While Bowie may have mostly reveled in identity as a "pose," rather than prompting liberation, this rootlessness more often terrified.[26] And by the time Bowie is reenacted in the 1990s, such terror had been baked in to the culture. In comparing the 1998 reenactment of Ziggy Stardust to the original 1973 performance, we find marked differences in understandings of time, change, identity, and loss.

Taking the name of their work from the final song on Bowie's 1972 album, *The Rise and Fall of Ziggy Stardust and the Spiders from Mars,* Forsyth and Pollard staged "A Rock 'n' Roll Suicide" at the Institute of Contemporary Arts in London, July 2 and 3, 1998. The typical characteristics of Replay are immediately recognizable in the description of the project. Their website states: "Exactly 25 years to the day since David Bowie's legendary 'farewell' performance as Ziggy Stardust, the artists re-created the entire show—in microscopic detail." It was "eighteen months in the making . . . perfecting an exact, move for move, replica of the original performance." Bootleg videos were consulted to fill out the original, which was only partially captured in D. A. Pennebaker's celebrated documentary: "Utilizing the, at times, patchy documentary of the original show made by D. A. Pennebaker as well as several bootleg recordings and sourcing first-hand accounts and recollections, Iain and Jane undertook piecing together everything that had taken place in 1973." They tout their connection to the original through real people, in this case a costume maker who had worked with Bowie and even Bowie himself, who congratulated them on their performance ("A Rock 'n' Roll Suicide," 1998).[27]

While Forsyth and Pollard take pains to distinguish their work from a clone band, their promotional materials reveal similar fetishizations and fascinations found in the Genesis and ABBA tributes described in the previous chapter. They fetishize time (reenacting on the twenty-fifth anniversary of the original performance) and material details (connecting with a Bowie costume designer to re-create the original costumes). They emphasize how hard they had to work (eighteen months) to dig through "patchy" remains in order to find the original ("perfecting an exact, move for move, replica"). They perpetuate the fantasy that we *can* have it all (ostensibly capturing "*everything* that had taken place in 1973"). And they stress their authenticity by getting "approval" from the original, citing David Bowie's congratulations.

Curator Vivienne Gaskin wrote in 1998 that in modern culture we have access to everything from the past—except the live experience. We have the records, the posters, the films and videos; however, "what none of these forms of mediation can convey . . . is the live experience, which was crucial to the mass impact of Bowie's theatre." She goes on, "Everything could be accessed from that era except the ambitious attempt to revive the live experience of the time—the essential part which moves people, which sets questions racing, which evokes memories." This overturns Allan Kaprow's call to bring real life into art. Bringing "real life" into art was meant to loosen the distinction between art and life with the emphasis on the aspect of "life." What Forsyth and Pollard were doing in the late 1990s, and what is understood as an advance and forward thinking by Gaskin, was to turn "real life" into a work, privileging the capture of life by turning it into an art object. In addition to having all of the memorabilia, now we would have the actual past itself too, reified and displayed—a return to the objectification that performance art initially sought to escape.

"Reality" as a hunk of time itself is therefore captured and presented as a "ready-made." Marcel Duchamp wrote that a ready-made is "an ordinary object elevated to the dignity of a work of art by the mere choice of an artist" (quoted in Breton and Eluard 1938, 23). Here Forsyth and Pollard take the "ordinary object" of a past live David Bowie concert and elevate it to the dignity of a work of art by choosing it. This echoes the description of performance art not as a lowly "performing art," but as *art* art—performed. As curator Vivienne Gaskin attempts to make clear, in contrast to a tribute band, Forsyth and Pollard were not focusing on Bowie-as-author-to-devotionally-re-create. Unlike the Musical Box's humble, invisible devotion to Genesis, the event was not to be about Bowie, but about Forsyth and Pollard, despite claims to their own invisibility in that they are not the "authors." Gaskin writes, "Unlike an act of nostalgic tribute, the event freed itself from the notion of authorship. This event was an idea created by Iain and Jane based on an idea of Bowie's enacted by a newly composed band, and so the need to assert authority through its dubiousness becomes irrelevant allowing the project a lifeblood of its own and a distinct status as art." Gaskin takes Bowie and Forsyth and Pollard out as authors, arguing that the chain of ideas makes the idea of the "author" moot and that somehow the project exists in and of itself, distinctly as art, without an author (creator) at all. This differentiates the work from pop music (enjoyed, "authored," and thus embedded in context and not understood as a thing-in-itself) or a "nostalgic tribute" (ditto). Forsyth and Pollard instigate a moment untethered from "authorship": a found object, a piece of art (but only because the artist has pointed at it).

As a "thing-in-itself," separated from its context through the pointing of the artist, the object is "free from heritage," a "distinct event in its own right." Gaskin writes:

> I may even go so far as to say that the re-enactment of Ziggy in '98 was, for those seven hundred or so of us who were there, the original. I am sure there are many thousands of devotees who would fervently argue to the contrary however [that] by re-enacting a piece of work which was itself a fictitious narrative the need for originality and indeed authorship are negated. "A Rock 'n' Roll Suicide" became an entity in its own right. By referencing an original so precisely and re-playing it in the live arena twenty-five years on[,] the experience of the night assumes its own identity and thus becomes an original experience free from heritage. (Gaskin 2003)

Gaskin seems to be arguing here that since Bowie's performance was through the fictional Ziggy, there is no origin to locate. The idea of no originary identity would be in line with Bowie's own view. Gaskin, however, goes on to establish an origin around Forsyth and Pollard. Rather than acknowledge the truth of the inability to find an origin,[28] Gaskin argues that the thing-in-itself can be perceived without any context and thus thought of as its own origin. To believe this, one has to willfully ignore the obvious, that (at minimum) Forsyth and Pollard are pointing and thus providing a context. But in accepting that the emperor has clothes, Forsyth and Pollard are omnipotent but invisible: the piece is not connected to anyone, but becomes itself an "original" with no connection to the past ("free from heritage") or author. This is, of course, the opposite of "signifying with a difference," as I will expand on in the next chapter. The notion of historical or cultural context at all is refuted. Gaskin says, "My feeling is that there probably wasn't any specific socio-political or cultural content which necessitated [Bowie's] work." But even if there were, Forsyth and Pollard are able to remove it. She states, "By removing context, authorship, nostalgia and trend[,] the projects devised by Iain and Jane remain expansive and powerful."[29]

Gaskin's view brings to mind media scholar John Fiske's work on whiteness. Her description of "A Rock 'n' Roll Suicide" strikes me as a particularly unalloyed example of exnominating whiteness. Fiskes writes, "Exnomination is the means by which whiteness avoids being named and thus keeps itself out of the field of interrogation and therefore off the agenda for change." Similar to the work of ABBA in constructing a vision of whiteness as an invisible universal, the impulse here is to put forward an event that is pure object, with no historicity and no context, and then to claim that somehow Forsyth and Pollard present this miraculously without really being there themselves. But meanwhile, the entire context of "Western Art and its genius" is behind them signing off on this as *art*, not, gasp, performing art. It is the privileging of abstraction, the Real, the thing-in-itself, free from any history or context, but invisibly tied to the values of the Western art tradition and implicitly, to whiteness as the invisible pointer, the arbiter, the knower, the definer. In this invisible move, "Whiteness constitutes itself as a universal set of norms by which to make sense of the world" (Fiske 1994, 42).

As part of the tradition that turned toward being in art, Forsyth and Pollard do not interpret and their work is not to be interpreted. Like historical reenactments described by Agnew, the work is presented as ahistorical and apolitical.[30] It is against interpretation. And like ABBA, there is no mess, no remainder, no polysemia, no change, and ostensibly then, no strain. The "author," that old-fashioned concept related to expressionism, who has something to express, is gone. What remains is the pointing and the status as art. The artist as pointer takes the author's place. What is not art is the tribute band, stuck in its old-fashioned belief in the expressive author.

Forsyth and Pollard's project of "removing context, authorship, nostalgia and trend" and presenting the thing-in-itself is part of performance art's insistence that it is showing us the Real, "to have things feel like they are really happening." But what remains is the artist who must point to it. The Real is separated, abstracted and objectified: "Here is the Real. Do you see it? I am showing it to you. I am performing it for you." Cotard attempted to capture the Real, but he had to stand outside of it to be the one who pointed at it. This is not to say that a powerful experience cannot be had in attending theater or performance art that focuses on the Real, often called, especially in relation to performance artist Marina Abramović, "presence." Indeed, these works often do provide a strong experience because they bring the audience into a more attentive, mindful state of being. But this is the *how.* This is the subjective experience that, in fact, is in our court, potentially stimulated by an artist's work, but ultimately our responsibility. The need to "authorize" presence qua real life furthers an ontology and epistemology that alienates through a reliance on symbols. We need to point to ephemerality and absence. The Western epistemology cannot *not* have the pointer. To not have the pointer would be to lose the self, and this is not acceptable. If we believed we could let go of the pointer, we would recognize that we're experiencing "real life" all the time, even when we're not attending an event of performance art. In performance art's most radical moments, it could be argued that the pointer (artist/author) disappears. But when the time comes for history's pen, disappearance dissolves in the shadow of the author, the spoke around which the Real ostensibly turns. It is the exact reverse of the promise of the 1960s and 1970s art of impermanence. And it is a complete turnabout from Kaprow's original statements about "happenings." Kaprow wanted to call into question the distinction between artist and nonartist. These artists reinstantiate this difference in order to maintain themselves as the ones who are able to point to the Real.

THE OBJECT AS THE "ONE WHO KNOWS"

We're living in a safety zone . . . there is no hell like an old hell.

David Bowie, "The Motel"

David Bowie himself recognized the "safety zone" mentality of the 1990s. His exhortations to abandon all the old gods did not get very far. While one new modern god is "the past," fetishized and obeyed in the manner of Replay described in this book, I'd like to take a closer look at another god that factors into our fetishization of the past—the "object."

Western culture has been critiqued for its sharp division between subject and object. Whether understood as beginning with the Greeks or taking substantial hold in modernity, twentieth- and twenty-first-century Western intellectuals have worked to reveal the ideology behind this long-held assumption.[31] Of course, we still live in a world that assumes a division between subject and object; and this should not be considered only a Western trait. Buddhist philosophy, for example, considers the tendency to split between subject and object to be a basic tendency of the human mind (which nonetheless can be understood and therefore surmounted). In the Western worldview, however, this split has been regarded as a way to gain objectivity and mastery of an object and therefore reinforced and stressed as the primary way to gain truth. I am interested in how this split has produced a certain love affair with the object that manifests in the desire to master or possess the object through a slavish precision to its contours. Since the proportional techniques introduced by Polykleitos in the fourth century BC, sculptors of Adonis, Aphrodite, or handsome "youths" strove to perfectly capture the proportions of the human body. This mimetic tradition and focus on "objectivity" has been so influential that 2500 years later surrealist artist André Breton would rail against "the realist attitude," which he "loathed" for its "mediocrity, hate, and dull conceit" (quoted in Holsinger 2005, 42). Or as Henry Louis Gates puts it, "Polemical traditions seem to valorize the literal" (2014 [1988], 26). The Greco-Roman emphasis on "objectivity" formed the basis of the scientific method and modern Western law by equating truth with examinable "facts" that could be verified and disfavoring accounts based on myth, metaphor, and subjective experience, which are not objectively measurable.

With this tradition of obeisance to the object(ive), the "subjective" has persistently been cause for concern within the Western tradition. While the subjective may have had its attenuated heyday during the rise of the "individual" in modernity—a time when the "individual" appears to make decisions based on his or her needs rather than the larger family or society—it was precisely in this era that a retrenchment of the object(ive) asserted itself. Desmond Manderson demonstrates this shift in eighteenth- and nineteenth-century Western law and music. Manderson suggests that the similar changes in law and music at that time reveal "two aspects of the same process and the same history," that is, the turn to modernity when "judgment" came to be replaced by "identity" (Manderson 2010, 1). While Manderson suggests that in the baroque era and before the question was of interpretation: "What do we *do* with this piece of music or with this law, at this particular unique moment or confronted with this particular context?" (2), it was in post-Enlightenment modernity that the question became: "Is this document an authentic statement of its author's intentions—whether we are talking about Shakespeare's First Folio or a sonata by Beethoven, a section of the Code Civil or an Act of Parliament" (2). Once the document is authenticated, the process then becomes relatively straightforward: one is simply "to obey the text 'as written'" (2).

Manderson relates this shift to efforts to avert the individual tyranny of kings or dictators. It can also be understood as "some individuals are more equal than others": the Shakespeares and the Beethovens. In my view, the important shift or solidification that occurred in this era was the entrenchment of the object-text as the "One Who Knows"—the One to whom we defer authority, the One who has the answers.[32] Musical scores became increasingly detailed in order to rein in the discretion of performers. Similarly, the law took on the status of a supreme text, moving away from individual discretion and interpretation by judges. Manderson describes this as a turn in the nineteenth century toward "a total subservience to the [musical work/legal text] as written" (2) and an elimination of improvisation (in music) or discretion (in law).

Richard Taruskin makes a similar point about a late-twentieth-century musical practice, suggesting that there is, indeed, a *fear* of "subjectivity." Writing in the 1990s during the height of the "historically-informed performance" (HIP) of Early Music debates, Taruskin compares HIP to a Robert Borkian–style of legal textualism. Robert Bork, the Supreme Court Justice nominee who practiced a "formalist" approach to law, stated that "a culture that engages itself to the interminable opening of possibility issues its own death warrant" (quoted in Taruskin 1995, 33). I believe Taruskin is correct when he argues that the root of this desire for objective certainty is "fear." Legal formalists "fear that 'subjective' legal interpretation will ultimately discredit the law and subvert its power to undergird the social fabric" (Taruskin 1995, 32). Likewise, subjective performance will undermine the authority of the canonical repertory (pace Marina Abramović). In discussing the modern approach to music history, he writes that we are "looking for . . . an authority that will save us from the onus of conjecture, . . . the onus of personal choice and responsibility. We can live with error as long as it is not our error. We cannot live with uncertainty, it seems" (45, 41). Leo Steinberg made a similar comment about art history in 1969. "With the disdain of subjectivity goes the demand that value judgments be eliminated from serious investigations of art since they cannot be objectified. Needless to say, much of the work art historians do is well done only in the objective mood, as in the physical examination of monuments, the searching of archives and texts, or tracing the provenance of an altarpiece by identifying its local saints" (Steinberg 1969, 828). In both music and art history, then, the fear of "sticking one's neck out" prevails; and the focus turns to verifiable objects: monuments, archives, texts, provenance, paintings, scores, and letters.[33] As Adorno puts it, it is "the neglect of interpretive thinking for the sake of fact-gathering" (2006 [1991], 16).

Understanding this history helps us understand Sontag's *Against Interpretation* as part of a longer turn away from subjective judgment. Sontag considers the split between form and content in art erroneous; however, she nonetheless argues for the need to focus on form as a way to blunt the impulse toward interpretation (2001, 2).[34] She argues that "more attention to form in art [is needed]. If excessive stress on content provokes the arrogance of interpretation, more extended and more thorough descriptions of form would silence." As such, critics should place their attention on appearance, creating "criticism which would supply a really accurate, sharp, loving description of the appearance of a work of art. . . . reveal the sensuous surface of art without mucking about in it" (13). Andy Warhol comes to mind as a salient example of this privileging of the object in mid-century art. Sontag would seem to have Warhol's repeating Campbell's soup cans, Marilyn Monroes, coke bottles, and dollar bills in mind when she wrote, "Ideally, it is possible to elude the interpreters . . . by making works of art whose surface is so unified and clean, whose momentum is so rapid, whose address is so direct that the work can be . . . just what it is" (11).[35] This is the lineage that informs Forsyth and Pollard's work when Gaskin claims that their efforts are "to persuade an audience in excess of 700 that they should and could suspend disbelief—to no longer approach the work as a piece of fiction but a shortcut to the authentic moment" (Gaskin 2003). I would argue that this turn away from interpretation must be understood as part of the general discomfort with the place of messy subjectivity in modernity. It is the privileging of the object as the locus of truth, as another "god," "unified and clean." It is the turn perpetually to the object and an abandonment of the subjective, which becomes more and more unknowable the more entrenched the Western model of knowing (based on separation, delineation, and boundary) becomes.

All of these various examples, from legal formalism to increasingly detailed musical scores to approaches to music and art history, demonstrate a desire to find the truth in objective fact and a distinct fear of subjective decision making, indeed, the fear of interpretation. Thus, while Sontag exhorts 1960s critics to stop interpreting, it would seem that the concern with our ability to interpret (or fear of the consequences of interpretation) had already taken hold. As I will investigate further in the next chapter, such obsessive formalism and textualism suggests a type of thinking that imagines the answers are anywhere but in our own decision-making capacity in the here and now. Replay extends this focus on the text and on the object to the live past itself, which now becomes the one to "obey."

LOSS

Perhaps one could argue that I am not accounting for enough complexity within the practice of rigorously mimetic reenactments. Indeed, while tribute bands are uncomplicated about their desire to capture the past in perfect detail, performance artists committed to reenactment will routinely highlight the impossibility and failure inherent in their task. In speaking of their reenactments to the writer Simon Reynolds, four different performance artists said: "In a way, the impossibility of recreating the event was part of it"; and "[I'm interested in] constructing a series of paradoxes . . . highlighting the contradictions that arise through trying to do something like that, the impossibility of it"; and "Failure is hugely important to us . . . Copying anything, the copy never reproduces the original completely. And this shortfall is where the Real emerges" (quoted in Reynolds, 52).[36] I can say only that I remain unimpressed.

First, as I note in the introduction, I find it uninteresting to ponder the truth that we fail to capture the past exactly—that the Symbolic fails to capture the Real. Reynolds writes that the performance artists with whom he spoke were "forthcoming and engaged" when discussing the intricate, meticulous, and arduous effort that went into re-creating the material detail of their chosen pasts as precisely as possible. They had no problem discussing with great animation the "how" of their work. "But," he states, "somehow the 'why' kept eluding us in our conversations" (52). The question is why do we keep trying to capture something we know we cannot capture? And why do we fetishize the intricate, meticulous, arduous work? The artists are not examining this question, but are fascinated by the impossibility of their projects because it is the titillating impossibility of the Real itself that we both fear and desire. The idea that the Real emerges at the shortfall of trying to capture the past is alluding to that gap—that inability of the Symbolic to fully signal the Real. But we know this already. Why must we keep, increasingly obsessively, showing that to ourselves?

While performance may highlight impermanence and unlocatability, it has generally moved in a direction that, like the tribute bands discussed in chapter 1 and like Caden Cotard, pretends to be capturing the Real while resisting the actual practice (of loss) that would allow for an engagement with the Real. While it follows many of the same ploys as tribute bands (fetishizing the material details, turning the flow of time into an object), the approach of performance art especially reveals the way that the artist must remain to point to the Real.

It is almost as if the embrace of loss touted by performance art was so frightening that a deep relapse into fantasy occurred. For indeed, as Gaskin asserted, if there is no context, no historicity, then why choose one event over another? Gaskin, Forsyth, and Pollard suggest that the allure is Bowie's own lack of authorship—their presentation of a contingent identity that was already the presentation of a contingent identity; a pointing to an identity that was already pointing to the surface of identity. But interestingly, they did decide to reenact Bowie's *killing off* of this identity.[37]

Vanessa Agnew has argued that historical reenactment can be used as an act of "coming to terms with the past" and "coming to terms with the present" (Agnew 2007, 302). While she is focusing on Civil War and other battle reenactments, I would argue that Forsyth and Pollard do something similar in reenacting Ziggy's demise. To indulge a psychoanalytic reading, couldn't we say that in reenacting the moment of Ziggy's demise the performance serves as a type of symbolic mastery of disappearance itself? In reenacting the moment that a (fake) identity is killed off, the trauma of (Ziggy's) death is repeated in order to attain symbolic mastery of this loss. Ziggy himself symbolized the loss of coherent identity, the "truth" of identity as a pose. Bowie killed him off, eventually to take on another persona. Bowie was ready to continue to fragment, to face the strain and evolve into Homo superior. But Forsyth and Pollard contain this moment, fetishize it, master it by capturing it, stop it, and point to it. But rather than creating a symbolic stand-in for the loss, for example, like Freud's grandson in the famous story of Fort-Da,[38] they claim to capture the loss itself. This is the fantasy that we are capturing the Real, while still completely lost in the Symbolic. We want to embrace the Real, yet fear real loss. And so we say we are capturing the Real, while actually cushioning ourselves from real loss (we think) by continuing to stand back and point at it. And by pointing at it, we establish and assure ourselves of our position: the one who sees and points.

Forsyth and Pollard are preoccupied with the same sense of control, containment, origin, and identity that I have elaborated in the re-creations of Genesis or ABBA. Gaskin says of Forsyth and Pollard: "I can only thank them all on behalf of the ICA for their neurosis." Indeed. The performance duo's attention to detail, to obsessively "capturing" the past in all of its realness, like Cotard, is the continued obeisance to the fundamental fantasy from which psychoanalysis wishes to free its neurotic subject. Whereas Ziggy was fantasy as fantasy—a recognition and acknowledgment of fantasy—reenacting Ziggy has been the pursuit of the Real. This is buying into the fantasy, *wanting* to believe. It is not fantasy as fantasy, but fantasy as, well, delusion.

Counter to Bowie, who was deconstructing the notion of truth and the authentic, Forsyth and Pollard try to find the truth again. Rather than embrace loss, the reenactment demonstrates the relentless belief that maybe we *can* have everything, including all of the time before us. This is more of the same for Western culture, which has been objectifying others for centuries. This capturing of "brute reality" cloaks universality in the assumption of the Western art and genius tradition as its unquestioned basis. Just as performance art has commandeered the name "performance" for itself,[39] Forsyth and Pollard's reenactment can be understood as centralizing the Western art tradition as the invisible curator and pointer to "real life" qua presence qua the past as ready-made. The Real is presented and curated by the genius-artist-master. The Western art tradition gets to decide what is *the* world thereby excluding itself from *this* world.

THREE

If I Should Lose You

Keeping Jazz Alive

Isn't it obvious that we're obsessed with death even as we preach that jazz is alive? That it's a constant feature of our thinking? We don't need more studies of the aging audience. What jazz lovers could really use is grief counseling and therapy. The debates that surround the music seem rooted in the problem that we still don't know how to come to terms with loving something so beautiful and yet so fragile.

Lara Pellegrinelli, "Dig Boy Dig"

In 1994 the renowned San Francisco radio station KJAZ went off the air after thirty-five years of playing jazz under its tagline of "Keeping Jazz Alive." There had been long and somber discussions. Then the life support system was disconnected. As Branford Marsalis claimed in Ken Burns's 2001 documentary *Jazz,* jazz music had "basically died" in 1975. According to the documentary, the strain of changes in jazz proved too much for the center to hold. Fusion and Latin styles pulled it in too many directions, and the avant-garde pushed audiences away. It seemed few people wanted to listen to jazz anymore. In 1994 KJAZ's passing was viewed as one of the last remaining nails left to hammer into the already well-sealed coffin of jazz.

But across the country, the enterprise of "keeping jazz alive" was rising like the proverbial phoenix in a newly established, institutional setting: Lincoln Center in New York City.[1] In 1991 Jazz at Lincoln Center (JALC) was formed, and by 1996 was inducted into Lincoln Center as a new "constituent." This eventually led to the construction of the one-hundred-thousand-square-foot Frederick P. Rose Hall in the Time Warner Center at Columbus Circle. In the 1990s then, while "keeping jazz alive" may have been a losing battle on radio stations across the country, it was also becoming a well-funded, national project that would soon create an edifice to present the "face of jazz" to an international audience. Jazz was becoming, quite literally, institutionalized.

This institutionalization of jazz takes place within the same era and context of live reenactments and the fears of loss surrounding performance's nonobject status generally. Like popular tribute bands and performance art, jazz has its particular set of histories and concerns that inflect its relationship to memory culture. Indeed, fears of the "loss" of jazz precede similar fears of losing "classic rock" or performance art, and have generally been more overt and far-reaching. Arguably, jazz is the Ur-lost object of music.[2] Efforts to "keep jazz alive" via Replay, however, are particularly astonishing. Based on improvisation and "repeating with a signal difference," approaching past music as something to re-create precisely is counter to jazz's understood philosophy.

This chapter investigates the significant turn to Replay in jazz performance and its ramifications. From precise reenactments of Paul Whiteman's 1924 "Experiment in Modern Music" and James Reese Europe's 1912 Carnegie Hall performance in the 1980s through JALC's "tribute" approach to Jason Moran's "revisiting" of Thelonious Monk's 1959 Town Hall concert in the twenty-first century, the jazz past is being brought "back to life" through various tactics of haunthenticity.[3]

While Jason Moran complicates the project, all of the previously mentioned events promote themselves via assorted aspects of Replay: they fetishize time and place; emphasize the hours spent researching and re-creating the intricate details; connect the project with some of the real original members (such as relatives); take the past as authority; and/or prize the material "authenticity," precision, and accuracy of their performances. As such, the re-performance of jazz moves from (re)interpretation to uncanny engagements with a particular, originary chunk of the past itself. Moving from a focus on interpretation, with the model of Replay an "original moment" is fetishized and reified.

What we are seeing with the institutionalization of jazz, then, is the collision of two different traditions of repetition and, relatedly, of the conception of musical form: one that conceives of form as an originary, locatable source and one that does not establish such boundaries. These two different understandings also create different understandings of preservation and loss. I will argue that while jazz has always been a combination of African-American and European American traditions, it was born from African-American understandings of form and repetition that differed markedly from a European tradition that values private ownership, necessitating a clear object (the work) and an author. As an American art form, jazz could not escape this ideology; nonetheless, its emphasis on improvisation, musical reuse, and "repetition with a signal difference" has at least attenuated the assumption of the fixed art object and single producer characteristic of the European tradition of art and "art music." It is important to consider the extent to which this African-American tradition may be declining as jazz is increasingly taught and performed under the aegis of various institutional structures.

That is, much jazz institutionalization has been involved in a certain "repetition without a difference" or "repetition-in-control." As stated in chapter 1, late-twentieth-century American politics stoked a "culture of fear" in order to move forward an aggressive international agenda. Faced with perpetual discourses of insecurity and fear, it is unsurprising that audiences were increasingly drawn to reenactments that offered performances of the *known:* performances that provide a sense of stability and mastery, a respite from the open-endedness, insecurity, and "loss of a sense of grounding" characteristic of postmodernity generally and fueled by political discourse. Rather than repetition-out-of-control, repetition-in-control provides a marked sense of mastery, stability, and boundary.

Various repetitions-in-control have various ramifications. After discussing different traditions of repetition and the relationship of jazz to loss, I investigate two jazz reenactments and their specific implications. Answering the general cultural desire to consume entertainment that provides the comfort of the known and the contained, JALC and the Yale Band offer audiences precise reconstructions of the jazz past. These ostensibly original and accurate pasts carry messages, of course. Examining JALC's tribute to Louis Armstrong's Hot Five recordings and Yale's Glenn Miller reenactment for the fiftieth anniversary of D-day, I demonstrate the ways in which Replay served to construct and ritualize ideas about jazz history, gender, and American nation.

MUSIC, REPETITION, AND FORM

The opening of chapter 1 offered a music reviewer's thoughts on the most inevitable way to keep classic rock music alive—through live reenactment. In focusing on the "live performance" aspect of classic rock, one could argue that keeping the music alive through continual performance is a laudable goal. But the desire for the original "analog instruments" suggests that the style is understood less as an approach or process than as a fetishized object or product. This way of imagining how to keep past music "alive" arises from the conception of music as an object to be preserved and displayed in a concert hall qua museum. Leaving behind the original instruments would be tantamount to death. The songs are not taken as texts that can then be reinterpreted. The music cannot change and transform and still be considered "the same." While "repeating with a signal difference" has been the hallmark of popular music since the early twentieth century, the Western tradition of understanding the past as an object is influencing popular music practice, turning events such as musical performance into objects. Replay is beginning to dominate forms of music that were once characterized by reinterpretation.

Scholars have pinpointed the latter half of the twentieth century as the beginning of a type of postmodern "memory culture." Within this context, repetition in music is often discussed as if it were a single phenomenon. George Plasketes characterizes late-twentieth- and early twenty-first-century Western culture as a "re-" culture with tributes, karaoke, reissues, sampling, and rap dominating musical production (Plasketes 2010, 12). But not all musical uses of repetition stem from the same tradition, nor do they have the same aims. Henry Louis Gates, Nathaniel Mackey, Ingrid Monson, and others have demonstrated how the African-American literary and musical practice of signifyin(g), or repeating with a signal difference, has characterized African-American artistic production for centuries, including most recently (in music) jazz, rap, sampling, and remix.[4] Zen has been a source of formal repetition in American music, most often showing up in Western classical styles, such as minimalism.[5] John Cage was probably the most vocal commentator on Zen's influence on his compositional thinking. Cage's famous statement on repetition was his advice that if you find something boring, do it four times, and if you're still bored, do it eight times. Keep multiplying and eventually you'll find what you are doing is extremely interesting.

Both Zen and African-American styles of repetition differ from Replay in a similar significant way. While Replay reifies form, both Zen and African-American traditions view form as more provisional, fluid, transient, and welded to content. In Zen calligraphy, for example, a movement of the hand is made following very traditional parameters, but only until the movement happens of itself. After careful and copious repetitions devoted to following form, at some point (if one achieves mastery) artist merges with form, doer and doing are one.

Indeed, Zen would describe that state as "no doer, nothing done, and no doing." No subject, no object, and no action. None of these has a permanent or separate existence. At that point, there is no more need to copy form. Form was a tool that was eventually abandoned as the student gained mastery in doing without doing. In the African-American tradition of repeating with a signal difference, there is not an original form that is used as a permanent template. The concern is not with retrieving or preserving an origin, but with responding according to current circumstances within an acknowledged context. Form is not separated from continually shifting and moving content. Both of these traditions seem to acknowledge that there is no origin, but rather perpetual play and movement.

While African-American music is a conglomeration of mostly European and African approaches, I want to turn to an example of West African music to further make my point about form. I do this not to equate African-American practices with African, but to underscore that the European practice of objectifying, locating, and establishing origin is, in many ways, the anomalous tradition from a world cultural standpoint. One can see similarities between the West African conception I am about to elucidate and African-American practices that do not objectify form, whether one wants to argue African-American practices stem from an African tradition or not.

In his study of West African drumming, John Miller Chernoff asked his teacher, Ibrahim Abdulai, about the origins of the Dagomba drumming/dance beat known as *Takai.* Abdulai responded:

> You want to know who introduced the beating, and I can tell you that no one introduced Takai. Any time you hear a dondon beater beating, and someone is dancing, then you must know that the dondon beater introduced the playing. He is the one who introduced the beating of the drum. (Chernoff 1979, 61)
>
> So as the Takai dancers who are dancing now are becoming old, they will train another set after them, and another set. . . . No one knows the original beat of Takai, and by that time the beat we take as Takai will die. It may be a new one altogether. By that time, I and the others will not be there. And those people who will be there at that time, they will think that they are dancing the real thing because they will not know the original beat as before. Before me Alhaji was leading the Takai group. . . . But Alhaji has not given it over to me. At present if we are drumming and he comes there, he says that we have changed the beat so much that we have spoiled it. And whatever happens, in

the future it will also change. Even in our time it is not the original beat. That is what will keep on happening.

So how do you feel about the fact that they will be changing the Takai beat?

To me, I feel it is better. The change is better because I have come to the stage that I feel that what we are drumming is good. If an old man says that at the time they were drumming, the beat was good, I don't know what the beat was at that time, so I feel that what we are doing at present is good. And in the future they will feel that what they are doing is better than what we have been doing now. That is what will keep on happening.

And what will you tell them?

I won't tell them anything because by that time I will not be there.

But if you are there, what will you say?

I'll tell them that they are spoiling it. (64–65)

Abdulai was at pains to describe a form that was always new, but not different; always changing, but not *really* changing. The difficulty in trying to describe what may have seemed self-evident to Abdulai was in the ethnomusicologist's tradition of understanding phenomena in terms of origin and ownership. There is no inventor or owner of a beat. It cannot be traced back to a certain source because one could always go back to something that influenced that particular incarnation of the beat. And while Abdulai may jokingly lament the change from his good beat to the new "spoiled" beat, there is no danger of the beat ever being lost. There is nothing separate to lose. The origin (or "introduction" as Abdulai puts it) happens with every beat, and therefore the beat does not recede out of our grasp. Such a relationship to form does not *create* an object that can then be lost. The past is in the present—the origin is always now. There is no object to slip further and further away from the subject.

It is illuminating to consider how the modern Western epistemology would understand this scenario. Because the beat would be construed as different from the earlier beat, there would now be two different beats. The different beat (despite the fact that it carries the past within it) separates from the old beat. As such, we have lost the "old" beat. Because we don't like losing, we must now go back, locate it, delineate it, and preserve it. And the way to do it is to capture it exactly, pinpointing it in some particular moment in time. With each change then, a new beat is created and an old beat is lost. Each old beat must then be preserved. We try to preserve more and more in the hope of losing less and less.

It is the sad irony that in preserving, we distance, separate, and alienate the past from the present and thereby experience a sense of loss more and more.

I am not making a through line from West African practice to African-American practice, but I do want to suggest that the Western propensity to separate subject and object has been the atypical view from a world cultural standpoint (while the dominant and now pervasive view). To the extent that enslaved Africans and African-Americans maintained a physical separation from the dominant European-influenced culture, they were able to maintain cosmologies that differed from the Western worldview. For example, African-American music began with a similar lack of concern with ownership seen in the West African example. Songs were not private property connected to an author, but a communal phenomenon.[6] Of course, by the time of the advent of jazz in the twentieth century, the idea of the individual composer was already an accepted practice by African-American musicians. Scott Joplin, Jelly Roll Morton, and W. C. Handy all claimed ownership of, and published, their music. This demonstrates the mix of traditions that has always made up the form. But the relationship to songs in the budding jazz tradition was one of reworking. As jazz developed, a key element of its practice became interpreting songs. Songs were not to be located and reperformed exactly as the composer had intended, but interpreted by the artists arranging and performing them. There was not a strong idea of locating the "original" song or the belief that the song would be lost if it were not reperformed exactly as originally intended.

In Nathaniel Mackey's terms, this reworking and signifyin(g) is a practice of "othering" and privileging the "verb" over the "noun." Mackey argues that such a practice reveals the African-American tradition to be "postmodern" before there was a postmodern. This is true if we define postmodernity as the late-to-the-game, poststructuralist recognition of the "X-ing" of the subject.[7] However, it is not true in terms of the different practices of memory and reuse used in postmodern cultural production. Indeed, the ways in which signifyin(g) is now butting up against postmodern reuse has not been recognized or discussed.

Before pursuing that line of thinking, however, I want to give one further example of a non-Western cosmology affecting jazz. A significant number of jazz musicians have been influenced by Eastern philosophies. Jazz musicians' interest in Eastern traditions to support their musical, personal, and spiritual lives can be traced back at least to the 1940s.[8] Herbie Hancock, Wayne Shorter, Joseph Jarman, Benny Maupin, and Buster Williams are just a handful of musicians who are long-term practitioners of Buddhism, for example. Buddhism's root teaching is of the "emptiness" of self and phenomena. As described regarding Zen, repetition is used not to capture an original form, but to eventually free oneself from form as a separate entity. This sense of no origin, no separation between doing and doer, and no separation between subject and object has been helpful to jazz musicians, many of whom describe copying the jazz masters before stepping off into their own "voice." It was through the studious attention to form that they eventually transcended that particular form (the musician being emulated) and launched into their own. To remain tethered to the master's form is to not develop one's own mastery. Musicians have used Buddhism and other Eastern philosophies to help establish cosmologies that support connection and paradox, rather than separation and "order."[9]

Buddhism, the West African tradition, and the African-American tradition use repetition in ways that demonstrate a different conception of subject and object, doer and doing, content and form, and the present and the past than the Western European tradition. Western postmodernity has collapsed into reuse under the weight of its teleological, delineating worldview that has nowhere else to go as it continues to hide from the Real, whereas these other traditions use reuse through an understanding of form that in fact aligns with the conditions of the Real. The separation of the past and present cannot be found, nor can the edges of the self.

Jazz has been moving away from its more non-Western influences and becoming subsumed within the Western epistemology, especially since the 1980s. Jazz styles aligned with "art music" have been absorbed into museum culture, while others, such as big band and "trad jazz," have been incorporated within the logic of memory culture. As fears of losing jazz took hold, the practice of signifyin(g) turned toward a practice of preservation and, therefore, an emphasis on origin. This is a shift from understanding the past in the present to conceiving of the past as a separate object receding into the distance. It is relatedly a shift from understanding musical form as highly interpretable and therefore inextricably connected with content, toward one that understands form and content (or score/work and performance) as separate, with the original form always establishing the ground for any interpretation (or lack thereof), much more in the tradition of Western classical music's work concept. Form moves from something that is always originating and introduced in the present to something that is separated in the past, locatable, and owned. While many scholars have already elucidated the discouraging tendency to "embalm" jazz,[10] my focus is to highlight how this move in jazz demonstrates a larger epistemological battle that encompasses questions of the subject, improvisation, loss, and the Real.

SAVING JAZZ

The 1980s is considered the era of neoclassicism in jazz and when jazz began to be canonized and museum-ified. But like other forms of memory culture, the neoclassicist movement can be traced to the 1970s. Scholars Gabriel Solis (2008), Alex Stewart (2007), and Ted Gioia (1997) have noted that the concept of preserving jazz's history through repertory companies gained momentum in that decade. In 1973 Chuck Israels founded his National Jazz Ensemble, and the following year George Wein promoted his New York Jazz Repertory Company. The Smithsonian Institution began taking an increasingly active role in preserving and promoting the jazz tradition, and Gunther Schuller pursued a wide range of activities, including concerts, recordings, and writings that furthered the repertory agenda. The 1970s also brought more reissues of earlier material by record companies, expanded attention to the jazz tradition at academic institutions, and the increased publication of jazz books and journals (Gioia 1997, 384–85).

Scholars such as John Gillis, Andreas Huyssen, and Svetlana Boym consider the 1970s the birth of our modern memory culture, linking it to feelings of loss—loss of home, of identity, and of faith in the future. While the booming post–World War II economy did not generate the urge to remember, the social changes of the 1960s and early 1970s and the decline of the prosperity enjoyed in the 1950s and 1960s fueled its rise. Changes in societal roles and expectations about gender, race, and the family as well as the increasing mobility necessary to find employment seemed to propel the desire to find some things that were "unchanging." As these scholars argue, the urge to commemorate one's past in order to establish one's identity grew out of a desire to locate a home in a world that often instilled a sense of homelessness (see Gillis 1994, esp. 15–16).

The "demise" of jazz can be understood as instigated not only by the proliferation of styles in the 1960s and 1970s, as is often argued, but also through the music's collision with an objectifying memory culture seeking security in a presumably fading past. As fears of losing jazz took hold, the practice of signifying turned toward a practice of preservation and an emphasis on origin. There was a fear of losing the "original beat." From something more akin to the West

African conception of form described, jazz moved toward the idea of form as something that is locatable and owned.[11]

Wynton Marsalis became the central figure, indeed "savior," in the project of keeping jazz alive. In 1987 Marsalis, writer Stanley Crouch, and scholar Albert Murray were the firebrands behind a Lincoln Center committee that concluded jazz could and should be a permanent and significant member of the large arts institution. After four summers of presenting "Classical Jazz," they officially linked to Lincoln Center in 1991 and eventually grew into a highly influential organization, the first to expand beyond Lincoln Center's walls. With 105 full-time staff members, a dozen interns, more than four hundred part-time employees, and roughly three-dozen members on its prestigious board, JALC now resides in the $131 million Frederick P. Rose Hall in the Time Warner Center, where it operates three performance venues and maintains an annual budget of $35 million. Marsalis describes the new hall as allowing JALC "to present a face [for jazz] to the world" (Pogrebin 2006).

Marsalis was dubbed one of the "Young Lions" of the 1980s—jazz musicians portrayed as "bringing back the tradition" by retrieving jazz from its foray into fusion in the 1970s and its experimentalism that many thought were taking it too far outside the "typical" jazz lover's taste. Consequently, the Young Lions were often hailed as the "saviors of jazz." Early on Marsalis was described as a "young player," virtuosic, but one who was still in the phase of copying the masters and had not yet found his own voice. He played as a collaborator first with Art Blakey and the Jazz Messengers, and later with pianist Herbie Hancock in a 1981 recording with the rhythm section that made up the stunning VSOP quartet of the 1960s (Ron Carter on bass and Tony Williams on drums). A critic described the nineteen-year-old Marsalis on that recording, writing "the technically fearless teenaged trumpeter mostly plays the eager student, imitating Miles, Freddie Hubbard, and Brownie McGhee, obviously relishing the challenge of keeping up with his world-class cohorts" (Ginell 1981). This album was initially to be released only in Japan, but the buzz on the young Marsalis was already so loud that CBS released it in the United States in 1982. Draped in the aura of the Young Lion mythology, Marsalis was proving more marketable than the jazz greats of Hancock, Carter, and Williams. Marsalis's 1985 release, *Black Codes (From the Underground),* is a model of the Young Lion sound, for both better and worse. This was the "neoclassicism" that many jazz artists and listeners found too imitative. As a critic wrote, "With his brother Branford often closely emulating Wayne Shorter and the rhythm section (pianist Kenny Kirkland, bassist Charnett Moffett, and drummer Jeff Tain Watts) sounding a bit like the famous Herbie Hancock-Ron Carter-Tony Williams trio, Wynton is heard at the head of what was essentially an updated version of the mid- to late-1960s Miles Davis Quintet" (Yanow n.d.).

At that time critics were still waiting for Marsalis to find his original voice and even starting to lose hope, considering the pastiche of *Black Codes.* To many, Marsalis's original trumpet voice never arrived.[12] Instead, his work continued in a re-creative vein, but began to mine deeper into the jazz past. Influenced by the philosophies of writers Albert Murray and Stanley Crouch, Marsalis became acutely concerned with jazz history and tradition, especially the work of Duke Ellington and Louis Armstrong. He began to go back to the 1910s, 1920s, and 1930s for inspiration. For example, in examining his tour journal from the 1990s, he and his septet bandmates were deeply involved in the styles of King Oliver and Jelly Roll Morton, discussing the nuances of the recordings in depth (Marsalis and Vigeland 2001, 126, 134). Marsalis has remained focused on this early period of jazz. His 2009 album *He and She,* predominantly in the style of Armstrong, was described by a critic as a "return to simpler times" (Nastos 2009). The majority of Marsalis's recordings since then are tribute albums, and his usual approach to performance is what I would describe as "demonstration jazz." Criticism of what many deem an overemphasis on the past has dogged Marsalis throughout his tenure at JALC. Even as he brings jazz into the schools, for example, students will ask, "Do you ever, you know, play anything contemporary?" (quoted in Marsalis and Vigeland 2001, 5).

Marsalis's accomplishments are legion; and his emotional, physical, and intellectual commitment to jazz and its place in America cannot be overstated. He works tirelessly, not only writing and recording, but touring nationally and internationally, speaking with young people as he goes. Charles Johnson has written that "to control the interpretation of the past is to control others" (Johnson 2013 [1988], 79), and jazz has been narrated to the American public and Europe by white men since its inception.[13] In 1924 European American Paul Whiteman sought to define jazz for the public by staging his "Experiment in Modern Music." The evening purported to trace the history of jazz from its "primitive" beginnings to its culmination in George Gershwin's jazz and classical music fusion premiere, *Rhapsody in Blue.* As described in the Introduction, the concert proffered an edifying tour through the assumed development of the music. The African-American composer, cornetist, and bandleader W. C. Handy answered Whiteman's performance with a concert of his own in 1928 at Carnegie Hall.

Tracing through the "evolution in Negro music" from "The Birth of Jazz" to a "Jazz Finale," Handy embraced jazz edification in order to name the story himself (Tackley 2012, 4–5). Thus, from its beginnings, and much like Wynton Marsalis's efforts, some African-Americans have attempted to use the "master's tools" to take control of the narrative themselves.

Thus, I sympathize with Marsalis's project and his drive to take charge of the narrative and the ongoing history. Giovanni Russonello notes that "many of the musicians who come through [JALC] programs as youngsters treat Marsalisite traditionalism as a launchpad, rather than an ideal," eventually moving into more experimental and creative approaches to jazz (Russonello 2017). In this, Marsalis's work has undeniably nourished jazz in the twenty-first century. Examining the repercussions and ramifications of Marsalis's traditionalist approach in terms of Replay and its prevalence at the turn of the millennium, however, illuminates conceptions of jazz as an image of America. Jazz critic Nate Chinen summarizes the still prevalent critique of Marsalis's vision held by many scholars, musicians and fans:

> Mr. Marsalis was armed with a big idea: that jazz is a model of democratic action, and a prism through which American culture can be understood. This notion, first articulated to him by [Albert] Murray and [Stanley] Crouch, has since been advanced by Jazz at Lincoln Center with the fervor of religious dogma and the adaptability of a political agenda. It served as a central conceit of *Jazz,* the 2001 Ken Burns PBS mini-series that spotlighted Mr. Marsalis not only as a commentator but also as a savior of the tradition. To a certain extent this has become the official story of jazz in the public sphere. (Chinen 2006)

Marsalis is the savior of the tradition not by bringing something new to jazz, but by becoming its champion preserver and border patroller.

In his efforts to build a "home for jazz" and create a "house of swing," as JALC promotional materials state, Marsalis has been unswerving in his definitions of what is and isn't jazz. Although he has opened up to different styles of music over the decades in answer to critics, demand, and what Francis Davis describes Marsalis's band's as his "canon-keeping duties," he has not changed his general view of what is *really* jazz. For example, in performing the music of Ornette Coleman, Davis described Marsalis's band's performance as the sonic statement "This Is Not Our Music," riffing on the famous 1960 Coleman album *This Is Our Music* (quoted in Teal 2014, 402). For Marsalis, the avant-garde signals the chaos of the modern world, something to which artists should be giving order. Fusion is considered a type of selling out to commercialism and lowbrow standards. Fusion and the avant-garde led to the near demise of jazz in the 1960s and 1970s, according to Marsalis. And the trumpeter saves his most vociferous comments for hip-hop, which he describes as degrading and a form of modern minstrelsy.[14]

While Marsalis's statements, especially on hip-hop, may be redolent of a type of "respectability politics" that has often been criticized as a bourgeois sensibility based in Western values, Marsalis in no way fits neatly into such a category. Certainly, he subscribes to an outdated distinction between high art and low entertainment. That Armstrong and Ellington were popular in their day only shows how culture has become increasingly degraded since that time. Current culture has sunk low, and artists need to give form to the chaos. The avant-garde is merely reflecting modern times—fractured, unlocatable, and lost. It offers no answer to this predicament. Hip-hop is an even more egregious acceptance of modern chaos and debauchery. But Marsalis's response is not to disavow black cultural practice or to distance himself from its rural and financially impoverished roots. In his view, it is hip-hop that is aligning with white values which led to and support a modern alienated world. What is needed is a return to the old-fashioned values found in the black community in an era even before Marsalis was born.

This narrative is most easily discernible in Ken Burns's *Jazz,* of which Marsalis was a central talking head. With his overriding focus on Armstrong and Ellington, Marsalis seems reluctant to bring into jazz's home even the post–World War II "modern era." A brief scan of the documentary gives a sense of the Marsalis-Crouch-Murray version of jazz history to which Marsalis still hews today.[15] An absolutely inordinate amount of time (that is, episodes 1 through 7, about 70 percent) is spent on the era before 1945. With the arrival of bebop in 1945, jazz begins moving into the realm of "chaos." In episode 8, "Risk," devoted to bebop, the music is alienating Armstrong, who remains, with Duke Ellington, the de facto center of jazz for every episode. In the ninth episode of ten, we arrive in 1956, where we hear about the innovations of Miles Davis, Sonny Rollins, and John Coltrane. The episode ends with an ominous section on "avant-gardist" Ornette Coleman, which plays his music over images of nuclear bombs, riots, and poverty—signals of modern anxiety and decline. And the final episode covers the last forty years of the hundred years covered (1900–2000), emphasizing the peril the avant-garde, Latin styles, and fusion posed to "jazz." The audience was either driven away or splintered into niche styles that weren't really representative of true "jazz." Marsalis emerges at the end of this episode as jazz's rescuer—able to return jazz to its true power. As Albert Murray put it in the documentary, jazz gives *form* to chaos, like all great art, and doesn't just follow whatever impulse pops into one's head, as he characterizes the approach of avant-garde musicians.

The triumvirate of Murray, Crouch, and Marsalis gave a version of jazz history unrecognizable to virtually every other jazz historian (as Scott Deveaux points out, the jazz "master narrative" before Ken Burns's *Jazz* focused on bebop as the beginning, not the end, of "real jazz" and generally moved on from there). But their version of jazz history has been compelling in the strong link they make between jazz and nation, a link aided and abetted by Ken Burns's syrupy treatment. As the founders and stewards of JALC, Murray, Crouch, and Marsalis promote jazz as a music that epitomizes the freedom and democracy of America. Jazz "objectifies" America, according to Marsalis in the documentary; it represents American freedom at its finest; jazz is democracy; jazz *is* America. It is a triumphant and heroic story of Americans (black men) overcoming incredible adversity to create the most beautiful art form America has produced. In order to inculcate this vision of jazz and democracy, Marsalis *fixes* jazz history in his listeners'—but really more accurately, viewers'—minds through Replay. As such, while Marsalis advocates for black values, his sense of their loss and his nostalgia propels a type of relationship to the past that is more in the Western vein of Replay than an African-American practice of signifying. It is a longing for a permanent and coherent identity.[16]

Fixing History: The Birth of Jazz

In 2006, Marsalis performed a tribute to Louis Armstrong's famous Hot Five recordings, recordings which Marsalis considered "the foundation of the organization of jazz improvisation, even as we know it today" (quoted in Schaefer 2006). The tribute took place over three evenings and included Marsalis on trumpet, Wycliffe Gordon on tuba and trombone, Vincent Gardner on trombone, Victor Goines on clarinet, Jonathan Batiste on piano, Carlos Henriquez on bass, Ali Jackson on drums, and "Papa" Don Vappie on banjo. In a typical response regarding Marsalis's tribute approach at JALC, a reviewer lamented the trumpeter's strict adherence to the past—his insistence on "getting it right" rather than taking chances. Of the Hot Five tribute, Chris Kelsey for *Jazztimes* wrote:

> The music worked as an homage or a revival. On a deeper level, however, it lacked. The ground covered was too familiar, the treatment clichéd and overly

> reverential. The wild and wooly spirit of discovery that speaks to us from the original Hot Five recordings was nowhere to be found. Therein resides the central point: That very air of adventure, that ineffable spark of inspiration provides the essence of what makes the best jazz great. It's what separates the original Hot Fives from a skillfully executed, well-meaning tribute. I wish Marsalis had made that point. Unfortunately, I'm not sure he understands it himself. (Kelsey 2006)

Kelsey here criticizes Marsalis for approaching jazz as an artifact that must be preserved, rather than a process that encourages engagement, exploration, risk taking, and openness to inspiration. Put in the terms of the Takai discussion mentioned previously, Marsalis treats these recordings as the "old beat" that must not be lost. Rather than understanding jazz today as built upon and still connected to these earlier recordings and their innovations, Marsalis feels that this old beat will be lost if it is not brought back in its "original" form.

Marsalis's approach to the jazz past is replete with characteristics of Replay. He takes the past as the authority, performing the music in its "original intent," rather than recognizing the "old beat" in the "new beat" and taking today's parameters as the authority. He is not primarily concerned with how the music or performance would best work now in relation to present-day circumstances—for example, accounting for popular taste regarding tempo or rhythmic feel. This is similar to discussions in a famous Duke Ellington tribute orchestra over whether to perform tempi as heard on the record or as remembered by players in the current band who had actually performed with Ellington. Choosing a tempo that might align with current trends is not considered.[17] The truth is in the past, not the present. Further, Marsalis emphasizes control. He stresses the ability to perform these past styles "correctly" as the hallmark of an authentic jazz player. This mastery involves painstaking, complex work. Only some people can do it. In presenting the music in this way, jazz is understood as a series of historic events, not as an approach or method. In this case, the recordings are the historic event and are therefore reenacted like a famous battle. As such, Marsalis "fixes" history in two senses of the term: he makes it permanent, and he "corrects it" through the implicit aspects of his performance, as I will demonstrate. Finally, there is the privileging of the "liveness" of the event—the audience will *be there* with the past. And this live embodied performance carries with it a truth.

Marsalis fixes history along the lines of the accepted master narrative of jazz by finding an origin in Armstrong's improvisation, thus serving to highlight the individual Great Man. In the program's musician biographies, in addition to the eight performers on the bill, only Armstrong's biography is given from the original Hot Five, suggesting that he is the only artist who matters in this origin story.[18] This particular Great Man narrative works well for the New Orleans born and bred, trumpet-playing Marsalis. As the playbill states, "Pops Armstrong always believed that New Orleans musicians had a special insight into the essence of jazz and nobody else could play it quite as well." Focusing on the importance of these New Orleans roots, the playbill stresses Marsalis's Crescent City heritage, making him ideally suited to be "the one to recreate the artistic achievement that Armstrong and these four musical pioneers put on record in those historic sessions" (Benjamin 2006). Marsalis promotes the Great Man tradition, with himself as the rightful heir to the tradition as a musician/improviser in this case (through Armstrong) and as a composer, through linking himself to Duke Ellington in other JALC performances and activities.

While Marsalis helps to fix the idea of jazz as the art of great individuals, he also fixes it by altering the original story to align with the gendered narrative of jazz that he promotes. That is, despite the fact that this group of "musical pioneers" who helped to lay the foundation of jazz contained a woman, there was no woman onstage with Marsalis. Like the vast majority of bands that perform at JALC, the ensemble was all male. Thus, while Marsalis is routinely criticized for being "too exact," such exactitude does not extend to representing the contributions of women to early jazz via a female performer.[19] Lil Hardin Armstrong was the pianist in the Hot Five and the composer and arranger for many of their songs. Indeed, of the eighteen songs chosen for the concert, three were composed or co-composed by Hardin. The only composer with more credits was Armstrong, with five written or cowritten. And of the total of fifty-four songs recorded by all Hot Five and Hot Seven ensembles, more than 25 percent are credited to Hardin.[20]

Marsalis, then, "repairs" the image of the foundation of jazz from one that includes a woman's significant contribution to one that is solely the work of men. And if we look at the review of that performance by Nate Chinen in the *New York Times*, we see how the ritual reenactment of jazz is taken as the "real" story, despite written contradiction of that narrative. As Chinen comments on how Marsalis "channels" the "Granddaddy of 'Skid Dat-de-Dat'" (2006), no mention is made in his review of Lil Hardin Armstrong, who is credited in the program as *the composer of the song*. Through the authority of the reenactment, the men on stage, performing Armstrong's ensemble so presumably exactly that they are criticized for it, produce the "truth" of jazz. This is the influence of performance and the command of Replay, that JALC can print the truth of Hardin's contribution, but the performance itself will give us the "real" message—that women are anomalous to jazz, a message Nate Chinen then reinforced in the *New York Times:* Grandmama supplanted by Granddaddy. Marsalis uses Replay to instantiate and perpetuate his vision and version of jazz history, fixing "errors" as he goes and fixing the history in his listeners' eyes and minds, if not always in their ears.

Another, more progressive example of fixing could be argued for Marsalis's embodied representation of Armstrong. In his many reincarnations of the trumpeter, Marsalis will perform in only a Brooks Brothers or equally stylish suit. Such a performance snubs the detail that from the mid-1940s on, Louis Armstrong was often ignored as a key force in jazz because of what some bebop musicians considered a form of "tomming." His grinning and mugging performance style was condemned by later trumpeters Dizzy Gillespie and Miles Davis. Biographer Terry Teachout describes the attitude held by Gillespie and others of Armstrong as "an artist, but also an old-time accommodationist who went along to get along" (Teachout 2009, 324). Of course, as Teachout and others have shown, this characterization was erroneous. Armstrong was often outspoken against racism and refused to perform as a jazz ambassador in protest of America's institutionalized racism. Further, his performance style was enjoyed by black audiences in all-black shows in the early twentieth century and was far from universally viewed as a form of "tomming" for a white audience. Nonetheless, Marsalis's work at JALC probably did much to retrieve Armstrong from the image of a mugging throwback to an overtly racist America. In the 1980s most people would have associated Armstrong with his vocal performances, such as "Hello, Dolly" and "It's a Wonderful World." For years his jazz performances were understood as pivotal for his time, but considered old-timey in the post-bebop period. Marsalis changed that. In re-performing the trumpeter with the dignity reserved for the classical concert of Armstrong's time, Marsalis "takes us back in time" to an Armstrong where the painful and degrading manifestations of racism in the 1920s are redacted.[21]

Marsalis is constructing a particular vision of the jazz past. But Marsalis also seems to long for a return to "old-fashioned" values of family, community, and responsibility. Marsalis routinely refers to black folk traditions centered around food, family, and the blues in his upbringing in New Orleans. His values are evident in interviews and workshops, JALC statements, and tour memoirs from his times on the road. The general storyline emphasizes hard work (exemplified in his work in jazz, but applicable to a variety of fields): to put exceptional effort and devotion into learning your instrument/art/craft and to avoid the easy, tempting, pandering approach to life represented by selling out or giving in to popular taste. By putting time and effort into your chosen endeavor, you will create something of high quality, and you will have developed a sense of dignity and self-esteem. This is the payoff for not taking the easy way of quick money through, for example, the modern-day "minstrelsy" of rap. It is cohering and maintaining an identity against a chaotic, fragmented, degraded world. This road of the great, hardworking, dignified artist, however, is a man's road. In Marsalis's many stories meant to pass on this wisdom, women are found in supporting roles—there to help the men in their quest toward excellence. Indeed, Marsalis proves himself to be very much behind the times in terms of modern gender relations, a fact that is unfortunate considering his position to declare both what jazz is and how it is a model of American nation.

Marsalis grew up in a household of six brothers with his father and mother. While the father and four of the six boys were involved in music, it was Marsalis's mother who did the cooking, cleaning, and disciplining. Thus, Marsalis was steeped in the environment of male camaraderie and artistry, with women in supporting roles, throughout his youth.[22] In *Jazz in the Bittersweet Blues of Life,* a tour memoir of his work with his septet in the 1990s, the importance Marsalis ascribes to the camaraderie of his all-male team is apparent. The banter that goes on incessantly during rehearsals, recording sessions, and on tour, as well as the pickup basketball games, are all a part of the glue that holds the band together, inspiring their performances and deepening their understanding of each other. The chronicle also reveals the place of women in Marsalis's vision of jazz. With one exception,[23] women appear in only the following forms in the account (quotes are from Marsalis):

- As an abstract muse: "[an idea may appear from] an exquisitely dangerous woman you just met" (142)
- As a metaphor: "[the trumpet] was like a woman that you had to go to. You couldn't wait for it, for her, to come to you . . . You got to get it. It doesn't just come because you want it" (130–31), or "[not improvising is like] having a plan for a woman. How do you know what she's going to do?" (56)
- As inspiration to practice: "It was a good way to get girls, being able to play the trumpet" (123), or "I'd be lying if I told you that beautiful women don't make you play better. Or try to play better." (19)
- As potential conquests: "We call him Sugar Rob. Because of his ability to communicate with the ladies." (54)

- In a joke: "Art Blakey used to say there's only two kinds of pussy. Good. And better." (110)

And in those instances when the women were actually specific people (though not always named):

- As musicians' wives who periodically join the tour
- As those who produce food: "my great-aunt Marguerite's house . . . lord help us for what came off of that stove" (41), or "their grandmother sending along fried chicken for the band" (132)

Whether muse, metaphor, joke, or provider of food, women in Marsalis's world of jazz are there to support the male musicians in their pursuit of excellence. The challenges, the inspiration, the triumph, the camaraderie, the pursuit of excellence—these areas are the domain of men.

In fact, a woman would disrupt one of Marsalis's primary concerns with his band, to establish and promote "the ease of interaction necessary for a group of men to live comfortably" (12). With women allotted to roles of metaphor and muse, admirer and food preparer, their transfer to role of musician will be hard to manage in Marsalis's strictly delineated environment.

Therefore, it is going to be interesting to watch the famous institution over the next several years. Inroads have recently been made to overturn the patriarchal and male-dominated nature of JALC. Responding to pressure from advocates for women in jazz, JALC instituted an annual JazzGirls Day in 2014 to focus on educating young female instrumentalists ("JazzGirls Day" 2016). More significantly, in 2016 JALC agreed to follow a specific procedure, including blind auditions, for positions in the Jazz at Lincoln Center Orchestra. A 2016 news release by Equal Rights Advocates states, "The new, more formalized selection procedures include blind auditions, formal job postings, and wider outreach about openings, all of which will help the Orchestra attract a broad and diverse pool of applicants" ("Jazz at Lincoln Center Adopts Blind Auditions" 2016). The release goes on to acknowledge that "blind auditions have been widely credited with increasing the representation of women in symphony orchestras from less than 5% of all players in the 1970s, to close to 50% today." There is very little turnover in the orchestra, and at present writing there have been no jobs to advertise. But a day will appear on the horizon when Marsalis's view of authentic jazz as a male province will be challenged by these changes. Fully integrating women instrumentalists into JALC will not feel natural to the prevailing culture at the institution. Women instrumentalists as regular members in the JALC Orchestra will be very different from the containment of one JazzGirls Day a year or a memorial tribute that allows JALC to present its version of "gender equality," as Kimberly Hannon Teal argues about their Mary Lou Williams tribute.[24] As the narrative currently stands, it might feel awkwardly modern, out of step with the general message of returning to old, lost values.

In her book *Yearning,* bell hooks recalls her childhood in rural, segregated Kentucky. Although she is fully aware of the injustice, limited opportunities, and overt racism that characterized and perpetuated that segregation, she also recognizes the deep benefits of growing up in this world, protected from mainstream society in many ways and nurtured by a support system that had been in place for generations. This safety and grounding was disrupted for hooks in the 1960s, however, when school integration bussed her to a predominantly white school. She writes, "That black world of my growing up began to fundamentally change. . . . What I remember most about that time is a deep sense of loss. . . . I . . . wondered why the grown black folks had acted as though they did not know we would be surrendering so much for so little, that we would be leaving behind a history" (34). While clearly not suggesting a return to the times of institutionalized segregation, hooks does convey the deep loss that much of the black community suffered *as community* in the wake of Civil Rights legislation and a concern with the loss of a history. An uprootedness and sense of alienation and homelessness could now be added to the continued experience of racism, which was not eradicated through the new laws. hooks also connects this experience to the larger sense of loss associated with postmodernity generally. She writes, "The overall impact of postmodernism is that many other groups now share with black folks a sense of deep alienation, despair, uncertainty, [and a] loss of a sense of grounding even if it is not informed by shared circumstance" (27).

I believe Marsalis's preoccupation with pre–World War II jazz is in part an answer to the type of longing described by hooks and seen across the United States in the 1980s and 1990s: the desire for a stronger sense of community and home that is imagined to reside in the past as a cure for modern alienation. In this, JALC was right on cue with the swing revival of the 1990s and an audience desire for "simpler times." Whereas hooks does not link those times with gender roles that place women in ancillary roles to men, in a more conservative vein, Marsalis does. Marsalis presented "simpler times" through the performance of his all-male ensemble that taught us the "origins of jazz," while it simultaneously presented us with a vision of "democracy." This can be viewed as a type of modern-day ritual return that serves to stabilize certain cultural themes, in this case the value of (black) men hard at work and the implicit assumption that women should be supporting them in behind-the-scenes ways. But I believe the appeal of reenactments involves more than nostalgia and the belief that times (as we imagine them) were better in the past. Audiences are drawn to performances of reenactments because they offer performances of the *known:* performances that provide a sense of stability and mastery, a respite from the open-endedness, insecurity, and "loss of a sense of grounding" characteristic of postmodernity. This element was especially prevalent in a 1994 reenactment of a Glenn Miller radio broadcast at Yale University and its ritual presentation of a unified nation.

GLENN MILLER AT YALE

On April 8, 1994, as part of America's yearlong fiftieth anniversary celebration of D-day, director Thomas Duffy and the Yale Concert Band presented a reenactment of a 1940s Glenn Miller "I Sustain the Wings" radio broadcast in Yale's Woolsey Hall, the site of the original performance. Yale Band personnel astoundingly recovered the original forty-eight-star American flag to again cascade down the back of the auditorium; band members donned simulated World War II–era uniforms appropriate to the rank of the musician they embodied, becoming Corporal "Peanuts" Hucko on clarinet or Private First Class Steven Steck on trumpet; and in a dramatic move by the perpetually barbate bandleader, Thomas Duffy returned after the intermission clean shaven (to the particular amazement of his musical charges), with slicked-back hair and wire-rimmed glasses, all the more to incarnate the famous bandleader. With the spirit of Miller upon him, Duffy led his band through the exact music and heroic war adventure skit performed decades ago for a World War II radio audience. The event was a huge success, leading to performances at the National Museum in Washington, DC, and at the international fiftieth anniversary D-day commemorations in France and England. Described by the band's business manager as their "cash cow," the event continued periodically over the next decade, culminating in a performance for 2004's sixtieth anniversary of D-day.[25]

This detailed reenactment occurred in the midst of the swing revival and the rise of the tribute band. Of course, by taking place at a venerated university, as well as the nation's capital and on an international stage, Yale's commemoration was not only popular cultural memory, but also a part of the sanctioned national memory of World War II. Fiftieth anniversary commemorations of World War II closely followed the First Gulf War and its supposed triumph over America's "Vietnam Syndrome."[26] Such remembrances served to supplant dissenting, plural, cacophonous 1960s wartime images with those of a "popular" World War II, and Yale's reenactment clearly participated in this widespread tendency. But the devil is in the details, and my focus here is on how the intricacies of Yale's production reveal important strategies for enacting and maintaining boundaries that speak to both political and musical gatekeeping. The Miller reenactment presents a unique opportunity to undress the cross-dressing and racial traversing that often attends such nostalgic performances of identity. Contemporary Yale women and men of color would not have been welcome in Miller's original orchestra; and yet in this reenactment, two men of color (trumpet and piano) and four white women (two cornets, trumpet, and tenor saxophone), along with their white male bandmates, now take on the identity of a particular white man, wear his uniform, and speak his words in a spectacle of national consonance. The recreation also enacts a precise gender ritual of big band and jazz performance that I describe as in-passing. I begin by demonstrating in-passing as it is performed by women playing jazz, follow with a dissection of Glenn Miller's constructed white masculinity and its mobilization as a synonym for American nation, and conclude by arguing how the reenactment serves to offer audiences performances of unity and identity. The Glenn Miller reenactment patches up feelings of loss while presenting images of an American nation with secure borders, benevolent patriarchal control, and the eradication of difference.

Women in Jazz and In-passing

When I discovered Yale's Glenn Miller reenactment, my immediate reaction as a female instrumentalist was to wonder how the women in the band felt. Tenor saxophonist Elizabeth Branch ('97), performing Private Vince Carbone, and trumpeter Else Festersen ('96), festooned in the chevrons of Private First Class Steve Steck, struck me as particularly unequivocal examples of the phenomenon I experienced playing saxophone in my faux tuxedo with the "other men" in the band. As the only woman instrumentalist in many swing bands, I was expected to blend in with its masculine veneer, while the woman vocalist in her beaded gown embodied the "feminine" in our (re)enactment of classic gender roles and heterosexual desire. Thus, I was in some way to "pass" as male, but this did not mean to be overtly butch (unacceptable) or to wear a disguise. Somehow obeisance to the tradition deeming this position as "male" was necessary without foreclosing my prescribed gender identity as female/feminine.[27] I have termed this move in-passing, as it bears some similarities with the action of "passing" in racial and gender contexts, an activity that has been productively unpacked and theorized by legal scholar Cheryl I. Harris and artist Adrian Piper regarding race and Jack Halberstam regarding gender (Harris 1993, Piper 1986–1990, 1992; Halberstam 1998).[28] In-passing relates to passing in that a privileged subject position retains proprietary status; but whereas "passing" entails an undetected and complete (albeit transitory and often uncomfortable)[29] assumption of the privileged subject position, in-passing is a signifying practice that asserts the authority and inevitability of the dominant position while simultaneously allowing the subordinate person to occupy it as a unique placeholder bestowed with honorary status. When placing syllabic emphasis on the *in*, *in*-passing suggests that the "noninevitable" person is *in*, and she or he participates in the dominant group and has some access to the concomitant privileges. However, by placing the emphasis on *passing*, the term acknowledges the temporary and contingent quality of this participation: the relation with the dominant group is only in passing, not assured or assumed, and must be continually remanufactured. Thus, in-passing is a form of liminal identity that does not disrupt unified identity, but rather "fashions unity" through its particular signifying practice.

In-passing can best be observed in the uniforms (uniformities) of a ritualized setting: a commemoration or a performance (and in our modern memory culture, many performances are commemorative in some way). For women in big bands, in-passing requires not calling attention to one's femaleness: in addition to wearing a faux suit, one does not blanch as the conductor calls attention with "Gentlemen!" or point out sexism when he exclaims, "You guys are swingin' like a pair of [tits]!"[30] Here women perform jazz musically while concurrently performing that performance as inevitably "masculine," reinscribing gender norms rather than embodying progressive action as is often assumed. The Miller recreation was therefore a ritualized enactment of how women in jazz have to "play [like] men" in order to play. However, this was not all that was played at Yale.

Glenn Miller, Swing, and Masculinity

As with the other reenactments described in this book, it is necessary to understand more fully what is being re-created. While the Hot Five recordings are arguably mostly important to music history, Miller's performance was pivotal not for its musical contribution, but for its embodiment of wartime America. And part of what Miller embodied was a particular idea of white masculinity, one that Miller himself created and sold to an eager public. As I've discussed elsewhere, aligning masculinity with popular music had been a successful formula in the years preceding Miller's rise (McMullen 2006). I described the masculinity of bandleader Paul Whiteman as white, cultured, and feminized, and that of Benny Goodman as of virility born from its relationship to blackness. It was Miller, however, who took swing and further commodified it for a mass audience. Miller's masculinity was that of the potent, authoritative white man, cut loose from any threat of blackness or femininity. Indeed, he kept swing's energy but eliminated overt references to blackness. Thus, much like Whiteman, Miller bleached jazz, but he retained the normative masculinity. Miller was a perfect fit for the segregated military, for unlike Goodman, Artie Shaw, Charlie Barnett, or Tommy Dorsey, Glenn Miller never hired a black musician or singer for his band; and his lyrics promoted images of rural, white America, replete with gendered and racial stereotypes that perfectly fed into wartime messages propagated by the Department of War Information selling the idea of the "idealized home front."[31]

Even before Miller became an enlisted man, he was described as a strict disciplinarian, maintaining a demeanor as authoritative and capable as a "General" (Erenberg 1998). Lewis Erenberg cites many such references to Miller's masculine image:

> Tall, "bespectacled and scholarly looking," he "was a commanding guy, youthful but mature," according to his press agent, Howard Richmond, who found that Miller "looked like security, like all the things I'd never found in a band leader." True, "Mickey Mouse band leaders looked like security. I'm talking about jazz leaders. To me they always looked like they didn't know where they were going to sleep the next night." Seventeen-year-old singer Marion Hutton concurred. As her legal guardian, Miller "was like a father. . . . He represented a source of strength. . . . He fulfilled the image of what a father ought to be." (Erenberg 1998, 187)

Much like the description of Genesis by Ron Ross in chapter 1, the naturalness and authenticity of white heteromasculinity is established through racial and gendered difference. Other "traveling bands" or "jazz leaders" clearly reference black jazz (either directly or as an inspiration for white jazz leaders) by opposing them to infantilized, "Mickey Mouse" bands of the popular white variety. By alluding to myths of black masculinity as excessive, profligate, and uncontrolled and thereby unable to provide adequate leadership, Miller's white masculinity is established as reasoned, controlled, and authoritative. Similarly, the "femininity" of Hutton is presented as childlike and in need of strength and guidance. It is Miller's firm patriarchal oversight that contains femininity and its threat of "emotionalism," "incompetence," and "vacuous commercialism" by disciplining it into the safe and only intermittently accessed arena of the beautiful and lyric spectacle.[32] Such analysis is nothing new, but it is important to understand with what desiderata we fulfill our appetite for reenactment.

Miller's patriarchal image was heightened when he enlisted in 1942 and led the 418th Army Air Forces Band stationed at Yale University. The Yale concert notes described Miller as "a man possessed of deep and genuine patriotic sentiment," but for him to enlist in the army was certainly as much a shrewd business move as any heartfelt allegiance (Ronzello 1994).[33] As Sherrie Tucker has written, men in big bands, as in other civilian work, would be "scrutinized with the ubiquitous, 'Why aren't you in uniform?'" (Tucker 2000, 42). The Glenn Miller Orchestra had been the most popular band in the nation since 1939; and given Erenberg's convincing analysis of swing bands as playing on patriarchal masculinity, it is impossible to imagine Miller's continued mass popularity without his connection to military service. And while Erenberg describes the move as a sacrifice, he also relates how the AAF Orchestra surpassed even its civilian predecessor in popularity (Erenberg 1998, 182). Indeed, Miller's priorities as an enlisted man leaned toward business over service. Although assigned to oversee all of the AAFTTC bands from Knollwood Field, North Carolina, Miller eventually convinced his superiors to allow him to remain full-time at the Yale campus, where his supposedly subsidiary position of leading the 418th AAF Band took place. This post band was to play for daily review formations, parades, luncheon sessions, weekly cadet dances and other cadet affairs, and enlisted men's dances, as well as march to and from ceremonies, and travel to nearby towns to recruit aviation cadets. In roughly eight months, however, Miller had extricated his band from any post duties (except special occasions); and in early December 1943, Miller transferred twenty-four of his twenty-eight band members into the 2nd AAFTC[34] Radio Unit, leaving the old 418th to be the post band with a new director and new name as the 718th. Miller's priorities for *his* band were gaining national radio shows, playing national war bond rallies (live concerts to huge audiences), attaining overseas radio shows, and eventually, touring Europe.[35]

While the stripped and restaffed 718th remained to provide post duties at Yale, Miller's band was now free to function much like a civilian band, but with free passage around the country and the world, free and regular radio play, and free promotion. Instead of playing local recruitment drives in Stamford and Bridgeport, Miller was now touring major American cities such as St. Louis and Chicago for national war loan drives; and he evaded the 1942–1944 AFM recording ban by recording V-Discs for the troops (distributed nationally and internationally by the War Department). Miller also recorded six local "test" broadcasts at Yale in the spring and summer of 1943 (the source of Duffy's re-creation). Played over WEEI Boston, "I Sustain the Wings" (after the AAFTTC motto, "Sustineo Alas") was soon broadcast nationally over CBS and later NBC under the aegis of the War Department. Miller also worked for months to get permission to travel overseas. On October 13, 1943, "Miller met with Lieutenant General Barton K. Yount to cover several points, the major one being his request that the 418th AAF Band be sent overseas to entertain the troops."[36] In June of 1944 the band made the trip and entertained "hundreds of thousands" of Allied soldiers (Ronzello 1994, 6). In describing his work with the bandleader during the war, saxophonist Hank Freeman recalled, "Glenn was sort of businesslike. It was like he was the head of a big corporation. He had that kind of mind" (quoted in Ronzello 1994, 5). And indeed, Miller seems to have situated his band in a way that would impress any CEO, guaranteeing huge exposure, a highly sellable image based on patriotism, and an overhead covered by the government. Of course, it cannot be denied that risk was also involved. In taking his band overseas during wartime, Miller did end up paying the ultimate price. He lost his life over the English Channel in what is now believed to be a case of "friendly fire."[37]

Despite evidence of such personal ambition, Miller's marshaling of normative white masculinity ensured that such endeavors would be read as "patriotic," or as capable and providing "business acumen," rather than the "crass commercialism" of sweet bandleaders. And it was under such aegis that Miller masterminded the formula for mass popularity perhaps before anyone: create a well-defined and desired image and then replay it, again and again. Miller's drummer Moe Purtill explained that in the early years of the band "we just . . . played [the] same twenty tunes over and over" (Erenberg 1998, 169). But also in the later years, playing for the troops in Europe, Miller continued the repetition. When asked about such repetitiveness, Miller responded: "We didn't come here to set any new fashions in music. . . . We play only the old tunes" (192). Already serving the function of nostalgia, Glenn Miller described his role as providing the fighting boys with a "hunk o' home." Furthermore, Miller insisted that every level of band uniformity be re-created night after night. A fine was levied if uniforms, socks, neckties, or handkerchiefs were not "just right." According to Miller's trumpeter, Billy May, "There was no room for inventiveness. Even the hot choruses were supposed to be the same" (187). Thus, Miller created and led America's most popular band (1939–1942), the first band ever awarded a gold record for a million records sold,[38] through the very deployment of repetition and identity. Miller tapped into the desire for the comfort and reassurance of repetition and indeed, of the identical, during troubled times. And what he repeated were images of white masculinity as reasoned and in charge.

Replay as Identity Spectacle

Thomas Duffy's obsession with repetition and identity and his fervent attention to detail, therefore, replayed not only the Miller broadcast, but Miller's own repetition compulsion. The reenactment included the songs "American Patrol," "The Volga Boatman," "In the Mood," and "Moonlight Serenade," and the radio play "Uncle Sam's Armorers" (a recruitment skit that featured the work of armorers and began with one of the two main characters singing, "I've got bombs that go jingle jangle jingle"). While the performance was a composite of different broadcasts, nonetheless, I would argue identity was in surplus: the identical space, the identical American flag, even Glenn Miller's original secretary was presented to the audience.[39] The Yale University performance, with its special claim to political memory through its institutional power, its status as a place of education where plurality is expected, and its sanctioning as a representative body overseas, is a particularly exemplary presentation of Replay. The reenactment fashions an identity against the pluralities of gender and race, subsuming these differences in a performance that plays unity through the medium of in-passing. Unlike battle reenactments, popular swing bands, tribute bands, or JALC, the Yale Band is not so self-selecting and must accommodate difference within its ranks. It is therefore faced with the dilemma of presenting women and people of color under the banner of unified white masculinity.

Such spectacles of national memory evidence the deep-rooted anxiety with plurality in American culture. In the 1990s, alluding to the Vietnam War became a touchstone for a generalized fear of postmodern pluralities. In the zealous proliferation of "United We Stand" bumper stickers, posters, and commentary, terrified Americans throughout the First Gulf War swore to learn from the lesson of Vietnam: that plurality can defeat a nation, a prospect the frightening specter of terrorism made more dire. As noted previously, America's victory in the First Gulf War was hailed as the corrective to America's "Vietnam Syndrome," and this "double victory" segued neatly into fiftieth anniversary celebrations of D-day and World War II. The Yale recreation served, like other World War II commemorations across the country, not only to return America to its old victorious self, but also to "return" it to a world of unity and identity.[40]

In its presentation of the World War II–era radio program, the Yale reenactment binds us together with its representations of nation—complete with a recruitment skit that could be viewed as recruiting a present "wartime" audience as well, since that was the beginning of the United States' now perpetual war on terror. And as Mircea Eliade describes in another context, such rituals cannot be of particulars, but enact "exemplary archetypes": in the Yale recreation's case, a particular vision of Western culture as white, teleological, unified, masculine, and strong.

Put another way, the Yale Replay is a ritual enactment of the "abstract citizen" of modernity. In her book *Immigrant Acts,* Lisa Lowe describes the contradiction inherent in Western capitalist countries between the need for "abstract labor" and for "abstract citizens":

> Theoretically, in a racially homogeneous nation, the needs of capital and the needs of the state complement each other. Yet in a racially differentiated nation such as the United States, capital and state imperatives may be contradictory: capital, with its supposed needs for "abstract labor," is said by Marx to be unconcerned by the "origins" of its labor force, whereas the nation-state, with its need for "abstract citizens" formed by a unified culture to participate in the political sphere, is precisely concerned to maintain a national citizenry bound by race, language, and culture. (Lowe, 13)

Lowe goes on to describe how the Asian immigrant[41] is a constant threat to the "abstract American citizen" by physiologically bearing the trace of a history (of racist immigration, employment, and social practices) that national memory wishes to forget, and of an Other (Asia) that must by definition remain outside for the West to establish itself as unified. Forever representing the "foreigner within," Asian immigrants and Asian Americans jeopardize the construction of the unified nation-state. It is spectacles of national memory such as Yale's, which attempt to "resolve" the contradiction of particularity (woman, Asian, black) into abstract (white male) by conscientiously enacting the ritual of "particularity" speaking "abstract."[42] Faced with the threat of an "incorrect" reading of the nation-state, national memory attempts to heal the gash through ritual Replay.[43]

Thus, the Miller reenactment fashions a message of unity that depends on women and people of color "becoming" white men, depicting the practice as completely commensurate. These moments of identity crossing are thus not "queering," following Butler, or "deviant details," following Lowe—they do not fray the seams of unity and perfect mimesis in their incommensurability, but are more often "obedient transvestism" employed to signify the opposite. Such a reenactment becomes a precise ritual seeking to salve the fear of plurality by presenting women and people of color as obedient "white men," a process that creates the illusion of "plurality within unity" but is in fact only the ceremonial spectacle of the dominant culture speaking itself through the mouths of others ritually vacated of their own positions.

However, in the realm of concert hall performance where the audience's gravitational pull always careens toward the past, Duffy's inclination toward Replay is not surprising. A look around the Yale Band room lined with past concert posters reveals how seductive the call of Replay is to a contemporary band director, who must not only prepare performances each year, but also sell them. Duffy frequently mined the patriotic spirit of aging Yale alumni to fill his seats, presenting "Music of the Civil War" or "Stars and Strife: Music of Conflict and Patriotism," but he also arranged music around other themes, as any band director would: school spirit ("Music from the Pens of Yale Composers"), movie themes, church music, or more awkwardly, "Memories of the Orient." Faced with a public resistant to new music, it is not much of a stretch for a music director to choose to make the old haunt us more palpably by re-creating historic details associated with earlier presentations, perhaps in a determined attempt to breathe new life into the endeavor (indeed, Duffy had already filled the post for twelve years in 1994). The director himself is a composer and presents several of his compositions with the concert band annually, obviously sharing in the desire to have new music programmed into concerts. Attempting to balance sales with aesthetic recompense, Duffy, like most of his contemporaries, probably partakes of a delicate game of bait-and-switch, now presenting the pop classics, now sneaking in a new or lesser-known work.

Therefore, I hope it is clear that this is not an inquisition into the personal motives of Thomas Duffy. However, as a highly successful band director and salesman, Duffy did divine what people wanted to hear and see, and he balanced that with his own desires as a director and composer. As the band's golden goose and a favorite for fund-raising campaigns (presented as "war bond rallies"), the Glenn Miller recreation obviously enthralled New Haven. But its national and international exposure also led to reviews in newspapers around the country, including the *New York Times* and the *Chicago Tribune*. Expressing the sentiment of the organizers as well as many who partook in national D-day commemoration events, World War II veteran Joseph Dawson told the *Washington Post*: "I thought Vietnam was a stupid war. . . . The whole purpose of this event is to show the world and to show our country that there was a time when our nation moved forward as one unit."[44] The article showed no evidence of soliciting comment on Vietnam; World War II commemorations bore this connection implicitly. Duffy, like other band directors—indeed, like Miller himself—found success by providing an image that spoke to certain mass sentiments.

In the examples I have discussed so far, the practice of Replay has had particular ramifications for the performing bodies onstage. In the case of the Genesis and ABBA tributes, having the "correctly" raced and gendered bodies of the original was necessary in order to create a "real Genesis" or "real ABBA" show. The all-black male performance of the Hot Five recordings pasted over Lil Hardin Armstrong and performed the "corrected," masculinist version of the birth of jazz proffered by JALC. In these examples, bodies were chosen in order to reenact the past performance "accurately." Not so self-selecting, the Yale reenactment turned the pluralizing women and men of color of the modern university into "obedient transvestites," performing whiteness and maleness as universal. The next chapter introduces a tribute band that, much like the first three examples, chooses its bodies in order to accurately and authentically re-create the original band. The all-female tribute to Led Zeppelin, Lez Zeppelin, claims to be performing an exact reenactment with the *correct* bodies. Taking androgyny as their way in, Lez Zeppelin performs Led with all the girly, ballsy, omnivorous pansexuality of the original.

FOUR

The Importance of White Women Being Earnest

Lez Zeppelin and the Performance of Cock Rock

In the days of my youth I was told what it means to be a man.

Sung by Shannon Conley in Lez Zeppelin

In the 1973 Madison Square Garden concert, Robert Plant, in tight, faded, "nut-hugger" jeans and a frilly blue unbuttoned blouse, leans back, with pelvis thrust forward, and belts out the lyrics to "Black Dog." His left hand holds the microphone as his right hand—near his face, with beautifully tapered long fingernails—twirls and points upward. As the screen zooms out, Plant appears to be a very sexy, lusty, powerful woman howling out her song. Viewed today, Plant resembles nothing less than the first wildly popular, internationally famous "chick with a dick."[1] He is a more refined Janis Joplin with tighter clothes, her crotch stuffed, and more traditional care put into her long wavy locks. Plant's "femininity" went largely unremarked on in the 1970s, however. Even with early comparisons of Plant to Joplin by critics, the "masculinity" of the band was enough to spur the moniker "cock rock." It was only decades later that a male fan's love of Led Zeppelin began to raise sexual suspicions. Indeed, despite the flamboyant femininity of Plant and the often delicately baroque pieces of the band, Led has remained the definitive and originary example of "cock rock."

Enter the twenty-first century and Lez Zeppelin, the all-women Led Zeppelin clone band. Lez's precise reenactment brings forward all of the repressed-in-plain-sight illogics of gender. For indeed, in a book which examines "rigorously mimetic" live musical reenactments, wouldn't such a tribute that reperforms an all-male band with all-female bodies be an example of signifying with a signal difference, not of Replay? In fact, Lez Zeppelin re-creates Led not through difference, but through identity. Following the 1 = 1 identity of the clone band, Lez Zeppelin mimics precise details of the original band, including instruments, equipment, clothing, and gestures. They consider themselves devoted and highly skilled musicians keeping a great band's flame alive through live performance.[2] They re-create specific, treasured concerts in their entirety and have recorded a painstaking re-creation of Led's first album in an analog studio ("to remain true to the vinyl version"), using the original instruments and effects. And a key part of this precision is the women's bodies: they perform the male bodies "for real." That is, they use the original band's "androgyny," gender ambiguity, and pansexuality as the way in to performing this music with bodies that are *the same* as Led's. According to fans, "These ladies are not trying to mess with a perfect recipe" and "You blur your eyes from far enough away, and you think you're seeing the real thing." Thus, while some may tout the band's "gender bending," in fact, in performing Led in earnest, they unveil the phantasmagorical quality of gender and the uncanniness of identity itself. Through their uncanny double, we glimpse that there is no there there at the base of gender and identity. Ultimately, I will argue that it is in recognizing this emptiness that we actually gain power and agency.

I begin by introducing Lez Zeppelin and their rise to international acclaim as a tribute band. I then turn to *Led* Zeppelin's "gender," investigating the type of band-body that they perform onstage and that Lez then re-creates "precisely." I argue that while men and women are always on the scene, it is the "origin stories" that cohere certain significant moments around a white male body. I therefore show how the origin story of rock music (via "cock rock") coheres around Led, eliding earlier influences, in particular that of Janis Joplin on Plant. I further investigate the rise of "androgyny" in rock music, tying it to white male concerns over stealing the musical black phallus and a need to make a sacrifice to appease this guilt. As such, pursued far enough, Lez's reenactment unveils the repressed racial longing beneath the love and theft of black music by white musicians. Ultimately, I elaborate the "conundrum of gender"—the problem of trying to overturn the hierarchies of gender within the system of gender itself. I assert that recognizing the emptiness of gender categories (careful not to confuse that with a retreat into a universalizing practice of whiteness) offers the best tactic to attenuate long-standing and ossified structures of dominance.

LEZ ZEPPELIN

Steph Paynes formed Lez Zeppelin in 2003, and by 2005 Chuck Klosterman of *Spin* magazine had already momentarily floated the possibility of it being "the most powerful all-female band in rock history" (Klosterman 2005).[3] With Paynes on guitars and theremin (as Page), Shannon Conley on vocals (Plant), Megan Thomas on bass and keyboards (Jones), and Leesa Harrington-Squyres on drums (Bonham), Lez Zeppelin released their sophomore CD in 2010, *Lez Zeppelin I*, a track-by-track re-creation of the first eponymous Led Zeppelin album. Their first release, *Lez Zeppelin* (2007), had Paynes with a different lineup, including the talented Lisa Brigantano on bass, mandolin, and keyboards. That CD was produced by Eddie Kramer (producer for Led Zeppelin, Jimi Hendrix, KISS, and many others) and mastered by George Marino (who remastered the original Led Zeppelin recordings with Jimmy Page). In terms of musicianship and presentation, Lez is considered one of the top tribute bands around.

Like the other examples of Replay in this book, Lez Zeppelin has gone to remarkable lengths to re-create precise details of the original band. Onstage, Lez members work to embody the original musicians. The two leads dress like Plant and Page of the early 1970s: Conley in tight, faded jeans and a frilly, torso-baring blouse and Paynes in a more stylized, coordinated outfit redolent of late-1960s psychedelia (see figure 4.1). They clearly revel in the sexually aggressive and swaggering embodiment typical of male rock stars of the "cock rock" era/genre and assuredly mimic the moves and stances of their respective originals (see figure 4.2). Paynes enacts the stylized gestures of Jimmy Page, lifting her arm up with a flourish after strumming a chord or leaning back resting the guitar against her forward-thrust pelvis, legs spread wide, as she offers pyrotechnics of guitar virtuosity. An early reviewer wrote, "Page's posture and moves are all studied—the placement of the legs, the bend of the neck, the swivel of the foot" (Carpenter 2005); and a former bandmate marveled, "She's got all the moves down. It's pretty outrageous" (quoted in Carpenter 2005). Conley swaggers and sways in the style of Plant, thrusting her hips out and shoulders back, stabbing the microphone into the air or kicking her head back to send her blonde curls flying.[4] In photos and videos, the drummer is often shown with a menacing grimace as she pounds her

FIGURE 4.1 Shannon Conley, Leesa Harrington Squyres, and Steph Paynes of Lez Zeppelin. Used by permission of Kyra Kverno Photography.

FIGURE 4.2 Robert Plant, Jimmy Page, and John Bonham of Led Zeppelin, Earls Court Arena, May 18, 1975. Photographer: Mick Gold. Used by permission of Getty Images.

toms, a type of wild wo/man persona that fits with the image of John Bonham, while the bassist is reserved and serious, focusing on the music, a propos of John Paul Jones. While the tribute band's first album comprised two originals and a compilation of songs from a variety of Led Zeppelin albums, *Lez Zeppelin I* (2010) was in the vein of the classic clone band: it re-created every track from Led's album in the original order.[5] As Paynes said of the album: "We did it in the way that we thought would be most authentic, which was basically to go into an analog studio, record to tape, do it with all the same vintage equipment that they used, I mean, down to every pedal, to the compressors that were used on the master mixes, everything."[6] In recent years they've taken up the practice of re-creating specific tour dates ("legendary Zep concerts in their entirety"), such as the Royal Albert Hall concert (January 9, 1970), "The Song Remains the Same" Madison Square Garden concert (July 27–29, 1973), and Knebworth (August 11, 1979). As such, their authenticity is the haunthenticity of the clone band devoted to precise mimicry, including the material details. In reenacting the men's gender performance precisely, Lez Zeppelin play on the figure-ground construction of gender that is always a dance within a binary—male body and female body, masculine and feminine (even inter-sex and trans bodies must define themselves via this binary). That is, their entrance into Replay is the apparently seamless, yet arousing, flip of androgyny to the gynandrous: it is the *same* band, with men in frilly clothes with high voices performed by women who strut and flaunt their rock phallus. As Steph Paynes has said of starting the band, "It just seemed so right—it was like an idea that's time had come" (quoted in Brandon 2006). To parse out the implications of this idea whose "time had come," I begin with a look at the gender performance they were precisely reenacting: Led Zeppelin.

LED ZEPPELIN'S GENDER

Led Zeppelin broke out in 1969 with their first album, "Led Zeppelin." From 1969 to 1979 the band produced eight albums, all of which were in the top ten in the United States and Great Britain (with six reaching number one in the United States and all but their first album hitting number one in Britain). In a testament to their continued influence and popularity, they are ranked number one on VH1's list of the one hundred greatest artists of hard rock.[7] Vocalist Robert Plant, guitarist Jimmy Page, and drummer John Bonham are considered "rock masters" who have spawned generations of imitators on their respective instruments, while John Paul Jones on bass, keyboards, mandolin, and other instruments is considered a master multi-instrumentalist. When still hugely popular, Led Zeppelin disbanded in 1980 after the death of drummer John Bonham at the age of 32. The surviving members pursued solo careers, and the band has reunited for "one-off" performances (usually benefits and tributes) on several occasions throughout the years, often with Bonham's son Jason on drums. Jimmy Page has been overseeing the remastering of their discography and re-released their first three albums in 2014.

Led Zeppelin's music and stage performance helped to solidify and define a new visual and sonic style of rock often referred to as "cock rock." With their bared chests, forward-thrust genitalia, often misogynist lyrics, and resident guitar hero in Page, the band has been cited by scholars as a quintessential model of the style. Using Led as an example, Simon Frith and Angela McRobbie describe cock rock as "music making in which the performance is an explicit, crude, and often aggressive expression of male sexuality" (Frith and McRobbie 1990, 319). Susan Fast (2001) argues, however, that understanding Led Zeppelin (and rock, in general) as only hypermasculine writes out female participation in the music.[8] To counter scholarly and critical assertions about the masculinist orientation of rock,[9] Fast brings to light the women who consumed the music and images of Led Zeppelin, arguing that such rock "power" was also a site of power for them.

Fast also highlights the "feminine" aspects of the band. One aspect of this femininity is inscribed through Plant's relation to guitarist Page's masculine persona as the "guitar hero" (Fast 2001, 45). Fast reads the song "Dazed and Confused" as a representation of heterosexual coitus between the musicians:

> During the fast section that follows the bow solo, all musical elements are subordinated to the dominance of the guitar . . . This solo would begin with Page playing a pitch, which Plant would imitate, this being repeated at increasingly higher intervals, forcing Plant to the uppermost reaches of his range. . . . Plant is at once mentored, musically, by Page, stretched to his limits, coaxed to go further and further, and also, ultimately, controlled by the guitarist. Plant also often ended this contest between himself and Page by saying, "Push; push" (which he was wont to do during many other of Page's solos as well). . . . It is possible to hear this comment as an imperative to Page, casting Plant in the role of receiver of sexual pleasure during intercourse, the "woman" who is asking for more, thus strengthening his role as feminine to Page. (45)[10]

Fast here aligns the feminine with "woman," thus possibly framing the "love making" onstage within a heterosexual matrix. Therefore, while having the advantage of placing women in the scene, it could serve to foreclose other readings. But one could read the roles being performed in a variety of ways.

Therefore, rather than framing this within a heterosexual matrix, I read Fast's passage as underscoring the omnisexuality of the band's performance: the performance of masculinity, femininity, male bodies, female bodies, or mixed bodies all in a jumble of sexual arousal that makes who's on top a difficult question to entertain, let alone (want, care, or need to) answer. As Fast uncovered in interviews, many consumers of Led equated their performance with sex, saying such things as "the band was performing sex on stage." But straight sex? Queer sex? Wasn't the titillation and power of Led Zeppelin in their performance of a plurality of sexualities? Couldn't Plant be the chick aroused by her own dick or Page the man aroused by Plant's dick or the woman aroused by Plant's "femininity" or . . .

The Aristophanic Band-Body

Couldn't part of the allure and titillation of Led Zeppelin's performance, the intensity of the sexual energy audiences felt emanating from the stage, be a type of bliss? A type of bodily enjoyment that surpasses even desire? To the extent that the band performs the complete body in no need of an other, it performs not desire, but bliss. Much like Aristophanes's account of love in the *Symposium*, where the beings' genitals are turned toward each other in order to help them return to their original state of oneness, the palindromic letters in ABBA were turned toward each other, as is *natural*, to form the complete whole. While ABBA performs this being in both a heteronormative and nonsexualized way—a type of sterile, almost noncorporeal representation of the body, Led Zeppelin performs the Aristophanic band-body as the continual excitement of union that is in no way limited to the hetero. It is a body before "sexual differentiation," but one that can still have sex. It is the fantasy of the all where we can have our cake and eat it, too.

In going back to Aristophanes's tale, the original complete being had a variety of combinations of body parts; some had two sets of female organs or two sets of male organs, some had one set of each.[11] Heterosexual coitus was not the only, or it seems, primary option. Indeed, the emphasis on a male and a female could intimate the procreation that revealed the subject's fall into "sexed reproduction," a fall from bliss (unity) and into desire (separation). In viewing the true Aristophanic body, all parts would be present, and no hint of separation (and therefore no need to (re)produce) is present. This plural being is representative of a "whole," of the space beyond desire—the space of bliss, of completion, of arrival, of immortality and utopia. Because Plant performs the dual role of feminine and masculine, his erotic musical relation with Page enacts a larger Aristophanic body for the group as a whole, which can be the body with two male organs or a body with male and female organs. And with the door already open, couldn't the "femininity" of the band perform, or threaten to perform, the body with all female organs? Indeed, once the differentiation is questioned, once the arbitrariness of gender threatens to come undone, couldn't we be left with the body that is undifferentiated because it is *all?*

I will return to the Aristophanic body when I discuss Lez Zeppelin's reenactment of Led. For indeed, this is the way Lez will uncannily perform the double. First, however, I want to trace the origins of the band's omnisexuality back a bit further. While this hypersexuality and plural gender performance may have cohered around Led Zeppelin as its originator, I believe it has a clear and definite precursor in the figure of Janis Joplin. By taking another step back and looking and listening to Joplin, we can see how origin stories cohere around the white male body and continually serve to write out the contributions of women and people of color. Just as "femininity" may be learned through the drag queens in the Harlem balls (as seen in *Paris Is Burning* (Livingston 2005)) or masculinity may be learned through the performances of drag kings (as argued by Jack Halberstam 1998), Plant's femininity/masculinity/cock rock performances do not necessarily trace back to a white male body. While the influences can always be traced back (from Joplin to Otis Redding, Tina Turner, Garnett Mimms, Bessie Smith . . .) and the gender story is always one of many crossings, the "song remains the same," however, in that the origin story seems to most often cohere around the body of a white man.

Janis Joplin and Cock Rock

In January 1969, introducing Led Zeppelin as the new group just on the scene, critic William Seavey wrote, "Robert Plant is the Janis Joplin of the group, a blues belter par excellence" (Seavey 1969). By summer (as their first album went to number ten on the Billboard Top 200 chart), many more critics were making this comparison. According to one, "[Plant] comes across with the funky finesse of a male Janis Joplin" (Scott 1969). Another avers that "lead singer Robert Plant, 21, comes on strong like a male Janis Joplin." A third tells us "[Robert Plant's] voice sounds like the male counterpart of blues screamer Janis Joplin"

(Hesse 1969). A fourth writes, "Robert Plant, the lead vocalist, went into his Janis Joplin dancing and screaming act" ("Led Zeppelin Makes Magic at the Arena" 1969). And a fifth describes, "Then the Zeppelin flew in, total theater of blues-rock, lead singer Robert Plant was the shrieking flight engineer, guiding the ship (imagine, if you will, a male Janis Joplin)" (Cobb 1969). By 1971, after Zeppelin had released two more albums and were about to drop their fourth, a reviewer for the *Oakland Tribune* writes: "It is well known that Led Zeppelin is a talented group. Jimmy Page is without a doubt one of the best guitarists in the musical world, John Bonham is a great drummer, bassist John Paul Jones is an above-average performer and Robert Plant, well, he has been called a male Janis Joplin" ("Led Zeppelin Bows in with a Roar" 1971). In 1972 (and another multiplatinum album later), a reviewer is somewhat more withering, writing, "Plant, by the way, tries to sing a lot of his songs like Janis Joplin might, and even the mannerisms are the same" (Mann 1972). The comparison still surfaces five years later, when P. Dewing writes of the 1977 twenty-thousand-arena concert in St. Louis, Missouri: "Plant's purgative, bleeding cries—so reminiscent of Janis Joplin—and the taunting, almost brutal exchange between his voice and the instruments brought the concert to its first of several climaxes" (Dewing 1977).[12] Unlike Viola Smith, Valaida Snow, or Nina Simone (described respectively as the "female Gene Krupa," the "female Louis Armstrong," and the "female Miles Davis"),[13] who often remained shadowed by the comparison, however, the "male Janis Joplin" would eventually become the prototype for a certain type of vocalizing associated "naturally" with white male rockers. And this even when the women just mentioned were associated with men simply because of the instruments they played (drums and trumpet) or presence they projected (Simone), and Plant was compared to Joplin for very specific stylistic reasons. Indeed, early reviewers continually fell back on the comparison when trying to describe Plant's sound and look to readers.

That is, despite the frequent correlation made between Plant and Joplin in early reviews of Led Zeppelin, Plant's "male Janis Joplin" designation has been dropped from the history books. In monographs on Zeppelin, with rare exceptions Joplin is never mentioned as an influence, and often she isn't mentioned at all. In *Led Zeppelin: The Stories behind Every Led Zeppelin Song* (Welch 2016 [1998]), *Whole Lotta Led Zeppelin* (Bream 2015), and *Hammer of the Gods: The Led Zeppelin Saga* (Davis 2008), there is no mention of Joplin. A few others mention her once or twice in passing, for example, attending a party, or two that provide one sentence comparing the Scottish blues-rock singer Maggie Bell to Joplin

(Cole 2002 [1992], Clayson 2006). A few do cite the influence Joplin may have had on Plant, but hold back on making a strong, supported connection and do no follow-up. In his 2005 book *Led Zeppelin: 1968–1980*, Keith Shadwick writes, "Plant's vocal . . . suggests close listening to Janis Joplin's approach, if not her style" (48). In his 2008 biography, Mick Wall writes that Plant's vocals in "Since I Been Loving You" from *Led Zeppelin III* "display[ed] his new Van Morrison and Janis Joplin influences" (2008, 192). Critic Barney Hoskyns makes two references to Joplin when reviewing Led Zeppelin reissues. In his 2003 review of the *Led Zeppelin III* reissue he writes, "It is surely Plant's greatest vocal performance—Janis Joplin reborn as a lovesick Black Country brickie" (Hoskyns 2003). And in 2006 he wrote of the *Led Zeppelin IV* reissue, "The sound of Plant's voice alone—like Janis Joplin with testosterone—was formidable" (Hoskyns 2006, 14). As this analysis proceeds, I exhort the reader to ponder what exactly this testosterone is that is purportedly added to Joplin.

Two books take Joplin's influence more seriously: Susan Fast's monograph on Zeppelin and Alice Echols's biography of Joplin. Fast argues that, although he has never acknowledged it, "One of Plant's strongest influences as a singer must have been . . . Janis Joplin since they share a similar emotional plane in their singing and since Plant draws on Joplin's specific licks and technical vocabulary" (45). Fast does not offer further specifics, but states that Plant's vocal characteristics exemplify the influence.[14] Alice Echols argues that Joplin has been an uncredited influence on male rock vocalists. She writes that "Janis disappeared from the airwaves soon after her death. But while she was curiously absent, her style was absorbed, without credit and in a way that obscured her influence." Echols cites Debbie Harry, who observes that "people do [Janis] even when they don't know they're doing her," especially male vocalists of heavy metal. Echols considers Plant the vocalist most responsible for bringing Joplin's style into heavy metal, though she, like Fast, notes that he has never cited Joplin's influence.[15] While I have found Jimmy Page discussing Joplin, I also have not found any reference to Joplin as a musical influence by Plant (although he name-drops her as a "friend" on several occasions).[16]

I have presented a detailed case elsewhere for the ways in which Plant was specifically influenced by Joplin.[17] In brief, Joplin's short international career from 1968 until her death on October 4, 1970, produced three remarkable and influential albums, many TV appearances, and near-constant live tours that offered material to influence the developing Led Zeppelin. Big Brother and the Holding Company formed in 1966 as part of the San Francisco "psychedelic rock" counterculture scene with bands such as Jefferson Airplane, the Grateful Dead, and Country Joe and the Fish. Big Brother garnered national attention after Joplin's stunning performance of Big Mama Thornton's "Ball and Chain" at the Monterey Pop Festival in 1967. Robert Plant acknowledged the early influence. Regarding that time, he told an interviewer, "I really just wanted to get to San Francisco and join up. I had so much empathy with the commentary in America at the time of Vietnam. I just wanted to be with Jack Casady and with Janis Joplin" (quoted in Hoskyns 2006). Indeed, Led Zeppelin would form in 1968, the year Big Brother released their second album, *Cheap Thrills.* Keith Shadwick considers the album an important "stylistic antecedent" to Led Zeppelin's first album, which came out the next year. According to Shadwick, these influences included "Janis Joplin's fever-pitched vocals, interludes of screaming guitars, pounding drums, and contrasting whisper-quiet passages" (48). In the Big Brother track "I Need a Man to Love" from *Cheap Thrills,* you can hear these qualities: the screams suddenly coming out of nowhere; the raspy, airy falsetto; and the quavering out-of-control melismas.

The reviewers early in Plant's career compared not only his voice, but also his general look and behavior to Joplin. This was noticed as far back as 1969 in Plant's Joplinesque "dancing and screaming," but it was in 1972 when a music critic noted how "even the mannerisms are the same" between the, by then, late Joplin and Plant. In the early seventies, the band started to dress more flamboyantly, influenced by glam rock.[18] This "androgyny" was read at the time as a type of hyperomnisexuality that, as Susan Fast has shown, was tantamount to the band performing an incarnation of sex on stage.[19] It was a largely unacknowledged homoeroticism that gave the sense of sex everywhere: sex was so present it could erupt anywhere, anytime. But this omnisexual homoeroticism had already been performed by Joplin, who, when singing "Summertime," would embellish the lyrics "and your mama's good-looking" with a suggestive "oh yeah, she's lookin' good now," which gave the distinct impression the vocalist was ogling your mother. In interviews, Joplin would often compare music making to sex in what Alice Echols views as Joplin's particular skill at marketing herself and enticing an interviewer.[20] Joplin's omnisexuality can be traced back to two of her influences, Ma Rainey and Bessie Smith, and summed up with the common phrase at the time, "If it moves, fondle it."[21] Thus the hypersexuality of so-called "cock rock" that finds its origin in Zeppelin can be traced back at least in part through three women's uninhibited sexual expressivity in music as inspiration.

While we can easily trace back the omnisexuality and the growling, wailing vocals of Led Zeppelin and Plant to earlier influences, it is Plant who has been cited as the originator of heavy metal vocals in popular and academic rock history. In MTV's *History of Heavy Metal,* Kurt Loder narrates, "The rising tide of heavy metal bands happily emulated Robert Plant's lead shriek and Jimmy Page's thick, murderous riffs as best they could." The program cuts to Robert Plant stating that every shrieking "ahh" could be heard all over the new genre, followed by a quick montage through a series of metal vocalists screaming with the assumption that it all goes back to Plant.[22] Andrew Cope takes as the starting point for his book on heavy metal the "strong consensus amongst academics and established journalists that heavy metal and hard rock emerged during the late 1960s/early 1970s in the industrial Midlands of England" (Cope 2010, 7). He goes on to say that "the vocal dexterity of Robert Plant provided the launching pad and inspiration for front line vocalists such as Rob Halford (Judas Priest) and Bruce Dickinson (Iron Maiden). These vocalists took Plant's dexterous but mild theatrics as the starting point to engineer a new level of performer status where the singer becomes the central figure in the band" (Cope 2010, 68). With a "launching pad" and "starting point" in Plant, Cope's book never mentions Janis Joplin. Nor Bessie Smith, Ray Charles, Otis Redding, Tina Turner, Aretha Franklin, Garnett Mimms, or Wynonie Harris.[23]

It is a bitter irony that the band which has been recently revealed as one of the most secretly derivative bands, Led Zeppelin, is continually noted for its *origin*ality and that Robert Plant is cited as the original heavy metal vocalist. As Plant is popularly lauded as authentic and worthy because of his originality,[24] his derivations are studiously ignored. Further, after white women and black women and men are written out of the story, the critical hand-wringing of various white male rock critics can begin, wondering out loud: "Why don't women rock? Why don't blacks rock?" as a way to further gaze at the now naturalized creativity and potency of white men.[25] Led Zeppelin could be the poster band for this phenomenon. Decades after their ascendance, the truth of the various origins of their songs has come to light. The band used the "borrowing" practice of the blues to excuse themselves from theft, assuming and expecting what did initially happen and continues to happen (even with emerging evidence to the contrary): *origin*ality will find them.[26]

If Joplin was a significant influence on Plant's vocal style, what could account for her consequent neglect in the story of cock rock? Certainly, the question is difficult to ask with a straight face. Women disappear from the origin myths of new artistic forms precisely through gender coding that would deem a music "cock rock." Chapter 3 detailed how Wynton Marsalis's jazz origin story elides Lil Armstrong's contributions to the "birth of jazz." Memphis Minnie is written out of the birth of the electric blues through that music's coding as "phallic"; Roberta Martin is forgotten as the innovator of gospel-styled organ because playing instruments is understood as the "masculine" role within musical production and innovation. Fast argues that the phallic coding of rock writes out women. Women are not understood as originators, but at best, they can demonstrate themselves to be good copiers—to be able to rock "just like men." But while I believe Joplin was overlooked because of gender stereotypes and bias, I don't think the phrase "cock rock" was invented in order to solidify this absencing. It would be too easy to argue that the moniker "cock rock" was invented in order to paste over the feminine origins of rock (in Rainey, Smith, Thornton, and so on)—that the repression of the feminine was replaced with this screen memory of Led Zeppelin's cock at the origin of rock. I believe this origin story of rock is a tangled web of love and theft that involves race and gender. Indeed, Fast argues that Led's complex compositions, abstract lyrics, and acoustic explorations do not even fit the definition of a cock rock band.[27] Further, the performance of "femininity" in the band belies its characterization as hypermasculine "cock rock." If Fast is correct in arguing that Led is not an example of cock rock and yet Led continues to be cited as the model and originator of cock rock, the fact that cock rock was invented as a narrative strategy, and subsequently widely accepted, even though a founding band of the alleged form cannot comfortably be considered an example, suggests a deeper complexity to the phrase "cock rock."[28]

THE BAND OF BROTHERS, THE RISE OF ROCK ANDROGYNY, AND THE BIRTH OF COCK ROCK

Popular music scholars have developed various ideas on the functions and motivations of androgyny in popular music. In his book *Performing Glam Rock*, Philip Auslander gives a brief historical sketch of androgyny in rock, identifying several contrasting stages (2006). He argues that early examples of cross-dressing and effeminacy in rock and roll (such as Esquerita and Little Richard) functioned more as markers of "iconoclasm" than as explicit commentaries on gender or sexuality. The later "soft masculinity" of the 1960s was a form of "counterculture androgyny" perceived at the time as authentic, "natural," and heterosexual. The androgyny of 1970s glam bands (David Bowie, T. Rex, and others) was a challenge to this authenticity, naturalness, and heteronormativity through their explicit artifice (focusing on "glamour") and open references to bi- or homosexuality (Auslander 2006, 33). Additionally, Robert Walser describes the androgyny of 1980s glam metal in the context of the exscription of women from rock. Walser argues that glam metal rockers harnessed "female erotic spectacle" to "male power," and that "male heavy metal fans and musicians sometimes assert masculinity by co-opting femininity" in an Oedipal desire to separate from earlier "fathers" of rock (1993, 134). I disagree with this reading primarily because the earlier "fathers" of rock were already androgynous, and therefore I see 1980s androgyny not so much as a transgression than as a continuation (and rereading) of earlier androgyny. I do agree with Walser, however, that the musicians' understandings of their androgyny will not always jibe with their audience's, something he demonstrates in his discussion of "gay metal" (115–16). Nonetheless, neither of these discussions addresses the androgyny of 1970s rock bands, such as Led Zeppelin, that found most of their early inspiration in the blues.

I believe a question remains as to the motivation behind the overt and pervasive androgyny of this rock style. Although the desire to further sexualize a music that had been considered sexual since rock 'n' roll is certainly one answer, I believe another inspiration may also underlie the entrance of the "feminine" into a music marked by its connection to the blues. Therefore, I would like to build on Auslander's history: as glam style responded to the authenticity of 1960s hippie culture, I believe late-1960s and 1970s rock androgyny was also a response to a perceived authenticity, that of the blues—however, it was a quite different response. For indeed, white rockers desired both proximity to and distance from "authentic blackness."

So much has been written on the co-optation of black blues music by white rockers that there is no need to retrace those investigations here.[29] I take as a given analyses such as Steve Waksman's of white rockers' response to Jimi Hendrix—that the black man has functioned in the white imaginary as a symbol of hypermasculinity and authenticity. The love and theft of black music by white rockers, however, often beleaguered white musicians with feelings of guilt and other emotions. Speaking of Jimi Hendrix's decision to play rock, Pete Townsend said, "There was a tremendous sense of [Hendrix] choosing to play in the white arena, that he was coming along and saying, 'You've taken this, Eric Clapton, and Mr. Townsend, you think you're a showman. This is how *we* do it. This is how we can do it when we take back what you've borrowed, if not stolen" (quoted in Waksman 1999, 106). Trapped in white fantasies about black behavior, I would argue that some white male rock musicians who appropriated black music found they could not manage its imputed masculine excess. As these musicians forged a new music bearing the desired sonic trace of blackness, they were inescapably waylaid by feelings of inadequacy, fear of what such a complete masculinity would be, as well as guilt over stealing it.[30]

If we were to consider this in Freudian terms, we might characterize this distress over stealing the musical phallus from a more masculine authority as the filial Oedipal guilt of a white band of brothers. In *Totem and Taboo,* Freud describes how the father is killed by a band of brothers in an Oedipal plot for power. Because there had always been love and admiration for the father, however, the brothers are filled with remorse. Therefore, while before the brothers felt prohibited from access to the superior masculinity of the father, now that they have stolen it, they, on their own, attempt to partially return it.[31] I suggest that the white rock brothers of bands such as the Rolling Stones and Led Zeppelin, early blues-influenced rock bands who made truckloads of money and embraced androgyny, made a "sacrifice" to partially revoke the deed of "killing the father" (Freud 1995 [1913]). They assuage the anxiety involved in stealing black masculinity, and the power that it purportedly yields, by ritually offering up some of their own. In doing so they signal their distance from blackness's masculine excess while simultaneously presenting white rockers' extra-potent masculinity, so potent it can even shoulder a heavy dose of femininity.

Indeed, as Led Zeppelin became more and more popular, their look shifted from jeans and leather jackets to one that heightened androgyny, especially in the figure of Robert Plant. Taking on the feminine provides a release valve for the hypermasculinity, the perceived excess that couldn't/wouldn't/shouldn't fully be taken on. This femininity allowed Plant to partake of hypermasculine excess, while still maintaining white masculinity as "normal" and unable to fully embody that excess. Because hard rock was coded as so sonically phallic, male effeminacy was like an arrogant challenge that stated, "Whatever we do (and we can hardly believe it ourselves) we still maintain the phallus." Such sonic excess provided space for all of this feminine play but also its necessity. Indeed, the power of rock music, its relentless reading as a hypermasculine form, continued to demand some type of response from burdened rockers wanting to redirect this imputation of excessive masculinity. The late sundress-wearing Kurt Cobain of the band Nirvana is a particularly trenchant example of a man wanting to redirect or siphon off some of the hypermasculinity associated with heavy rock.[32] Ultimately, a sacrifice must be made in "deferred obedience" to the black father, because did the sons really believe they could wield that much phallus? The increase of overt femininity and hidden homoeroticism-in-plain-sight in heavy-rocking "hypermasculine" rock bands such as Led Zeppelin is a symbolic relinquishment and admission that white male rockers could or would not perform the hypermasculinity they had inscribed onto black men.

But if white male rockers negotiated their masculinity to be both powerful and still within the bounds of normative white masculinity for themselves, critics and audience members may not have had the same excess masculinity to spare. The majority of mainstream fans were unaware of the black origins of Led Zeppelin and had no need to assuage any guilty consciences. As the rock era pressed on, simultaneously with the glam era, audience anxieties over rock's androgyny grew, as a 1973 *Creem* article "Androgyny in Rock: A Short Introduction" attests in its need to address the issue for its readers. While white rockers could perform the feminine while still being read as masculine, what did this mean for the male consumer of androgyny? Rather than devotedly accepting the definition that cock rock describes a hypermasculine band, I suggest entertaining the possibility of another meaning. To wit: the male consumer of androgynous rock performances repressed the feminine and homoerotic, often in quite plain sight, with his new designation of the music as hypermasculine and decidedly heterosexual "cock rock."[33] It wasn't the bands, but the male consumers and critics who coined the phrase "cock rock."

In this origin myth of cock rock, we find a double absence of women: it is a story of men negotiating the phallus. Women are not seen or heard in this story, even when their contributions form the material of the genre. Black men are the fathers from whom the blues were stolen and then improved. White men were able to wield the hypermasculine phallus of this sonic blackness, but made nods to their inability to seriously or "naturally" be this phallic. Women really can't be part of the story—femininity can be appropriated only by dress; women cannot be acknowledged as a legitimate and "natural" influence. Janis Joplin has to be understood as a fairly freakish anomaly. Ma Rainey, Bessie Smith, Big Mama Thornton, and other black female originators have to be swept under the rug. On seeing the effeminacy of the performances, male critics and audience members may have been even more concerned to downplay any female involvement in the production of this music. Thus, the musicians deny female involvement because they see their story as one negotiated through the black father, whom they love and honor, but want to surpass and at least partially erase. While some critics and audience members also partook of this view, others oblivious to black origins of rock had to claim the hypermasculinity of a form of music that had two men simulating sex between vocals and guitar in "girly" clothes.

Twenty-First-Century Readings of Led Zeppelin's Androgyny

What are the various ways that women musicians *can* enter a rock world so committed to naturalizing the form around the white man? Lez Zeppelin found a few ways, and the first was through the sexual fears of its presumed core audience—straight white men.

The meanings of rock androgyny changed between the 1970s and 2000s, not only in the various new music styles that used androgyny, but also in the way we read the old styles. In the 1970s, "free and exploring" (hetero)sexuality was a mainstream preoccupation. And with the 1970s women's movement, gender was also a topic. Gender in the 1970s was generally an essential category, with the idea that if a man was doing anything, it was some form of masculinity, and if a woman had "masculine" tendencies, she was "male-identified." Therefore, the long hair, loose clothing, and jewelry of men in the seventies was primarily read as "swinging" attire that presented the man as (hetero)sexually available. In this context (combined with the stories of his appetite for female groupies), Plant's effeminacy did not hit homophobic anxiety buttons in mainstream American culture. However, as Walser demonstrated with gay metal, different audiences read the cues according to their own desires. In her research, Fast found one openly gay respondent who gave his thoughts on Zeppelin in the 1970s:

> [L]ike a lot of hard-rock bands, Zep drew its share of white male homophobes. Odd, considering the fact that the band was fronted by two foppish, somewhat androgynous intellectuals! I was always aware of that contradiction, and as I've learned from some other gay and bisexual males in their thirties, I wasn't the only one so aware. Certainly the fact that the band happily frequented gay clubs for the pleasure of simply being left alone and had their adventures [dressing] in drag (such as their infamous dinner with George Harrison and Stevie Wonder) made an impression. I would guess that the sexual nature of so much blues-based music (this of course including both Led Zeppelin and the Rolling Stones) couldn't help but appeal to horny people of whatever orientation. Robert and Jimmy always struck me as a more dangerous and more androgynous "version" of Mick and Keith, anyway. (quoted in Fast 2001, 175)

Though kept under the radar, homoerotic titillation was clearly part of the thrill for at least some consumers of Led Zeppelin in the 1970s.

Walser recounted how many 1980s metal fans denounced its androgyny, such as a female fan who wrote in to a metal magazine that "real men don't wear makeup" (quoted in Walser 1993, 130).[34] Although Walser does not make the connection, it is clear that androgyny in the 1980s was read differently from the "swinging sexuality"-informed androgyny of the 1970s. Although 1980s glam androgyny was stylistically different from 1970s rock forms, in an era transformed by the AIDS crisis and the increased visibility of gay men and lesbians in mainstream culture, one wonders if the same type of commentary would have been directed toward Led Zeppelin if they had continued to play into the 1980s. If the change in David Bowie's comments about his own sexuality are any indication (in the 1980s he retracted some of his earlier statements about his bisexuality), one can wager a guess that Plant's very effeminate corporeality on stage would have been subjected to greater policing than it was in the 1970s.

Certainly, young consumers in the 2000s appeared to be reading the band's sexuality differently from in the 1970s. Consumption of earlier rock eras was rabid, with CD reissues and live concert DVDs, as well as YouTube videos, fansites, and blogs readily available. The rock of the 1970s was being recontextualized by young listeners of the twenty-first century. A 2006 web article in a student-run online magazine, *Hooked,* presumes to be humorous but speaks to many of the issues and anxieties around the reading of 1970s rock music, in particular Led Zeppelin.

> HOOKED has just stumbled upon a startling discovery—some might call it the greatest cover-up in human history. To put it simply, if you like rock music, you might just be gay. What you are about to see might shock you, and challenge previous conceptions, but the evidence is overwhelming. . . . The gayness of the rock band emanates from the lead singer, with his subliminal relationship with the lead guitarist and the unsuspecting audience. Let us now take exhibit A—the mightiest of all rock bands—Led Zeppelin. The duo exemplified rock cred, with Page's mind-blowing guitar solos and Plant's banshee howl. But they were also the most skin-crawlingly gay rock stars ever. . . . Now if you worshipped at the feet of Robert Plant, with his flowing blonde locks, I-dream-of-Genie top and ball-shrinkingly high-pitched yodeling, then yes, you might be gay. What's more, this goes way beyond the way Plant looks. Onstage, he pranced around like a fairy, while canoodling with Page like a girl possessed. (Shawn 2006)

And so the online poster reveals the greatest cover-up in human history. Indeed, hiding in plain sight is the vagina rather than the cock, the gay rather the hyper-hetero, the fairy rather than the ideal example of masculinity. It is the return of the repressed. And Lez Zeppelin is here to help.

"AN IDEA THAT'S TIME HAD COME"

Given the consensus on Plant's femininity, the sexual dynamic between the vocalist and Page, and the overall androgyny of the band, the all-women Lez Zeppelin's representation of cock rock in fact appears more accurate than the phrase's more forced definition as extreme and exclusive heteromasculinity. As such, their performance can be read as confirming the worst fears of straight male Led Zeppelin fans. By (re)performing the sexual and gender ambiguity extant in the original band, Lez Zeppelin re-creates originary rock codes that are usually willfully ignored. They are the return of the repressed that the term "cock rock" sought to cover over and which was already being picked up by twenty-first-century audiences.

In interviews, however, Steph Paynes attempts to ameliorate any such discomfort with a different story. Paynes suggests that Lez Zeppelin provides resolution for the discomfort of the straight male listener always presumed to be the main audience of rock. She has said, "Plant and Page were beautiful, and they looked like girls with their long hair. Guys wanted to kiss them back then, they just didn't know it. They were turned on by them. Let's face it, the band were wearing girls' clothes" (Stanley 2005). "Now they can lust after us without having any sort of sexual conflict" (Doster 2005). Paynes's brilliance here could be in the marketing campaign: claiming to be the resolution to men's homophobic hysteria rather than its cause—and in this, not necessarily a progressive move. Indeed, an unfortunate exhortation from male audience members at a Lez Zeppelin show is the ubiquitous "Show us your tits"; and the band's coy sexuality (revealed in their promo, "All girls. All Zeppelin.") has been criticized as stereotypical marketing of women, and as pandering to straight male fantasies of lesbian eroticism.

Lez-bianism as a Marketing Tool

Most press on Lez Zeppelin will at some point circle around to the sexuality of the band members. Playing off of the plural sexuality of Led, Lez re-creates the homoeroticism through their performance and their name, which has attracted a substantial lesbian following for the group. Most of this press stems from the straight male fan's perspective, however, and the eroticism of the powerfully sexual music of Zeppelin being performed by women. Reviewer John Adamian offers a typical analysis in the *Hartford Advocate,* writing, "Lez Zeppelin, a New York-based all-girl Led Zeppelin tribute band, has engineered a perfect realization of the male fantasy and brought it to life, amplified and on stage: chicks kicking out the jams of the greatest rock band ever" (Adamian 2004). As such, the homoeroticism can be viewed as pandering to straight male desire. In her article "Women's 'Cock Rock' Goes Mainstream," Jennie Ruby asks of Lez Zeppelin's performance, "With a predominantly male audience what did it all mean? . . . When the performers threw in a little lezzie action—as when the singer began to touch the guitarist's hair seductively—how much was that pandering to the male audience?" (Ruby n.d.). Ruby argues that rather than creating their own expression, the women of Lez Zeppelin are simply performing to the needs of straight men.

This reading is supported by the fact that it is likely that most of the band members throughout the years have been straight women. Definitely, they are not all lesbians. In her article for *Between the Lines: Michigan's Weekly News for Lesbians, Gays, Bisexuals, Transgenders and Friends,* D'Anne Witkowski writes,

> No, the women of Lez Zeppelin, the all-female Led Zeppelin tribute band, are not all lesbians. At least, they aren't saying and, frankly, it's doubtful. Of course, with a name like Lez Zeppelin, questions about the band's sexuality are bound to crop up. In fact, said Paynes, many people make the assumption that the band is all lesbian, but she doesn't care. "Our policy really is to say it's strict Clintonian 'don't ask don't tell.' Whatever assumptions are made is really fine with us, but it's just something we don't feel we want to divulge. It's not really about that." (Witkowski 2005)

This is a bit of a strict reenactment itself. Led Zeppelin was famous for their mystery, keeping their private lives private and teasing with oblique answers in their interviews. Lez Zeppelin re-creates this mystery to further the sexual intrigue of their own band. For example, part of their "merch" includes a pink pair of "Lez Zeppelin" panties with the "barn door" of men's underwear. One reading of the panties suggests the "sexy tomboy as object of male desire." But indeed, a variety of consumers could want these panties. And it is true that for a straight woman, her male partner could be vaguely threatened by them: "Is she 'going' lesbian? Or worse: butch? What does it say about me if I like these panties that invoke male underwear?"

Perhaps it is best to understand Lez Zeppelin as soliciting "an unholy alliance between a male gaze and a more queer . . . gaze" (Halberstam 1998, 176). Because Lez brings out many layers of sexuality and sexual partnering inherent in the original band, Lez's audience can partake of a variety of readings according to their desires. Although acknowledging that the band probably was not composed of lesbians, D'Anne Witkowski did admit that their performance was a great show for "lesbian rock fans" (2005). In re-creating the Aristophanic body of Led Zeppelin, arguably Lez foregrounds these many readings both by bringing women's bodies into the mix and by performing in an era when mainstream culture is much more attuned to homosexuality. Their plural body highlights the many forms of the original: male/male, male/female, female/female.

I am reluctant to call their re-creation a form of "queering," however, because the focus of their project is not on difference, but on identity. In focusing on identification, they are performing an important ramification of the fact that gender is not fixed. They bring out how cross-identification occurs—how characteristics and practices flow across bodies even as these practices are read as coherent racial and gender categories through systems of power. This I do find a "brilliant" concept.[35] Unfortunately, however, the "brilliance" of Lez Zeppelin perceived by journalists and others generally refers to the marketing brilliance of taking the sexuality and power of Led Zeppelin and re-performing it with women's bodies. By doing this, Lez was able to find a strong market niche that served to salve cultural anxieties and displeasures: they neutralized the discomfort of Led's homoeroticism, and they also allowed men to be attracted to the power of women who are nonetheless still, in their minds, just copying men. Lez thus can provide entertainment for an audience who wants to see women rockin' hard, but without the threat of women's originality or ownership. But while some audience members may see them as copying men, their performance can be understood as undoing the origin story that establishes the male body as the origin and the female body as the copy.

The Conundrum of Gender

Gender analysis is fraught. We think we know what "masculine" and "feminine" refer to, but if we trace these words down to what we actually think they are describing, they reveal themselves as impossibly elusive. This is because gender itself is a system of power, a sleight of hand used to construct a hierarchy that if examined will be found to be built upon sand. To use its terms is to necessarily invoke and inscribe the very hierarchy we wish to dismantle. The categories of masculine and feminine, and even of female and male, are the construction of a system that "sorts human bodies into binary categories in order to assign labor, responsibilities, moral attributes, and emotional styles" (Halberstam 2014, 117).[36] This system of power hierarchizes gender with men and masculinity on top. As Judith Butler puts it, "The category of woman is socially constructed in such a way that to be a woman is, by definition, to be in an oppressed situation" (2017 [1988], 485). This presents us with a conundrum. To stake a claim around the category of woman, while at times arguably politically necessary, also risks continuing to reify a category constructed precisely to delegitimize the authority and power of its bearer. To not claim this category risks the continued naturalized dominance of patriarchy and the elision of the subaltern experiences and lives that exist within it.

To answer this sticky situation that is impossibly loaded from the outset, scholars and cultural workers often emphasize the "fictional" nature of gender. Gender's main weapon is its ability to present itself as natural, deeply "felt" and real. The exhortation then is to play with the fictions of gender, not as the monadic subject who can choose her or his destiny with impunity, but in a type of chiasmic relation with the world, an inside/outside co-construction of self with other.

While progress has certainly been made in the acceptance of a wider array of gender expressions and sexual identities via this tactic, the reification and solidification of the hierarchies of gender continue to be reinstantiated and re-performed. Indeed, how could it be otherwise? Gender operates through a figure-ground system between the alleged "body" and its alleged "gender performance"—it can only function when one of its poles holds its ground. Take the idea of masculinity. A male body can be described as performing an "alternative" masculinity. David Ake describes saxophonist and composer Ornette Coleman's nonteleological compositional style as representative of a type of nonnormative masculinity in jazz. Approaching gender from this vantage solidifies the male body as the ground and the idea of "masculinity" as the figure, which then takes different forms as it plays out against the male body. The other vantage point on gender takes the term "masculinity" or "femininity" as the ground; for example, "masculine" characteristics remain stable, around which the body is now the figure—female or male bodies can and do perform "masculinity." Jack Halberstam offers the salient example here in his work on "female masculinity." By definition, because gender is a binary (there are only two terms: masculine and feminine; androgynous, for example, is conceived of as a combination of these two terms), the only way to make sense of gender is to negotiate this binary in different ways. This is certainly a conundrum, in particular because "male" and "masculinity" continue to be the esteemed qualities in this figure-ground dance. What I believe is crucial to understand is that this privileging is not going to change *precisely because gender itself is a system of power fabricated to forge this type of hierarchical relationship.* Nonetheless, many scholars and cultural workers put tremendous hope in the possibility of reworking this hierarchy through alternative expressions of "gender." While I deeply appreciate the motivation for this view and understand and support the desire to create spaces of "livability" and "recognition" for those who, to follow Butler, may not have access to a viable subjectivity, I do question the methods for getting to this "livability."

For example, I stated that Lil Armstrong, Memphis Minnie, and Roberta Martin have been written out of the story because of the masculine coding of jazz, blues, and instrumental performance. Understanding these performances as "female masculinity" would do little to change the story. In such a case, the ground would be "masculinity" around which the female body rotates, but the privileging of masculinity (here equated with excellent musicianship) remains. However, Fast argues that because women are attracted to the sexuality and aggressiveness of rock, it is problematic to call rock "masculine." Rock needs to be understood as also commensurate with the "feminine." In this way, the activity (rock) is coded via gender because of the bodies that participate in it and enjoy it. It is now also "feminine" because women enjoy activities that are associated with it (just like men). But in this scenario, the masculine will also still predominate. If rock really were to become more fully associated with the feminine, it would experience the fate of other activities that moved from a masculine to a feminine coding, for example, secondary school teachers (see Cacouault-Bitaud 2001). As they become more associated with women and the feminine, they lose the cultural prestige reserved for the masculine.[37]

Attempting to enact alternative genders involves a lot of running around. We chase our tail hoping to overturn a hierarchy that is enacted through the very terms we want to redeploy. Sometimes it appears that the goal is to "thoroughly scramble gender relations" (Halberstam 2005, 85). To the extent that that might be the approach, it can't help but remind me of that story of power by one of our great political commentators, Dr. Seuss. In Dr. Seuss's story, the Star-bellied Sneetches finally learn the lesson of tolerance and acceptance based on two factors: (1) They run out of money to pay for their star-on/star-off procedures. They can no longer afford to pay Sylvester McMonkey McBean his money to add or remove a star in order to be in the valued group. (2) They get so mixed up they can no longer tell "which kind is what, or the other way 'round?" So while I like the idea that through the eventual realization that one's efforts toward self-regard are actually leading to a type of suffering and not the happiness one presumes (that is, the original Star-bellies may realize that their preoccupation with being better is actually detrimental (costly) to them rather than beneficial), the idea that we can overcome power hierarchies only by confusing ourselves into it—by no longer being able to tell who should legitimately hold power and who should not—is a very dystopian view of the world. Can we only live in a world of equality when we are confused into it? And let's be real, none of these hierarchies make logical sense. Confusion is not the antidote but the cause of relentless systems of power over others.

This story illustrates for me the conundrum of conceptualizing "alternative" masculinities or femininities. Indeed, based on the figure-ground, binary system of gender, every alternative masculinity could equally or logically be described as an alternative femininity. Further, masculinity is preferred because to use the word femininity is taken as an insult or degradation in so many scenarios. (Indeed, how often do we even hear "alternative femininity"? Why wouldn't Halberstam use that terminology, rather than female masculinity?) We remain trapped in this system of power as we motor through our gender-crunching machines getting stars and taking them off—"this is alternative masculinity, this is alternative femininity"—all the while perpetuating the system of gender. It also can make gender into a category that seems to stand alone, outside of other desires—for example, the desire to make music. The women of Lez are not first and foremost out to create a specific gender identity for themselves, but they are trying to negotiate a space for themselves and their desires—the deep desire to make music on an instrument and in a format that is still relentlessly described as "male/masculine territory." Gender circumscribes their relationship to music. I am stating the obvious here, but sometimes I wonder if gender is somehow understood and theorized apart from the activities that make up its very definition (including here the idea that bodies are activities, that is, bodies are "bodying").

In the previous chapter, I described the gender performance of the women in the Glenn Miller Orchestra reenactment as "in-passing." As stated, in-passing is a signifying practice that asserts the authority and inevitability of the dominant position while simultaneously allowing the subordinate person to occupy it as a unique placeholder bestowed with honorary status. In-passing can now be understood in the context of the Sneetches. Whether the star is on or off (that is, whether we argue these women are performing an alternative masculinity or an alternative femininity), power still coheres around the male/masculine as the appropriate normative Sneetch while she temporarily wears, or doesn't, the star. The specific conundrum of women in the big band—do you wear gowns? tuxes?—reveals that there is no appropriate answer. It reveals the always already hierarchy of gender where, to quote Janis, "Men always seem to end up on top."

It is interesting, then, that the women of Lez Zeppelin are not in-passing. They are not taking on a "male" identity, but performing the men's gender identities as completely commensurate with their own. Further, they are not "queering" gender identity. They take on these roles as fully commensurate and "natural" for their female bodies. They are laying claim to this space in earnest, with a stress on the "no difference" aspect of their reenactment. And most important, this identification is *not* with masculinity. Which brings back into the discussion a term that is considered passé these days: "androgyny." Jack Halberstam warns that the term "androgyny" can signify a type of complete liberal humanist, equally male and female—a type of skirting, if I may, of the gender issue. The idea of androgyny, however, provided a way in for Lez to re-perform Led in earnest. Performing their algebraic equation where male femininity equates with female masculinity, they perform Led Zeppelin not as ironic, not as "queer," not as in-passers, but "for real." They perform femininity as fully commensurate with the "real Led Zeppelin" and rock masculinity as fully commensurate with their performance as women. Their performance can be viewed not as a fall back into the liberal humanist individual, then, but as a way to reveal the phantasmagorical quality of the "individual." In their strict doubling, they open up the uncanny emptiness of gender, and as such, identity itself.

THE IMPORTANCE OF (WHITE) WOMEN BEING EARNEST

So what's a poor "girl" to do? What are "women's" options if gender is a system of power that will always already place them in the attenuated position? (And now that we're in the land of scare quotes, we can see that we don't know where we are, but we're not free. We're in the opposite situation of the Sex Pistols' Johnny Rotten on anarchy: "Don't know what I want, but I know how to get it." Gender: "I know what I want, don't know how to get it.")

I have argued that Lez Zeppelin performs a more "accurate" representation of the script of cock rock by returning to the center the since-marginalized femininity and homoeroticism in the early form. But I cannot stop there. To contend that they have captured the actual, real past would clearly go against the argument presented in this book. They illuminated some repressions, they demonstrated the myth of origin, but they did not capture the "real past." Thus, while I think it is important that we understand how Janis influenced Robert and how homoeroticism was a part of cock rock, I don't find these insurrections the most significant ramifications of Lez. The most important aspect of taking Lez as a rigorously mimetic repetition is how they open up an engagement with identity that is based not on interpretation, but on the eruption of the uncanny that comes from our encounter with the double. Instead of interpreting identity—trying to imagine its "realities," its changes, its options, its sameness, its difference—the sense of the uncanny is that brush with the inherent emptiness of identity itself.

The Uncanny versus Interpretation

In chapter 2 I discussed the turn to the object as the one who knows. Fearing "subjectivity," there was a turn to the object in itself, not to be interpreted but experienced as it is. While heralded by Susan Sontag, Fredric Jameson views this as a type of postmodern depthlessness that evacuates meaning—meaning that Jameson believes we need. As I have shown, however, the reenactors discussed in this book are not trying to perform depthlessness, but quite the opposite. They view their project as a precise answer to this vacating of meaning. Like Caden Cotard, the reenactors are trying to capture the Real. In a world of only signifiers, they attempt to embody the signified, to get to the real thing by actually becoming it.

Of course, the practice does not work. It does not succeed in "accessing" the Real in the ways the reenactors tell themselves it will. It does disrupt "meaning," however. And in this there is a brush with the Real that erupts outside of the reenactors' explicit intentions and desires. As Walter Benjamin has put it, "A literal rendering [is] a direct threat to comprehensibility. [. . .] it is self-evident how greatly fidelity in reproducing the form impedes the rendering of the sense" (quoted in Schneider 2011, 113). That is, while the reenactors may have failed at capturing the signified, they do succeed in short-circuiting the signifier. Their exact replications undercut the figure-ground difference that makes "meaning" possible. One term is no longer stabilized around which another term can have meaning. All terms become clones; there is no difference, no "this" distinguished from "that." And it is this glimpsed realization that produces the sensation of the uncanny. While Lez is not obsessed with capturing the Real in the same way as the Musical Box (if only because they are also concerned with female bodies being able to "naturally" reenact this past), Benjamin's general result pertains. While Lez may have used the form as a way in to perform as natural rockers with their female bodies, ultimately their uncanny performance reveals the emptiness of the meanings of gender.

It is fruitful to consider Lez Zeppelin in relation to a subset of earnest re-creators: white women artists, influenced by the tradition of performance and conceptual art, re-creating the renowned work of white men. Famous examples include Elaine Sturtevant's copies of Roy Lichtenstein, Claes Oldenburg, Jasper Johns, Andy Warhol, Joseph Beuys, and Marcel Duchamp beginning in the 1960s; Sherrie Levine's 1980 *After Walker Evans,* in which Levine rephotographed Evans's work and called it her own; and Elizabeth LeCompte's 2004 reenactment of Jerzy Grotowski's work in *Poor Theater: A Series of Simulacra.* While a detailed analysis of these works is beyond the scope of this study, I do want to entertain some thoughts about the motives and ramifications of these works. These works have all been recognized as interrogations of the idea of "origin" and "originality."[38] As argued previously, the myth of origin is in fact a power play that will find certain bodies. There is a clear advantage for women in highlighting the "no origin" aspect of work through a reenactment. For one, it confronts the "in-passing" problem head-on. Rather than reaffirming the correctness of a particular subject-position—the white male as authoritative swing musician as seen in the Glenn Miller reenactment—these women take on the role of "women as copiers," bringing forward the privileging of male authority. Further, in performing "in earnest," I believe these works can accomplish more than re-performances using irony or drag. While Judith Butler claims the practice of drag reveals gender as a construct, I believe these strict reenactments bring to light the complete fantasy of identity itself.

That is, in their doubling, these works brush the uncanny. Moving away from interpretation and therefore "truth," their fidelity undermines the structure of meaning. As art critic Andrea Kroksnes has written, Sherrie Levine's copies and appropriations highlight the "absent figure of meaning . . . or some other projected story." Speaking of an early work of Levine's that involved photographing and selling shoes in New York (photographs that Kroksnes argues are reminiscent of Van Gogh's painting), Kroksnes writes:

> [H]ow can we find out the truth about Levine's shoes, borrowed from Van Gogh, or maybe just from Evans' "Floyd Burroughs' Work Shoes," itself prob-

> ably an homage to Van Gogh's "A Pair of Boots." . . . Or what is the meaning of her 'After Walker Evans' . . . stolen for sure? Already in the originals—Van Gogh's shoes—it is hard to find and fix meaning. . . . Already in Van Gogh's paintings we trace meaning back to some origin outside the picture—be it peasant woman or city dweller. In this process of interpretation, the depicted shoes become straw men, stand-ins, fetishes, for the absent figure of meaning—be it the artist/author him- [or her-]self or some other projected story. (2001, 6)

Levine's appropriations and strict copies open up the ways we solidify and cohere around the (great white male genius) artist as the point of origin, but not all of the steps before, including the world that supported him and that he is "capturing"—the influences, inhabitants, the specific time, and all of the time that led up to the work's momentary materialization at the instant of the photograph or painting. The revelation of the ways that we cohere, stabilize, and in fact, impute significance onto the object is revealed in the uncanny when the rug is pulled out and our fantasies are made plain.[39]

Thus, in a postmodern world without interpretation, the depthless reenactment erupts with the most basic of our repressions: the phantasmagorical quality of the self itself. In Lez this is initially understood in terms of "gender." In taking legitimate entrance into the plural band-body of Led Zeppelin, in performing the moves of Plant and Page (who performed the moves of Joplin and Big Brother who performed the moves of Redding who performed the moves of Thornton who . . .), Lez reveals "gender" to be an imputation—a set of characteristics that actually can and do float across bodies, but only cohere based on the stories we tell ("some other projected story"). In seeing Paynes embody Page, see and hear her wield her sexy guitar, watch as she gives a shy smile to the audience, tosses her hair, and then sinks into a power chord followed by a blistering riff, the uncanny of gender identity is revealed—there is no masculine or feminine. Whether stories of "female machisma" that would claim Suzi Quatro and Chrissie Hynde are identifying with men, stories of "female masculinity" that consider masculinity stable, or stories of "alternative femininity" that view women as sexual and aggressive—all of these stories are revealed as interpretations of characteristics that have no ultimate ground.

But this absence of gender, and ultimately, absence of identity must not be confused with a type of invisibility and universality that is the hallmark of whiteness. It is important to note that Sturtevant, Levine, LeCompte, and Lez are all white women reenacting famous white men. Sturtevant, Levine, and LeCompte are clearly progeny of the Western tradition of Replay as described in this book. While all of that is problematic, Lez is perhaps even more problematic because the music of Led also has roots in a different tradition that Led worked to erase. Thus, in claiming that Lez reveals there is no origin—well, this can sound a lot like Led Zeppelin claiming there is no origin and knowing all along that the origin will find them. The race of the women in Lez is not taken into account, but taken for granted as universal. They can take on Led naturally both because of their gender and because of their race. They could reveal the emptiness of gender while solidifying the "naturalness" of whiteness as universal.

Therefore, I want to be clear that the privileging of whiteness is not tantamount to the acknowledgment of no origin. Invisibility as a tactic of whiteness is pretending there is not an origin, while secretly solidifying originary naturalness around whiteness. This is ignorance—ignoring. I am arguing for the opposite, as I will develop in the conclusion.

In not being able to trace back to a founding origin, we can see how we impute a subject that is inherently not there—that we are filling shoes which, in fact, always remain empty. As Judith Butler writes in opposition to theoretical models that "take the gendered self to be prior to its acts, I . . . understand constituting acts not only as constituting the identity of the actor, but constituting that identity as a compelling illusion, an object of *belief*" (Butler 2017 [1988], 482; italic in original). Not only is "gender" a compelling illusion, but the whole of identity itself. In my view, this is why "letting go" of gender categories may be so terrifying. It is part and parcel of our belief in our identity itself. More than not knowing how to solve the gender problem, I believe we are highly ambivalent as to whether we want to.

Lez's rigorous reenactment reveals the ways women contribute to the formation of what Halberstam would say are "masculinities" and what I would say eventually are *called* "masculinities" (for example, Joplin's influence on Plant). They undo the origin story that establishes the male body as the origin and the female body as the copy. And they help to uncover the greatest cover-up in human history—the queer core at the heart of cock rock. They do so not through a method that could fall under a broad rubric of "identity politics," but through Replay. In claiming to be re-creating Led precisely, they reveal the uncanny emptiness of gender and identity. Their practice is not one of staking an (even provisional) claim around an identity in order to find a place from which to speak. It is in missing the memo that tells you a certain identity is different from you. Accepting provisional truths may be necessary, but it can also be a way to defer knowledge of the inherent emptiness of the subject. We have to be honest about our commitment to provisionality: commitment to provisionality is not an easy task.[40] I think there is room for both approaches: indeed, we can be more effective in reworking identity if we can practice recognizing the inherent void of all identity.

CONCLUSION

A Different Lean

On Intimacy and Emptiness

> Not everything that is faced can be changed. But nothing can be changed until it is faced.
>
> *James Baldwin, "As Much Truth as One Can Bear"*

> All the bits and pieces—the screams and cries, the silences, the density of the nation's history, the ideological justifications, . . . the courageous political resistance, and so on—do not quite add up. They can be isolated and laid bare, and they can be put to the political task of exposure, but it seems as if in that very act the ghosts return, demanding a different kind of knowledge, a different kind of acknowledgement.
>
> *Avery Gordon,* Ghostly Matters

I have argued that the sense of the uncanny arises when we startlingly encounter the emptiness of identity. I now explore this emptiness further and argue for the need to lean in its direction. Embracing the emptiness of identity and phenomena does not elide political or historical questions in favor of apolitical and ahistorical navel-gazing. On the contrary, acknowledging emptiness destabilizes erroneous Western ideologies and offers the best chance to first survive and, then, dislodge them. I begin by discussing emptiness, eventually connecting it to relationship and intimacy as modes of engaging with the world. I offer Jason Moran's *In My Mind: Monk at Town Hall 1959* as an example of intimacy and emptiness in Moran's handling of the past. Although a reenactment of sorts,

Moran's work was more evocative of Toni Morrison's definition of art as "the fully realized presence of haunting" (quoted in Bhabha 1994, 18). As we continue to recognize this world as interdependent and in continual movement, we need a new way to conceive of ourselves within it. In the final section of this book, I argue for a new theorization of the subject within critical theory. I believe our long-standing model of the subject constituted through desire/recognition perpetuates a cycle of alienation, fear, separation, and disempowerment. I suggest we lean away from the recognized subject and toward the subject who gives.

Emptiness is the most common English word used to translate the Sanskrit word *Shunyata*, from Buddhism. *Shunyata* points to the reality that nothing has a permanent, locatable existence. Therefore, not only do phenomena come into existence and also at some point cease to exist, but even when they are existing one cannot find their exact boundary. The Madhyamaka logics illustrate this in great detail. Whatever object we take—be it a person, a tree, a cloud, any phenomenon—we can always break it down into smaller and smaller particles. We will never find its essence. Further, nothing is free of the conditions that support it. The tree cannot be separated from sunlight, water, dirt, all the constituents that make up its being. For those unfamiliar with Buddhism, the word "emptiness" can sound cold and barren, but this is a misunderstanding. A warmer translation, which also may be more descriptive for English speakers, is Vietnamese monk Thich Nhat Hanh's word, "interbeing." Another helpful translation for emptiness is relationship. Everything is emptiness means that everything is relationship. The word "relationship" can be confusing in that it may give the sense that there are separate things *in* relation with each other. No. Everything *is* relationship. Everything is interbeing, nothing can be found to stand alone. As Thich Nhat Hanh says, we all inter-are. Everything inter-is (Thich 2003).

Emptiness, therefore, is also the Real as I've described it in this book: impermanence and interdependence—an understanding of which is both feared and desired. Timothy Morton describes this Western fear of the Real using a different term: Buddhaphobia. Morton exhorts us to face this fear, suggesting that "thinking Buddhism is a way to think [critical] theory beyond certain deadlocks" (2015, 250). For Morton, Buddhist philosophy can help resolve the antinomies of Western philosophy that arise from the subject-object split and its plethora of binaries. Other scholars have offered counterepistemologies that similarly privilege the relational and the intimate as a way of characterizing and understanding the world. Homi Bhabha focuses on the "unhomely" as an aspect of the uncanny to highlight relationship as a counter to Western separation and location. Linking unhomely to a literal translation of *unheimlich,* the Freudian uncanny, Bhabha articulates how the modern postcolonial condition elicits the unhomely in ways that unsettle public/private, self/other, and other binaries that maintain "civil society." The (post)colonized subject in particular "creates an uncertainty at the heart of the generalizing subject of civil society, compromising the 'individual' that is the support for its universalist aspiration" (1994, 15). The unhomely triggers the startling recognition of the ultimate impotence of hegemonic knowledge regimes. Through this, one's world can "expand enormously" (13). The uncanny is also a characteristic of haunting as described by Avery Gordon. To use James Baldwin's phrase, haunting offers "the evidence of things not seen" (quoted in Gordon 2008 [1997], 195). Gordon tells us, "If you let it, the ghost can lead you toward what has been missing, which is sometimes everything" (58). Far from a past that is lost, Gordon demonstrates how the past remains and cannot be separated from the present. Not literal, but subtle and pervasive, the ghost upsets the modern Western view's "monopolistic hold on culture, which forbids anything that cannot be grasped" (Adorno 2006 [1991], 65).

All of this work is encouraging an understanding of the world that recognizes its relationality and intimacy. Morton's discussion of Buddhaphobia, Bhabha's of the unhomely, and Gordon's of haunting all suggest that the world is complex, relational, and uncanny. And this is frightening from the perspective of the Western epistemology. As Morton puts it, "What Buddhaphobia really fears is . . . *the intimacy of life*" (215; italic in original). For one, this intimacy disrupts Western knowledge regimes that maintain cultural hierarchies. For Bhabha, the unhomely reveals an "interstitial intimacy" that questions boundaries between self and other, inner and outer, "binary divisions through which such spheres of social experience are often spatially opposed" (19). And Gordon beautifully articulates how the past is deeply intimate with the present—far from lost, stories continue to haunt, stories that ache to be heard. This intimacy, this connection, this emptiness of self "is just what Western philosophy has mostly been designed to ward off" (Morton 2015, 228).

But as I've argued, we also deeply crave this intimacy, this connection. And this can be our way in to face our fear of it. As such, I join with these scholars and others to advocate for a different way to conceive of our world. To ask if "the perplexity of the unhomely, intrapersonal world [can] lead to an international theme?" (Bhabha 1994, 17). Can we develop ways to accept this perplexing blur of an intimate, uncanny, interdependent, unlocatable, but fully here, world as a basis for living? This intimacy of the past and the present, of the other and the self, is found in my final example of live musical reenactment. In many ways, jazz music itself can be recognized as art as "the fully realized presence of haunting." Jason Moran brings out these qualities of acceptance and incorporation of the past into one's body and performance in his interaction with Thelonious Monk.

JASON MORAN'S *IN MY MIND: MONK AT TOWN HALL, 1959*

As part of a "Monk-at-90" tribute in 2007, the San Francisco Jazz Festival approached jazz pianist, composer, and MacArthur Fellow Jason Moran with the idea of doing a "historical re-creation" of Thelonious Monk's 1959 Town Hall concert: "To recreate the historic Thelonious Monk concert. . . . The idea was that I would play the piano part, and Thelonious's son, T. S. Monk, would play drums" (Moran 2008). Moran demurred on an exact re-creation, remarking in an interview that "technical re-creations can be a recipe for disaster" via quick allusion to Gus Van Sant's shot-by-shot remake of *Psycho* (Johnson 2009). But he was intrigued and soon secured a co-commission from Duke University, the San Francisco Jazz Festival, Chicago Symphony Hall, and the Washington Performance Arts Society to create a compromise: a "making of" combined with a "historical re-creation."[1] With his ensemble the Big Bandwagon, and in collaboration with visual artist Glenn Ligon and video artist David Dempewolf, Moran presented a multimedia re-creation developed from archival material of preparations for Monk's original concert that, in part, examined the making of the Town Hall concert (Moran 2008).[2] He premiered it in 2007, took it on a sixteen-city international tour, and has performed it intermittently since. It did not sidestep all of the fetishistic landmines associated with strict reenactments. As part of the Duke University "Monk Festival," it was staged for almost the exact fiftieth anniversary on February 27, 2009, at the original venue of Town Hall in New York (the original performance took place on February 28).

I attended a performance of *In My Mind* in the Eisenhower Theater at the Kennedy Center on March 28, 2015. The evening did not begin auspiciously. As the audience filed in, a screen at the back of the stage filtered through a series of black-and-white television clips framed by the representation of a mid-century television set. Flashing by were 1950s-era film and TV images: commercials; Major League Baseball; white men surfing; male hands of unidentifiable race playing the piano; news or military footage of warplanes; other news footage I did not recognize, but some including Rosa Parks; the headline to a documentary, "The

Story of Television"; and news footage of Richard Nixon in the USSR, referencing, I imagine, his 1959 Kitchen Debate with Nikita Khrushchev. I was hoping the material was not all from 1959, but the Kitchen Debate footage led me to believe it was. This fetishizing of the year and the unironic presentation of nostalgia all framed within the 1950s-era television set gave me the Disneyland feel that I get from many reenactments. It is as if the images taken from "That. Very. Year." are what should be thrilling and interesting for us. Positivistic, flat-footed, literalist fun, I'm thinking. I was preparing myself for disappointment.

But this fetishistic interaction with the past dropped away when Moran entered from stage right, took his place at the piano, and donned a pair of extra-large headphones. Soon we heard the original recording of *Monk at Town Hall* "leaking" the first track from Moran's headphones: "Thelonious." Moran dove into the piano, scrawling all over the partially audible-to-us, but we get the impression very-loud-to-him "Thelonious." The pianist did not treat the original "reverently." He was not dutifully re-performing the master's licks, but getting funky here, atonal there, gospelly in another moment. For me, it evoked Moran's youth, his private practice at home, experimenting, pretending to be a grown-up "great artist," being free, unrestrained: playing. Moran seemed to be saying, this is how jazz artists interact with the jazz past—they *play* with it. Playing with the past is how they learn jazz. Perhaps overly excited, I read it as a critique of this whole reenactment thing. It was a call to arms, a statement of what this "historical recreation" would and would not be: Moran *playing with* the past. *Playing.* WITH. Monk. Here's the *with* that all of these reenactments have been vainly trying to capture. Here's the connection. The past *is* here when we stop trying so hard to locate it. Monk *is* here. I was relieved.

As the performance unfolded, I was pleased to find that I was not overly excited; I was as excited as I should have been. The performance was not only an answer to the reenactment approach, but an argument for a way to think about the past and about art. It was a case for a way of knowing that favors connecting and allowing, not copying and conquering. After the Monk/Moran "duet," the band entered, joining Moran for a full band version of "Thelonious." Like many of the evening's musical arrangements, at a certain point the song began to fragment into bits of melody-turned-riff that looped and overlapped by different sections of the band. These loops continued to repeat beyond the point of "overdoing it." The effect was a type of implosion of the song with different sections of the band obsessively repeating different riffs in kaleidophonic splendor. It seemed to be another comment on the issue of copying, tradition, influence, and repetition.

You want tribute? You want the past?—here it is. Over and over and over and over and over and. . . . It was making copying so obsessive that something else came out the other side. Indeed, songs subjected to this approach disintegrated out, sending constituent particles of the melody into the ether as atonal solos or group improvisation sidled in. Although not an exact technique that Monk employed, it was redolent of a certain brilliant obsession I find in Monk's work. A starkness and complex simplicity. An adamantine quality that marks Monk's idiosyncrasy.

With the exception of the video prelude, David Dempewolf's contribution further supported the overall approach to engaging *Monk at Town Hall.* Moran collected archival sound and visual material from the original rehearsals for the Town Hall concert as well as images from Monk's family history. Dempewolf manipulated and played with those images. Photographs of the rehearsals for the Town Hall concert jumped around and changed with color filters or were partially obscured. They were "ruined" so as not to remain clear representations of a locatable past. The visual backdrop behind the performance of "Monk's Mood" displayed photos with subtitles. From my seat the subtitles were partially obscured, but what I could read—"This is my room, my piano, I started piano lessons when . . . "—I initially took to be statements from Monk. The song is called "*Monk's* Mood," after all. But I started to think that these were statements from Moran and the photos probably of Moran's childhood home. This was further supported when we heard a recording of what I took to be Moran describing listening to a Monk record with his family in his childhood living room. The TV set was on with the volume down, and his parents were discussing the recent tragic news of some friend or relative dying in an accident. While I do not clearly remember the details of the story, the effect remained with me—it was a story of Moran learning the importance of music—its power to help us survive in a world full of unknowns.[3] This "arrangement" of "Monk's Mood" was an example of how Moran blurred the "my" in his title: *In My Mind.* While beginning with "*Monk*'s Mood," we are led through a complex interaction that leaves everything unclear as to whose mood, whose mind, whose song. Who is Monk here and who is Moran? As we listen, where, precisely, could we find that boundary?

And isn't "blurred" just another word for "connection"? The visuals behind the performance of "Off Minor" included old newspapers flashing by quickly. There were no images of Monk or even jazz, but simply newspapers that gave the impression of "the past" more generally, not some specific Monk past or jazz past. Live shots of the band currently playing in Eisenhower Theater were then superimposed on these images. Throughout the song we had these two worlds coming together, the present concert smeared into the representation of the past, playing and interacting with it, blurring and connecting. It is the antithesis of the idea that we here in the present can somehow capture the past as a separate object. There was no separation and therefore no this to capture that. As "Off Minor" came to a close, we heard a recording of Monk talking about the song "Crepuscule with Nellie." At a certain point Monk intones, "Let me see you play it," and Moran begins playing, immediately creating the strong impression that Monk's statement (asked in rehearsal) was a generous invitation. Moran responds to that invitation with alacrity, offering his own version of "Crepuscule." Moran is listening to Monk and responding. He is not copying him exactly. He is taking up the invitation offered by a jazz elder. Moran is honoring the artist by listening hard enough that I/you/Monk/he can verify that he has heard by his own response. To mimic the man would be to demonstrate that, indeed, he has not really heard him. He has not heard what needs to be heard.

The performance made a final case for connection in the last number. In the middle of the song, the musicians rose and left the stage while still playing. The audience followed the sound of the players growing fainter as they filed into the wings. It was unclear what was happening, but then the audience heard the sound coming nearer again. The music grew stronger until a side door to the auditorium opened and the band paraded through, crossing the audience aisle and then turning right toward the lobby. On exiting the back of the theater, the band continued to play until the song was finished and the audience offered its hearty applause. As we exited into the lobby, we found the musicians there waiting to interact with us.

I requested one, but Moran did not have a recording of the entire performance to offer me. There are so many specifics of this performance that I don't remember. But this is apt. Things are lost. We don't retain everything. But what is it that is important to retain? For example, I was fascinated by the musicians getting up and leaving the stage while still playing. But I don't recall what the song was. Was it still "Crepuscule"? I don't think so. Was it a reprise of "Little Rootie Tootie"? I also don't think that. I recall being pleased that Moran did not reprise "Rootie Tootie," which was so fetishistically performed by trumpeter Charles Tolliver and rewarded with critical praise.[4] But I wouldn't stake my life on that memory. How I remember the music now (and I think "incorrectly") is as a kind of second line style. Perhaps because they were walking and playing I am now remembering it as the sound of a New Orleans second line process. Or perhaps it really was. I like the truth of this imperfect recollection. I cannot fix the performance in my mind—it cannot be fixed (neither frozen nor my memory "fixed" by listening to a recording).

Indeed, the phrase "in my mind" was taken from a recorded comment by Monk during one of the rehearsals that Moran had, in fact, misheard. What Monk actually said while discussing some music was "*for* my mind." As Moran stated in an interview, he remembered it as "in my mind" and began to ponder the phrase, listening when other people in his life stated this phrase. He then created a sound collage in which he tried to repeat the particular cadence of the way each person said "in my mind" (quoted in Hawkins 2009). Moran misremembers "for my mind," turning it into "in my mind." I can't perfectly remember the Kennedy Center performance. Moran's misremembering, like mine, is acknowledged. The point for myself, and I believe for Moran, is the impact the "misremembered" moment had. We are not relying on some perfect accuracy, but on how we are affected by something. Moran's "reenactment" highlights how the past cannot be "said" in the positivistic, pointing-to, obsessive way of strict reenactments. It is an uncapturable influence, which is to say it is here and not here. Of course, the Town Hall concert is no longer what it was exactly. That time, that whatever-it-was (which could never be captured anyway, even then)—that is the "not here." But it is here in the influence. Moran is *connecting* with the past. He is demonstrating how the past is a *relationship* of which we are made.

What is important to copy? What is it we want to know wanting to know the other? A discussion between the two artists Jason Moran and Glenn Ligon offers a perspective:

LIGON: "What drew me to your work was when I heard you playing Monk. I heard Jason Moran playing Monk—I didn't hear someone trying to re-create Monk in a straightforward, note-for-note, this-is-how-he-would've-done-it way. I realize that it's the result of an incredibly intense research project. You figure out how he played as the base, and then you build your own vocabulary up.

MORAN: For me, Monk is the best example. When he plays someone else's work, it just sounds like him. I discovered Monk in the '80s. . . . I was like 13. . . . He had his eyes set and he never wavered, and I thought, That's how you're supposed to do it—period. When I try to approach Monk's work, I have to make sure that I have reckless abandon within it. I try to make sure I don't let that sandcastle just stand. It should start getting demolished from

> the bottom and move its way up to the top, dissolving into something else. I think that's the problem with jazz in general. It's still a young art form—a little over 100 years old now—and there's the idea like, shit, we've only had a couple of golden eras, and we really want to keep looking back at them. That will just get us stuck. (Moran n.d.)

In My Mind does not display the many fetishistic qualities of Replay, yet in many ways it is a type of "exact" reenactment of Monk. It simply assumes different things are important to copy. From this interview one could say that Moran is trying to imitate Monk quite seriously, in fact. But what he is trying to imitate/learn from/know is something not so easily located. It is something about determination, about devotion, about self-worth. Something about recognizing the importance and validity of making one's own contribution while understanding that that "you" is also a part of the "them" you embrace as your ancestors. Perhaps it is something akin to what Timothy Morton describes as "intimacy without ego" (240), which may also be "the fully realized presence of haunting." The blur between past and present, self and other, makes ego hard to maintain, let alone locate. The experience is fraught with (mis)remembering and messy subjectivity. "The 'past-present' becomes part of the necessity, not the nostalgia, of living" (Bhabha 1994, 10). Monk's story is past-present in that it both was and is still here. The continued ripples from the atrocity of slavery: racism, discrimination, the Civil Rights movement, and other acts of beauty to counter injustice and put forth humanity—they are all here. The past is not over, and therefore it is not lost. In fact, it needs to be recognized and heard. As Moran acknowledges this history, musical and social, as integral to *now*, he performs a type of past-present that can allow for connection and promote an acceptance of our unlocatable but deeply interdependent state of being.

THE GIVING SUBJECT

Moran's performance offers a model of the past and the present as blurred, connected, and intimate. New models for understanding our world are acutely necessary at this time. After a long, slow decline that began almost as soon as the idea developed as Western ideology, the concept of the self-standing individual is no longer tenable for anyone. Whether in philosophy, science, or our current environmental challenges, the truth that we do not stand alone in mind or body is becoming impossible to ignore. In this book, I have described this truth in terms of the encroachment of the Real. The question is: What models of living can help us encounter this Real rather than continue to fear/desire it and push it away? I offer a model of thinking of the "self" in a continually fluctuating and interdependent world. If the self and other are constructions, the models we use to conceive of this constructedness nonetheless profoundly influence how we think of ourselves. In my view, it is all in where we place the lean.

The Subject of Critical Theory: The Desiring/Recognized Subject

The dominant model of subjectivity in critical theory comes from Hegel, as interpreted primarily through the work of Judith Butler. Butler introduced the idea of gender performativity in her 1990 book *Gender Trouble*, and since then, performativity has become a central theorization of the subject in cultural studies. As Butler has acknowledged, "In a sense, all of my work remains within the orbit of a certain set of Hegelian questions: What is the relation between desire and recognition, and how is it that the constitution of the subject entails a radical and constitutive relation to alterity?" (quoted in Salih 2004, 47). Butler's subject is very similar to the Hegelian "self-consciousness" outlined in the "Lordship and Bondage" section of his *Phenomenology of Spirit*. Hegel writes that "self-consciousness exists in and for itself when, and by the fact that, it so exists for another; that is, it exists only in being acknowledged" (Hegel 1977 [1807], 111). In a similar passage, Butler writes, "One comes to 'exist' by virtue of [the] fundamental dependency on the address of the Other. One 'exists' not only by virtue of being recognized, but, in a prior sense, by being recognizable" (Butler 1997, 5). For Butler, the subject will be acknowledged (or recognized) to the extent that it is "recognizable." Subjects are compelled to operate within the confines of intelligibility or suffer the consequences of illegibility, including the possibility of "exclusion and violence."

The Hegelian/Butlerian subject, therefore, is constituted in its desire. As Butler writes, "This subject neither has nor suffers its desire, but is the very action of desire as it perpetually displaces the subject." The subject's desire "for and by another" brings forth a "struggle for recognition." Like the man waiting outside looking for recognition and acknowledgment by the Law in Franz Kafka's story "Before the Law," the subject is both constituted through and delimited by this struggle for recognition.[5] Rather than a discrete, self-contained, and unified subject that is impinged upon by outer forces, the subject's constitution, its very condition of possibility, is through this desire. The Butlerian subject, then, is one that only comes into existence in relation to a "larger cultural order." Butler writes, "Hegel developed the view that the struggle for recognition gave rise to a concept of the individual essentially defined in terms of a larger cultural order, which, rather than limiting the individual's freedom, provided for its concrete determination and expression."

Given this view of the subject's constitution, Butler then asks: What types of subjects are "thinkable"? Can we expand the thinkability of who is recognizable (by the Law, the cultural order) as a subject? How do we expand the conditions of possibility, indeed the "livability" for subjects—in particular, those subjects who are marginalized, or even unintelligible, and thus open to "exclusion and violence"? For Butler, the idea of iterability is key to expanding these conditions of possibility. The iterability of the subject ensures that drift and context will counteract the foreclosure of meaning. This theory has been taken up by other theorists of identity, for example, in the work of José Esteban Muñoz. Muñoz argues that marginalized subjects practice a type of "disidentification" in order to manage "an identity that has been 'spoiled' in the majoritarian public sphere" by re-performing the "spoiled" identity with a type of conscious embrace and an eye toward subversive context. These subjects use the iterability of language to reiterate the terms and expand their conditions of possibility as recognized subjects.

Butler and Muñoz give convincing arguments for the ways in which marginalized subjects can expand their conditions of livability. My concern, however, is that this particular post-Hegelian approach has become an ideology that grounds contemporary cultural theory and naturalizes one way of conceiving of the subject's "conditions of possibility." My concern with the current ideology of thinking about the subject is that while we generally recognize the contingency of the subject, the "Other" is often implicitly credited with great stability and power. Butler acknowledges the equally co-constitutive nature of the self and the Other in Hegel's account. She writes, "The self is not its own, . . . it is given over to the Other in advance of any further relation but in such a way that the Other does not own it either. And the ethical content of its relationship to the Other is to be found in this fundamental and reciprocal state of being 'given over.'" I would agree that the self and the Other are in a "fundamental and reciprocal state of being 'given over'" to each other. Yet in my view, in contemporary cultural theory this lack of ownership of the Other is not adequately investigated. For indeed, we could imagine that rather than a state of being "given over," we could operate from a state of "giving to."

In current critical theory, however, the lean is toward the Other as a point of origin. I believe that it is the focus on recognition that serves to erroneously solidify the Other. Particularly in theories of performativity, there is an emphasis on the Other who gives or withholds recognition. Even if that other is only myself watching myself, the idea of performance always entails the idea of an other who is watching. But what if we had a different conception of the other—not the one for which we always perform, for which we want recognition and acknowledgment? What if we conceived of the other as the one to which we give? There is a leap in Hegel's statement: "Self-consciousness exists in and for itself when, and by the fact that, it so exists for another; that is, it exists only in being acknowledged." How does existing for another seamlessly become "it exists only in being acknowledged"? Is that the only way that a self can exist for another? It is not. The idea of wanting recognition from the other actually imputes a specious solidity to this other (making it "an Other"). We could conceive of the other as that to which we give. This encourages a type of selflessness that is, in fact, the reality with which we begin—the already acknowledged lack of the subject.

The Giving Subject

If the self and other are co-constituted, there is no need to deduce that the self exists for the other "only in being acknowledged." Since the "self" is what we each have access to (our mind, our body—problematic, complex, and constructed as that may be), we start from that phantasmagorical place with a model of self-other that both aligns more with the ultimate reality of the situation and also (as it turns out) gives us agency. That is, we can rewrite Hegel's description thus: self-consciousness exists in and for itself when, and by the fact that, it so exists for another; that is, *it exists only in its giving to the other.* This is the next step in conceiving of the self. The first view—the lean toward an other who delimits us through its recognition—may indeed be the default in Western culture as it is so lived. But as we have entered a phase in which the constructedness of this self and other is so eminently apparent, we can turn to a different model, which in fact may take more effort to conceive. While I may have accepted the "other's" inducements to perform a legible role in this society, I do not need to continue to believe in what I am now beginning to understand is a phantasmagorical display with no essential reality. As I give up that fantasy, I must take responsibility and find a way to locate myself anew. It is impossible to simply live without an orientation. Taking the constructed self as the one who gives as my orientation aligns with the reality of no real self. Complete giving would be complete selflessness, which would be a manifestation of the reality of the self. It is not there. And what a relief. The focus changes from the concern for recognition from the other to the concern to give to the other. The lean turns toward the emptiness of the self that can nonetheless give, rather than toward the emptiness of the other which we imagine can nonetheless take (by not recognizing us). But this is a practice and it is not easy. It involves letting go of conceptions of self in which we still implicitly believe, particularly in the West.

Jason Moran's performance offered this different epistemology, which can be especially recognized in relation to the other reenactments examined in this book. Asked to perform a strict reenactment, Moran countered the very premises of that desire in his encounter with Thelonious Monk. He dissolved boundaries rather than worked to instantiate them, and he improvised, which demands generosity—listening, communicating *with,* and responding *to.* Ultimately, his performance represented a type of intimacy that acknowledges the inseparability of past and present and of self and other.

Moran's performance was intent on dissolving the boundaries that are established in the Western performance tradition of classical music. Moran found ways to dissolve the stage edge that separates audience from performance. Working against the Eisenhower Theater, where the stage is raised up from the first rows of seats and demarcated through lighting and curtains, the Big Bandwagon meandered off and on while continuing to play and ultimately came in through side entrances into the audience to play in the aisles and then out into the foyer. Live performance of the Big Bandwagon was superimposed onto the images of the past displayed on the back screen, performing a type of past-present. Such staging echoes the blurring of the identities of Moran and Monk as described previously.

The practice of improvisation can be a direct repudiation of an epistemology of boundaries. Scholars, artists, and laypeople define improvisation in many ways. Wynton Marsalis privileges improvisation, yet his definition is much narrower than mine. Many of his performances I would describe as Replay, the opposite of improvisation. I therefore use the specific term "improvisative" (in counter to the performative) to describe improvisation as a practice of generosity, one that works to dissolve the specious boundaries instantiated in our modern world. The improvisative denotes improvisation as an act of giving to the singular other.[6] It is a practice that involves deep listening. This deep listening is necessary to counter a long-standing habit of dulling our listening (and other sensibilities). Already in the mid-twentieth century, Adorno was speaking directly of listening when he described the modern Westerner as "childish; their primitivism is not that of the undeveloped, but that of the forcibly retarded. Whenever they have a chance, they display the pinched hatred of those who really sense the other but exclude it in order to live in peace, and who therefore would like best to root out the nagging possibility" (2006 [1991], 46–47). This "forcibly retarded" listening in an attempt to live in "peace" continues today, even as the "nagging possibility" of others is ever apparent. And a "pinched hatred" is no sign of peace. Real peace could come with an acceptance of a complex world and when effort and responsibility take the place of timidity and dulled senses. In this way, Moran listened and responded to Monk, opening himself to what would occur. To follow Gordon, Moran listened for what the "ghost" would say "out of a concern for justice" (Derrida, quoted in Gordon 2008, 58).

Jason Moran demonstrates this type of generous responsiveness that I associate with the improvisative. His work as a composer, pianist, and Kennedy Center artistic director for jazz displays a tremendous openness and bigheartedness. Not only does his conception of jazz and improvisation include music from the avant-garde to hip-hop, it also includes visual and sound artists, choreographers, and skateboarders. His work with the Betty Carter Jazz Ahead program nurtures young musicians, and he programs a diverse array of performers, including a much richer representation of women instrumentalists than can be found at JALC and other jazz festivals. Finally, Moran's approach to improvisation exemplifies this responsive generosity. To a question about improvising with different musicians, Moran replies, "My approach can change drastically depending on who is on the gig. When I play with Tarus [Mateen] and Nasheet [Waits] (bassist and drummer with his trio, Bandwagon) we really do understand how each other fly. Like 3 kites circling one another from 40 feet high. When I play with other folks, I try to have empathy the way they do. And I want to support people's goals and sounds" (quoted in Harris 2016). Moran describes a particular, situated, empathic responsiveness to the singular other. What Moran offers in comparison to the other reenactments described in this book is "a story that is no longer located in the vice of the morality of verisimilitude" (Gordon 2008, 164). It allows for "knowing the things behind the things" (Morrison, quoted in Gordon, 164). It is a type of knowing that is subjective, nonconceptual, ineffable. Yet this deep knowing seems to have an ethical impulse. Emmanuel Levinas argues that in sincerely becoming aware of an other, we experience a profound ethical response to help the other. Ignoring the sense of the other leads to psychic and physical violence. Acknowledging this sense makes violence very difficult to enact.[7] In

In My Mind, as Moran interacted with other musicians in the Big Bandwagon, and with Monk himself, a type of intimacy of self and other, past and present is acknowledged. This intimacy is "nearer than breathing and closer than hands and feet" (George Morrison, quoted in Morton 2015, 252). Which is to say, it is also an intimacy with ourselves and the unanswerable mystery of who we are.

A New Lean

Most current critical and cultural theory continues to have difficulty with the subjective.[8] But scholars such as Morton, Boon, Gordon, and others are pushing back, calling for an acknowledgment of the real complexity of life as subjective, blurred, connected, impermanent, and unlocatable. This is an acknowledgment of the Real, a way to take all that normally "escapes [us] . . . this, here, now, alive, active" as a basis, rather than ignore and malign it as opaque, unknowable "personal" or "subjective" experience (Williams (128), quoted in Gordon 2008, 199). We need to recognize and rethink our deep and erroneous fear of the Real—its causes and its ramifications (including our quixotic attempts to triumph over death and impermanence). Boon asks, "What if we face our fear? Could we do without [phantasmagorical] framings entirely?" In my view, the short-term answer is no. We need mental structures or models that can help us move toward a more honest relationship with the world as it is. We need an orientation. I have suggested the giving subject. Certainly there are other framings and structures that, while provisional, can help orient us in a healthy and honest direction which aligns with an impermanent and interdependent world. We cannot drop our mind's desire to frame the world, but we can develop strategies and practices that will move us in the direction of a less phobic response to the Real.[9] Replay is a phobic response to the Real. As a cultural practice, or even ritual, it exemplifies a culture that deeply fears loss and longs for connection. But in order to have such connection we need to come to terms with reality. We need to acknowledge the past in the present, the other in the self, and the poignant, necessary loss at the heart of every experience.

NOTES

Introduction

1. Based on audience surveys conducted by the author. Description taken from my attendance at the Musical Box concerts in Los Angeles, San Francisco, and Montreal from 2011 to 2012. Quote from Phil Collins on the Musical Box taken from the Musical Box website, accessed July 12, 2012, www.themusicalbox.net.

2. The Gabriel, Banks, Hackett, Rutherford, and Collins lineup.

3. From their website, "The Musical Box," accessed July 2, 2012, www.themusicalbox.net.

4. In the 1970s, the historically informed performance (HIP) movement in classical music was composed of performers of early music who attempted to re-create music as "accurately" as possible on instruments of the time.

5. Taken from audience surveys conducted by the author and author interview with the Musical Box bandleader Sébastien Lamothe, October 3, 2011.

6. I was eventually fired from the band for a reason that I can describe only as "playing saxophone while female." Over after-gig drinks with some members of the band and the bandleader, I asked the leader what he thought was the weakest aspect of the sax section. "[The second alto] can't find 'do,'" he replied, referring to "do-re-mi" and meaning the second alto was out of tune. I nodded. This was the problem I had heard and, being the only woman in the group, worried about how to redress. Apparently, the bandleader then relayed the discussion (although I had only nodded my head) to the first, and maybe second, alto, clearly mentioning me as perhaps saying it or noticing it, because the following happened. In a section of a tune where I knew we were always egregiously out of tune, I did not play. After the song, the first alto leaned over to tell me I was out of tune in that section. I told him I had not played that section because I knew it was always out of tune. The bandleader called me the next day and told me I was fired. In his words, once these problems in a horn section start, they can only be resolved by firing someone. I was deemed the difficult member to be fired.

7. See Sturken (1997, 123).

8. Haunthenticity is not the same as the haunting described by Avery Gordon (2008 [1997]) regarding sociology and by Ethan Kleinberg (2016) regarding history. These authors conceive of haunting as that which lingers, erupts, slips away, and is feared and denied. The haunthenticity of Replay is, in fact, a way to continue denying all that haunts us sociologically and historically.

9. Clifford Geertz (1973), Victor Turner (1982), Marshall McLuhan (2001 [1967]). Richard Schechner describes performance as a space of ritual where spectators buy into the illusion (Schechner 2006, 64).

10. Seen most clearly in the influential scholarship of Homi Bhabha (1994).

11. See Ozment (2014); Woolfork (2009, 9); Gallagher (2008, 2).

12. Writing in 2004, Vanessa Agnew states that historical reenactments occupy "vast numbers of reenactors, government agencies, academic advisers, event planners, corporate sponsors, merchants, and spectators" (Agnew 2004, 328). Describing two of these events, Agnew writes, "Tens of thousands participated in the reenacted Battle of Gettysburg (1998), while English Heritage's 'History in Action' (2000), a so-called multi-period event, is reported to have featured '3000 performers from 100 top groups, 150 displays a day in 8 performance areas plus within a huge living history area, large-scale battles, including one featuring 3 World War II Spitfires, plus drill and military displays, armored vehicles, earth fortifications, massive living history encampments, medieval falconry, drama, comedy, music, dance, cooking, photographic and art exhibits, authors' talks and book-signings, historical traders' market and a huge grand parade'" (328–29).

13. "In March, 1967, the Ampex HS-100 color video magnetic disc recorder was used for rapid playback in normal, slow, or stop action, for the 'World Series of Skiing' program from the US Ski Championships in Vail, Colorado, marking the beginning of instant replay on commercial television." Ampex Data Systems, accessed March 15, 2017, http://www.ampex.com/ampex-history/.

14. It is particularly used to see if shots were made before or after the end of a period. Light often flashes to end a period now, replacing the much slower and imprecise sonic mechanism of the horn.

15. Both have been analyzed in terms of repetition and trauma in contemporary culture. See Fink (2005) on the Twin Towers, Phelan (1997) on Rodney King.

16. It was argued that the police were acquitted in the Simi Valley trial because of the way the video was presented to the jury (in small chunks that were then narrativized by the defense). Again, see Fink (2005) and Phelan (1997).

17. As described by Huyssen (2003), Jameson (2003 [1991]).

18. As I elaborate in chapter 2, I use the term "Real" to designate the impermanence and nonlocatability of all phenomena. Therefore, the Real does describe these brute facts—for example, in my analysis, the brute fact of death is Real. The Real also becomes an idea—something we fear and desire. Thus, linking the feminine, music, etc., with the

Real is an example of conceiving of the Real as an idea. I alert the reader to be cognizant of these two contexts as I use this term.

19. Charles Johnson "[indicates] how Western ontological divisions between higher (spirit) and lower (body) coupled with Christian symbologies for light and dark develop the black body as being in a state of 'stain.' 'The Negro suffers in his body quite differently from the white man,' Fanon wrote, and this is so insofar as we have attributed to blacks the contents that white consciousness itself fears to contain and confront: bestiality, uncleanliness, criminality, all the purported 'dark things'" (Johnson 2013 [1988], 27).

20. Jankélévitch is also arguing for a way of knowing that is subjective, rather than objective.

21. Indeed, Richard Leppert writes that "at least since the eighteenth century, music and femininity were viewed interchangeably" (Leppert 1993, 155). Leppert tells us: "By far the most consistent suspicion, in fact fear, about music in the West, going back to Plato (*The Republic*) and continuing to this moment in the anxieties of Allan Bloom (*The Closing of the American Mind*), revolves around music's connection to the body, notably its sexual parts, and the closely related paranoia that the sexuality awakened by music and becoming addictive (Bloom's word) will weaken men, make them womanish" (1993, 219). Lawrence Kramer writes that music, as an already feminized, "othered" form, has an element of horror, of abjection, in its "feminine" ability to "dissolve the listener's ego boundaries" (Kramer 1995, 55). In this, Kramer argues, music is "symbolically castrating for the normatively masculine subject" (55). This music-woman nexus threatens the listener with "[inheriting] the uncontrollable subjectivity of the always-already mesmerized female body" (56). All of these scholars highlight how music and the feminine/body/sexuality are conflated in their nonsignifiable excess, their resistance to the Symbolic, and their consequent challenge to well-defended boundaries, particularly the coherent identities of men. Further, music's conveyance through sound is one of its most distrusted characteristics. As Dale Chapman writes, there is an "inadequate sense of music 'being there'" (2003, 156). Music cannot be seen. John Shepherd and Peter Wicke have emphasized how sound's distinct qualities differ from those of vision, which serve to "separate and locate" objects in a field (Shepherd and Wicke 1997, 126–27). Thus, music problematizes the search for certainty that characterizes the Western paradigm. If the subject is searching for its certainty by separating and delineating a separate other, music is a direct threat to this project.

22. This emphasis on music's ephemerality can also be found in the work of Richard Leppert.

23. As I will discuss further in chapter 2, the Real is brutal in its resistance to our appeals through language. It is this that we fear, and it is this that music speaks to: that which is impossible to contain within the Symbolic and yet acts upon us continuously and often brutally. See also Phelan (1993) for a discussion of performance in terms of its ephemerality.

24. Thus, while Kramer positions music within Lacan's Imaginary register, I argue that although we may attempt to contain music through the practices of the Imaginary, it is culturally construed as dangerously close to the realm of the Real. Quoting his earlier work, Kramer suggests, "Musical immediacy behaves like the Lacanian imaginary. Like the process of imaginary identification, music offers a seamless band of pleasure and presence, but nonetheless one 'open to disruption by recurrent intimations that the supposedly self-present ego is always already alienated, that its desire is the desire of (desire for, desire determined by) the Other'" (Kramer 1995, 19).

25. Desmond Manderson also describes the decline in improvisation in Western art music at this time, which he links to contemporary judicial changes. He writes, "Just as nineteenth century musical practice began to condemn any exercise of improvisational judgment in favour of a total subservience to the work as written, so too the exercise of judicial discretion was increasingly condemned in favour of a total subservience to the legal text as written" (Manderson 2010, 2). It is a turn to a type of positivism that resonates deeply with Richard Taruskin's critique.

26. Richard Taruskin places the advent of the "work concept" in the nineteenth century within the "fallacy of reification" in modernity. Turning ideas into objects and putting objects ahead of people exemplifies the fallacy of modernism—that of reification ("it fosters the further fallacy of forgetting that performances . . . are not things but acts" (1995, 24)).

27. To follow Taruskin. Taruskin is not using the term "text" in the postmodern sense, but referring to music's representation in scores.

28. To the surprise of many, ABBA reunited in 2018 and is set to release two new songs at the time of this writing.

29. For an example of how taxonomy works as part of the liberal humanist tradition, see McClintock 1995.

30. See, for example, Trinh (1989), Hurston (1990 [1935]), and Anzaldua (2010 [1987]) on the Western gaze as taming and naming.

31. Thomas Duffy used all ten cornet and trumpet players from the Yale Band in the re-creation, alternating them into the big band's five slots for each performance. This accounts for the higher number of women in the trumpet section. This personnel breakdown is representative of subsequent re-creations of the "Glenn Miller AAFTTC Band" over the next ten years; that is, predominantly white and male with a few racial minorities and/or women.

32. As Svetlana Boym writes in *The Future of Nostalgia* (2001), "It is as if the ritual of commemoration could help patch up the irreversibility of time." I will say more about time and repetition in the conclusion.

33. This synonym was used in a lecture I attended by the Buddhist teacher Elizabeth Mattis Nyamgel in 2015.

34. Timothy Morton writes that, "Within Left theory there is something of a taboo

on the notion of interior life" (2015, 251). In our world "of technocratic utilitarianism, obsessed with 'objects' and 'outcomes' . . . the inner life [is] a phrase that now sounds absurd in many ears" (252). We find that not only the sciences, but even the humanities have relinquished the realm of subjectivity. "The way the humanities regularly express contempt for subjectivity as a mere construct, and a dangerous one at that, might be a classic instance of Stockholm Syndrome" (252). "Buddhaphobia is nothing but a fear of subjectivity as such" (252).

35. Robin James makes a similar argument when she argues for the revolutionary power of "caring." James writes, "Caring, as I understand it, is investing in others without expecting or receiving a return" (2015, 174). This orientation disinvests from the capitalist logic of self-interest. "Caring is a bad investment" from capitalism's point of view, "because it doesn't build your human capital" (174). She offers as an example the "Rolling Jubilee," which developed out of the Occupy movement. "The Rolling Jubilee buys debt (medical debt, credit card debt) not to collect it at a profit, as is customary, but to forgive it" (173). This selfless generosity undoes the capitalist logic of self-interest and competition, defusing it with a focus on giving to the other.

ONE Performing Security

1. See, for example, James (2015).

2. Huyssen, Boym, and Sturken have been especially influential for my understanding of memory culture.

3. Using irony to repeat with a difference is a topic covered by numerous scholars of performance. My interests lie with those reenactments that claim to be as exact as possible. For more on the tribute band phenomenon, see Oakes (2005), Homan (2006), and Gregory (2012).

4. Elvis, of course, is a case in itself. For an interesting article on female Elvis impersonators, see Brittan (2006).

5. Both Peter Gabriel and Michael Rutherford attended TMB concerts in England in 2002, and Steve Hackett even joined TMB onstage at the majestic Royal Albert Hall in London to play guitar for an extra encore of "Firth of Fifth." In February 2005, Phil Collins attended the "Lamb" concert in Geneva and joined TMB on drums for the encore of "The Musical Box." TMB thanks Mike Rutherford himself for lending them the original "'Coral Sitar' . . . which was used by Steve Hackett in 'I Know What I Like.'"

6. The members of Genesis have welcomed the reenactment. Peter Gabriel said, "The Musical Box re[-]created, very accurately I must say, what Genesis was doing. I saw them in Bristol with my children, so they could see what their father did back then" (from interview in *Voir Montreal,* in Gabriel 2002). Phil Collins notes, "This is the only way to see it because it was never filmed. So . . . if you want to experience what it was like . . . and

certainly musically they get very close and I think these guys play it better than we did" (Collins 2005). Steve Hackett remarks, "I cannot imagine that you could have a better tribute for any act. They not only manage to sound, but look virtually identical. It seems as though nothing is too difficult for them. I think they're the closest thing to seeing us back in either 1973, 1974, or 1975. They spend a tremendous amount of time re-creating the whole thing and probably play it better than we did at the time! It was better than the real thing actually. It was great, that was fantastic." Tony Banks declares, "The guy who does Gabriel is brilliant" (Gabriel 2002).

7. See Robison (2002, 236n17) and Covach (1997).

8. Genesis continued on with Collins replacing Gabriel on lead vocals until 1999, when the band went on an indefinite hiatus. Collins, Rutherford, and Banks reunited for a tour in 2006.

9. They have also toured with *A Trick of the Tail,* the first post-Gabriel album with Phil Collins as lead vocalist.

10. Unfortunately, examining the ramifications of French Canadians reenacting a hyperanglophone band is beyond the scope of this project.

11. In 2016 the Musical Box began touring with "The Black Show," a 1974 version of the Selling England by the Pound performance that toured in only North America. TMB's website describes the original performance: "Genesis returns to America in 1974 with a re-imagined performance. A pitchblack stage illuminated with two giant circle screens. Peter Gabriel had now morphed into an eerie stage presence with shaved temples and elaborate make-up. The band ventures into a more live and improvised rendition of the songs, with Phil Collins' drumming skills imposing a new level of musicianship. This performance, only done in America, is wildly [*sic*] known amongst early Genesis fans and captured on SUPER 8 amateur films at the now famous Montreal CEPSUM performances of April 1974" ("The Musical Box: 'The Black Show,'" 2017).

12. Characteristic 7 of Replay is "emphasis on the painstaking work involved." Here is an example from TMB's promotional material: "The first task was to find the instruments and equipment to re[-]create the sound, including: an RMI keyboard, a Synthi Hi-Fly, and various percussion instruments. Another double neck guitar had to be made. Access to Michael Rutherford's original guitar and the acquisition of a rare Micro-Fret 6 string bass allowed an exact reproduction to be made. The visual reconstruction was based on more than a 1000 photos and slides. A few Super-8mm films gave a better understanding of the choreography and the general atmosphere of the show. Finally, thanks to Genesis and to people who worked on the original tour, the remaining questions were answered.

"All the elements of the show have been re[-]created with meticulous precision. The 'Slipperman' alone required nearly 2 months of work, with each detail being scrupulously reproduced by hand. The re-creation of the 'Lamia' brought other difficulties. First, it was necessary to figure out the drawings on the cone. This was then reproduced on a special type of fabric. Many models, including one of the real size, were necessary. The Musical Box received a copy of the 1120 slides used in the original Genesis tour. More than a month was necessary to put them back in order and locate them in the songs. A month of pre-production was necessary to put everything together and rehearse the show in its entirety. Modern technology was used to synchronize the slides during the show and to add some tracks and sound effects. The show is still very complex. The crew members have to follow a precise synopsis, and some costume changes imply specific logistics" ("Background Lamb," 2007).

13. Further, their documentary about their process explains how they piece together bootleg videos from different shows, gleaning new bits of information from new angles discovered in continually unearthed bootlegs.

14. This complicates the logic of the simulacra in postmodern society described, for example, by Fredric Jameson. At first glance, the Musical Box might seem to be a classic example of postmodern cultural production, performing mere simulacra of the past in a type of depthless performance of "pop history" as entertainment. Jameson associates the flatness and depthlessness characteristic of postmodernity with a "fundamental mutation" in the "object world itself," where works have turned into "texts or simulacra" (2003, 9). Employing Andy Warhol's art as exemplary of a focus on "surface," Jameson describes the postmodern turn from the "work" in art to that of the "text." TMB's desire is to turn the text as signifier back into a work that is so true it is Real.

15. In E. T. A. Hoffman's 1816 tale "The Sandman," a quite suggestible young student, Nathanael, falls in love with the daughter of a prominent scientist (in fact, a very wooden automaton that the scientist invented). Rejecting his initial love interest, Klara, Nathanael chooses Olimpia, whom he discovers is the only person who "truly understands [him]" (Hoffmann 1969, 118).

16. Hitchen says, "They really don't know what to do. They want to meet you, but we don't exactly look like the Beatles when we don't have all our gear on . . . we walk in and they don't quite know what to do. It freaks them out a little bit" (quoted in Inglis 2006, 131). In Hoffmann's short story, "The eyes, however, seemed to him to have a singular look of fixity and lifelessness. But as he continued to look closer and more carefully through the glass he fancied a light like humid moonbeams came into them. It seemed as if their power of vision was now being enkindled; their glances shone with ever-increasing vivacity" (Hoffmann 1967, 203).

17. "Perhaps more than at any other juncture, the indispensable incompleteness, ceaseless displacement, and abundant contradictions of social and political life that we witness daily suggest the limits of calculability and management have been reached. If so, the fervent hope that rationalist discourse can instantiate and secure homogeneous, stable

identities can only be frustrated" (Campbell, 19). The late-modern period is marked by "the increasing tendencies toward ambiguity, indeterminacy, and uncertainty on our horizon," for example, with the persistent threat of terrorism (17).

18. Much of the material I cite on TMB has been removed from their website. Lamothe stated that the band took down information about the band members, wanting to make the performance as much as possible just about Genesis (Lamothe 2011).

19. And in November 1998, the Musical Box "performed at the Montreal University Sports Center to commemorate the 25th anniversary of the original concert [bringing in fans] from all over the world, including North America, Europe and Australia." From their promotional website, WIV Entertainment, accessed July 5, 2007, http://www.wiventertainment.de/.

20. For an interesting discussion of both, see Kondo (2000).

21. And perhaps dangerously "not real." As Gabriel was quoted saying previously, a brown-skinned New York character named Rael made it all seem more "real."

22. A sequel, *Mamma Mia! Here We Go Again*, was released in July 2018.

23. Stig Anderson, the band's manager, said, "We soon agreed that it was an excellent name in an international perspective. You can say it in any language" (210).

24. Directed by Lasse Halstrom, who directed their "music videos." Thus, Halstrom was part of the promotion machine. These particular interview clips were chosen to define and promote the band.

25. As Palm writes, "The ABBA/Australia phenomenon was probably the first instance where a pop act achieved superstar status solely through pre-filmed television performances of their songs" (273).

26. ABBA did not perform musical palindromes. Such a structure is uncommon in Western art music, let alone popular music. Berg is probably the Western classical music composer most famous for his use of palindromes. ABBA does not have any song lyrics in the form of a palindrome, but its song "SOS" earned the band a place on the Wikipedia entry for "palindrome" as the rare occasion of a band's name and one of its songs both being palindromes. Other videos also accentuate the "two groups of doubles" of the group: the 1974 music video for *Mamma Mia* (director Lasse Hallström) separates out the women from the men and turns each set into a doubling.

27. Definition from the *Oxford English Dictionary*. The word "palindrome" comes from the Hellenistic Greek word *palindromes*, meaning "running back again" (*palin* "again" plus *drom* from *dramein* "to run").

28. The article further defines this understanding of symmetry through these examples: "Time translation symmetry: Physical laws do not change with time. Translational symmetry: The laws of physics are the same whether they are acting in our solar system or at the far end of the universe. Rotational symmetry: The laws of physics don't change if we turn around."

29. Björn states, "In the 80's ABBA was 'distinctly uncool' . . . But in some strange way we still remained popular in the gay scene . . . When we got a revival in the late 80's, early 90's, I'm sure it's because we were still popular in the gay scene. That was the most important factor" ("Björn Thanks Gay Fans" 2011).

30. The hypervisible surface of ABBA excluded them from the canon of good music. Seeing that ABBA is in the company of the Beatles and Elvis, however, some critics have felt the need to explain why ABBA has withstood the test of time. These critics have found the blues and melancholy in ABBA, focusing on their divorces and difficulties, thus maintaining the classic rock definition of authenticity that comes from the rough and rugged, tough-times blues. See Harrison (2014) and Walters (2015).

31. The tracks include "Lay All Your Love on Me," "SOS," "Take a Chance on Me," and "Voulez-Vous." Both comments from Erasure's *Abba-esque* video on YouTube, accessed August 1, 2017, https://www.youtube.com/watch?v=3TROaIJ30Ww.

32. Taken from their website, "The Concert," accessed December 26, 2017, http://theconcert.se/biography/.

33. They "bring one of the GREATEST pop phenomenons [*sic*] in the history of music back to life." "The Concert," accessed December 26, 2017, http://theconcert.se/biography/.

34. Britt Music and Arts Festival, accessed July 12, 2013, http://www.brittfest.org/archives/abbaarrival. For more reviews see, "Arrival from Sweden: The Music of ABBA," accessed May 24, 2018, http://www.themusicofabba.com/gallery/reviews/.

35. ABBA the Concert, http://www.theconcert.se/biography: saxophone players Johan Stengård and Ulf Andersson; bass players Mike Watson and Rutger Gunnarsson (who died in 2015); guitarists Lasse Wellander and Janne Schaffer; and drummers Ola Brunkert (died in 2008) and Roger Palm. Arrival from Sweden, http://www.themusicofabba.com/abba-musicians/. In addition to Andersson, Watson, Gunnarsson, Schaffer, Brunkert, and Palm, Arrival from Sweden also employs Finn Sjöberg and Mats Ronander on guitar; Åke Sundqvist on percussion and drums; and Janne Kling on saxophone. Indeed, it could be an ABBA-off with Arrival from Sweden claiming they are "the closest you ever will get to see ABBA!" and ABBA the Concert declaring, "This is the closest to ABBA you'll ever get."

36. From Arrival from Sweden: The Music of ABBA, accessed June 12, 2018, http://themusicofabba.com/biography/.

37. From Arrival from Sweden: The Music of ABBA, accessed June 12, 2018, http://www.themusicofabba.com/biography/.

38. Two well-known exceptions that prove the rule, however, are the bands Journey and Judas Priest, both of which famously hired lead singers taken from their respective tribute bands. The 2001 film *Rock Star,* starring Mark Wahlberg, was inspired by Tim (Ripper) Owen's rise from a Judas Priest tribute band to Judas Priest itself.

39. With the most prominent story being the successful birth of a cloned sheep, Dolly, in 1997.

40. Ernst Jentsch describes the uncanny as, in part, a feeling of sudden "intellectual uncertainty" (Freud 2003 [1919], 138).

41. In "Signature Event Context," Derrida uses insightful imagery to describe J. L. Austin's "successful performative." For Austin, the many unsuccessful operations of the performative must be ignored in order to understand the performative's "true" or "real" function as speech that carries out a particular action (rather than representing an action). In response to this, Derrida asks, "[D]oes the generality of the risk admitted by Austin *surround* language like a kind of *ditch,* a place of external perdition into which locution might never venture, that it might avoid by remaining at home, in itself, sheltered by its essence or *telos?*" (Derrida 1991 [1972], 103; italics in original). Just as Lacan's analysand dreamed of a "fortified camp" or a "stadium," Derrida describes "protected" language as surrounded by a ditch; indeed, he emphasizes this image with italics. Such language avoids disruption, imperfection, "unhappiness," sheltered in its home by its essence and its *telos,* its final goal reached. In this, what I would call *perfect* performative, "No remainder escapes the present totalization. . . . no irreducible polysemia, that is no 'dissemination' escaping the horizon of the unity of meaning" (99).

TWO Capturing the Real

1. This act of postponing our encounter with enjoyment—such as obsessive photo taking while on vacation, tweeting one's experience, or uploading photos and videos to Instagram while attending a rock concert—reveals our sense that we aren't quite anywhere unless we can show another, or watch ourselves showing another by observing our life on our own social media page. Whereas in the past we may have had a vague sense that we would enjoy the photos later, today the experience itself is almost thoroughly evacuated in the course of immediately representing it. The Palm Pilot was advertised with the phrase: "Life Moves Fast. Don't Miss a Thing." Which is to say, capture it all, find it all, by burying your head in your Palm Pilot—that is how you will not miss life.

2. My colleague in theater studies, Sarah Bay-Cheng, also shared an insight from a director's point of view. Cotard's endless project represents a director's fantasy in which the director never need let go of the production, but will remain forever involved.

3. Cotard's Syndrome (also known as Cotard's Delusion and Walking Corpse Syndrome) is a mental illness in which one believes one is dead or has lost one's soul. "In its most profound form, the delusion takes the form of a professed belief that one does not exist." PubMed.gov, "Jules Cotard (1840–1889)," May 14, 2002, http://www.ncbi.nlm.nih.gov/pubmed/12011289.

4. At the funeral of Claire's mother, where in hearing the pastor describe her infancy, Claire (Cotard's lover at the time and mother of one of his daughters) exclaims wistfully and a little airheadedly to Caden, "I used to be a baaaby." The thought of oneself as a baby

is indeed unthinkable. We know it and yet we cannot really believe it: We are told it is true, but we don't feel it, we can't intuit it, we can't understand it. It is in this same way that we know we will die, but we cannot feel it to be true. It remains unassimilable. Another instance of the Real of impermanence is when Caden wishes that Hazel would look at him the way she used to. The past—when she so fully and *really* desired him, flirted with him, and gave her undivided attention to him—is revealed to be only a passing memory. Now she loves, is married to, and has children with another man. Caden longs for that time when Hazel's desire seemed so real it would continue forever—and yet that time and that desire have passed and are gone.

5. Cage regularly cited his historic decision to give up "communication" through music. He held this belief throughout his life, as demonstrated in a late interview with Larner (2015 [1989]).

6. Kaprow took John Cage's classes at the New School between 1956 and 1958.

7. In discussing Kaprow, Richard Schechner writes that "the avant-garde from the Italian Futurists through the Dadaists, surrealists, and on to practitioners of earth art and other kinds of avant-gardists, introduces us to the idea that art is not a way of imitating reality or expressing states of mind . . . but [the] altogether upsetting idea of art as an event—an 'actual'" (Schechner, quoted in Schneider, 125).

8. Robyn Brentano writes that "the term 'performance art' first appeared around 1970 to describe the ephemeral, time-based, and process-oriented work of conceptual ('body') and feminist artists that was emerging at the time. It was applied retrospectively to Happenings, Fluxus events, and other intermedia performances of the 1960s" (Brentano 1994, 31–32, quoted in Schechner 2002).

9. Further, Sontag writes, "What is important now is to recover our sense. We must learn to *see* more, to *hear* more, to *feel* more" (14; italics in original) and "Our task is to cut back content so that we can see the thing at all" (14).

10. Other types of performance art, such as that of Carolee Schneemann and Adrian Piper, interrogated the racialized and gendered body; however, I will focus on the type of performance art that made particular claims about brute reality (often "presence") and ephemerality. The initial happenings of Kaprow influenced many artists, and performance art was taken up by feminist artists and artists concerned with representations of the racialized and gendered body. With its focus on the constructedness of identity, this work is quite dissimilar to work that wants to connect itself to the Real. There is a racial issue here, especially seen in Abramović, as I will show.

11. Lozano's "General Strike Piece" (1969) consists of these instructions: "Gradually but determinedly avoid being present at official or public 'uptown' functions or gatherings related to the 'art world' in order to pursue investigations of total personal and public revolution. Exhibit in public only pieces which further sharing of ideas & information related to total personal and public revolution." Art critic Roberta Smith writes that, "Sometimes

[Lozano] designated everyday activities like thought, conversation or marijuana smoking as art, attracted by the idea that they were unsaleable and democratic" (Smith 1999).

12. Lozano's "General Strike Piece" and "Dropout" were both highly critical of the art scene, but she agreed to retrospectives of her work when she found out she was dying of cervical cancer. Roberta Smith writes, "In 1998 her work, long absent from the New York scene, returned when three SoHo galleries, Mitchell Algus, Rosen & Van Liere and Margarete Roeder, each showed a different phase of her painting. At the same time the Wadsworth Atheneum in Hartford exhibited her 'Wave' paintings and notebooks." Lozano did remain committed to one constraint she had imposed decades earlier—a prohibition against speaking with women. As Smith writes, "All the dealers and curators involved with these exhibitions were men" (Smith 1999).

13. *A Little Bit of History Repeated* (2001) at Kunstwerke in Berlin showcased some of Marina Abramović's students re-performing "classic" works of performance art. *A Short History of Performance* was launched in 2002 at the Whitechapel Art Gallery and included Carolee Schneemann's reenactment of her 1964 performance piece, *Meat Joy,* and other performance artists' works. *A Short History of Performance: Part Two, Part Three,* and *Part Four* between 2003 and 2006 continued the practice of reenacting "classic" works of performance art.

14. Over the course of six nights, Abramović re-performed *Body Pressure* (1974) by Bruce Nauman; *Seedbed* (1972) by Vito Acconci; *Action Pants: Genital Panic* (1969) by VALIE EXPORT; "The Conditioning" (the first part of *Self-Portrait(s)* (1965)) by Gina Pane; *How to Explain Pictures to a Dead Hare* (1965) by Joseph Beuys; and *Lips of Thomas* (1975) by Abramović. The seventh and final evening was a performance of Abramović's new work for the occasion: *Entering the Other Side* (2005). Abramović's accompanying book for the performance was dedicated to Susan Sontag.

15. As Rebecca Schneider has put it, quoting from Abramović's *Seven Easy Pieces:* "Marina Abramović herself is interested in the 'correct' transmission of 'seminal' works, including 'extremely strict instructions,' payment of copyright, and permissions to re-perform" (Schneider 2011, 4). Abramović writes, "I think it's very important to have total control over the concept" of what will be reenacted (2007, 23).

16. Further, "In *Seven Easy Pieces,* I reenacted seminal works that had been performed by my contemporaries in a prior time and space. My focus was on performances that took place in the late sixties and seventies. I interpreted them as one would a musical score" (2007, 11). And Nancy Spector states: "The model you and I have always referred to is that of the musical cover, which allows an artist to reinterpret a piece of music, but the composer must be acknowledged (and compensated). You've always pointed out that one has to be specially trained in a certain way to be able to perform your work responsibly . . . you offered SEP as an example of how to do this—it was almost pedagogical in its intentions" (quoted in Abramović 2007, 20).

17. Regarding performance, Amelia Jones writes, "In the context of the visual arts, the live body in action always already, in the words of Robert Legorreta, becomes 'frozen art'" (in Flores Sternad 2006). All the most interesting artists deploying performance, in my view, understand this and play with it self-reflexively" (2011, 26). She gives Chris Burden as a salient example, including the ways in which he deals with reenactment.

18. Examples of early performance reenactment work include Andrea Fraser's *Art Must Hang* (2001) and Jeremy Deller's *The Battle of Orgreave* (2001). Exhibitions include *A Little Bit of History Repeated* (Kunstwerke, Berlin, 2001); *Life, Once More* (Witte de With, Rotterdam, 2004); Re- (Site Gallery, Sheffield, 2007); *History Will Repeat Itself: Strategies of Re-Enactment in Contemporary (Media) Art and Performance* (Hartware MedienKunstVerein [HMKV], Dortmund, and Kunstwerke, Berlin, 2007). *Experience, Memory, Reenactment* at the Piet Zwart Institute (2004); *Once More . . . With Feeling* at Reg Vardy Gallery (2005); *Ahistoric Occasion: Artists Making History* at MASS MoCA (2006); *Now Again the Past: Rewind, Replay, Resound* at Carnegie Art Center (2006); and *Playback_Simulated Realities* at Edith-Russ-House (2006). In an example of how these reenactments are linked with the Real as opposed to the mediated, *History Will Repeat Itself* curator Inke Arnes wrote in 2007, "In the last five or ten years, there has been a growing interest in the strategy or logic of reenactment, which means taking things out of history books and making them happen again to allow for a different kind of experience that is neither reading nor looking at images. It has to do with the fact that, in a media-saturated society, you are more and more unable to relate to what's been going on" (Kollectiv 2007, 10).

19. Attributed to Lord Snowdon by Victoria Broackes and Geoffrey Marsh, curators of *David Bowie Is* (2013), an exhibition devoted to the pop star. (Also quoted in Menkes 2013.)

20. For example, see Echols 2010.

21. As Bowie put it, "I can't stand the premise of putting on jeans and being real. I mean it's not normal" (quoted in Hale 2012).

22. Nietzsche 1977, 124.

23. See, for example, Auslander 2006, chapter 4.

24. Stevenson writes that "David Bowie above all was about change. Bowie articulated the pleasures of mutation" (Stevenson 2006, 2).

25. Lyrics by George Clinton, Bernie Worrell, and Leon Ware (1977).

26. Bowie: "If anything maybe I've helped establish that rock 'n' roll is a pose" (quoted in Stevenson 2006, viii).

27. All quotes from "A Rock 'n' Roll Suicide," 1998.

28. I examine this inability to find an origin in McMullen (2014).

29. This context is removed by mimicking the event exactly. According to Gaskin, "It's by creating what I can only describe as a 'virtual' environment—an environment where everything is a signifier that will take you back to that original event, and nothing can be

a distraction" (Gaskin 2004). The distraction would be any infiltrating context. It is as if Forsyth and Pollard are attempting the perfectly thrilled performative (following Austin). It is perfect repetition. There is no "distraction," nothing to change or recontextualize the original that is now understood as the original again, here with us. Not surprisingly, "cultural context" will return later. In speaking of the various performance art reenactors she has worked with, Gaskin says, "For me each of the artist's projects have in their converse ways exceeded the precedents and limits, which have framed/constrained live performance in recent times. By harnessing the mass appeal of pop performance and reframing it in a cultural context they have successfully, to re-cite the words of Mr. Rock, 'upped the visual ante'" (Gaskin 2003). Cultural context here means high art. And this visual ante has been upped, it seems, by placing it in the new uncontext context of the European high art tradition. That is, by presenting Bowie's performance as an art object, the visuals are upped because now they are perceived within the art tradition, rather than within the more mundane tradition of popular music.

30. Agnew writes, "Reenactment's emancipatory gesture is to allow participants to select their own past in reaction to a conflicted present. Paradoxically, it is the very ahistoricity of reenactment that is the precondition for its engagement with historical subject matter" (Agnew 2004, 328). Agnew argues that these reenactments are usually avowedly apolitical. She critiques this stance by arguing that privileging experience sacrifices broader interpretive questions (334).

31. For example, Anzaldua 2010, Trinh 1989.

32. Lacan describes a "transfer of powers from the subject to the [One Who Knows], the locus of speech and, potentially, the locus of truth" (Lacan 1998 [1973], 129). In my view, the object becomes the locus of speech/truth because it is the one that gives the answers. We are to accept these answers without interpretation.

33. "Order is a kind of compulsion to repeat," Freud remarks in *Civilization and Its Discontents*, a normalizing practice of "regularization" that determines, once it has been laid down, "when, where and how a thing shall be done, so that in every similar circumstance one is spared hesitation and indecision" (Freud 1995 [1930], 739).

34. As Sontag argues in her essay, the mimetic theory of art set the stage for the necessity to defend art's existence. In an attempt to secure its importance, defenders of art split form from content and placed an emphasis on content. "It is the defense of art which gives birth to the odd vision by which something we have learned to call 'form' is separated off from something we have learned to call 'content,' and to the well-intentioned move which makes content essential and form accessory." Even in modernity, which may have placed an emphasis on the artist's individual expression, "It is still assumed that a work of art is its content" (Sontag 2001, 2).

35. Further, Sontag writes: "Pop Art works . . . [to break the habit of interpretation by] using a content so blatant, so 'what it is,' it . . . ends by being uninterpretable" (2001, 10).

Roland Barthes describes this as "pop art['s desire] to desymbolize the object." Hal Foster puts this into his words, writing that "[pop art wants] to relinquish the meaningfulness of the object to its surface visibility" (quoted in Foster 2001 [1996], 128).

36. The artists are Jo Mitchell, Rod Dickinson, and Iain Forsyth and Jane Pollard.

37. Why reenact Bowie's incarnation, and elimination, of Ziggy Stardust? One obvious answer is Bowie's general theatricality. As Nick Stevenson writes, David Bowie "brought a level of performativity and theatricality to popular music that had rarely been seen before" (2006, 2). Bowie wanted to move away from the "authenticity" of rock and reveled in taking on characters such as Ziggy Stardust, Aladdin Sane, and the Thin White Duke. Much like the progressive rock of Genesis, the theatricality and highly stylized visual aspect of these performances give reenactors much to bite into. The theatricality is easier to reenact (like TMB). We can *see* it. The figure of Andy Warhol offers another enticing reason to reenact Bowie as a work of performance art. Bowie was interested in Warhol's emphasis on surface. Doggett writes that Bowie's song "Andy Warhol" was "like Warhol's art, [hinging] around the act of repetition, and the haphazard consequences of reproducing an original concept" (Doggett 2012, 139). Bowie's famous claim that he wanted to be like a "Photostat machine," which merely captured the surface with no depth of its own, was influenced by Warhol's obsession with surface (137).

38. Freud famously described how his grandson came to master the "disappearance" of his mother when she would leave on errands. He observed his grandson playing a game that he had developed, "Gone (*fort*)." This game consisted of the little boy throwing his toys around the room and yelling "Gone!," leaving his room in quite some disarray. Eventually, the boy discovered that he could throw a toy that was connected to a string over his crib, say "Gone," and then bring the toy back to him, exclaiming with glee, "Here (*da*)!" Freud described this game as his nephew's way of mastering the pain and loss he felt on his mother's absence.

39. Performance artists and scholars of performance art now commonly refer to performance art simply as "performance."

THREE If I Should Lose You

1. These two tired metaphors in a row indicate a certain weariness with the project of keeping jazz alive in the neoclassical vein.

2. If not the Ur-lost object itself of modern times. This is how I read the film *La La Land*, which is not "about" jazz, but about dreamers who dream the impossible dream (aka, a love letter to Hollywood). "Real jazz" is used as the impossible lost object *par excellence* of which our hero, Seb, cannot let go.

3. See Peress 2004 on James Reese Europe and Paul Whiteman reenactments.

4. Gates 2014 [1988], Mackey 1998, Monson 1996, Walser 1995.

5. See Fink 2005.

6. For example, see Robert Palmer's description of early blues (1981).

7. "New Black Music is this: find the self, then kill it," Nathaniel Mackey writes. "The emphasis on self-expression is also an emphasis on self-transformation, an othering or, as [Edward] Brathwaite has it, an X-ing of the self, the self not as noun but as verb . . . To kill the self is to show it to be fractured, unfixed" (Mackey 1998, 522).

8. See, for example, Monson 2003.

9. For more on jazz and Buddhism, see McMullen 2013 and 2014.

10. Much of this critique has centered on the approach taken at JALC. See Porter 2002, Gray 2005, Gennari 2006.

11. The appropriation of African-American styles by whites contributes to concerns about "losing jazz." Kembrew McLeod's argument that claims of "authenticity" often are generated from a desire to protect a tradition from those who would appropriate it is especially pertinent (McLeod 1999). This does not mean, however, that one needs to reify the form in order to not "lose it." Pianist Jason Moran, for example, takes a different approach, as described in the conclusion.

12. While Marsalis is widely recognized as a highly skilled performer and improviser, reviews of his recordings and performances regularly lament his decision to hew so closely to ideas of "classic" jazz. Nate Chinen, for example, will praise Marsalis's work, but the term "nostalgic" frequently appears. See Chinen 2016, 2013, 2010. Giovanni Russonello writes, in 2017, of "Jazz at Lincoln Center's decision to stay the traditionalist course." Scott Yanow, however, writes that Marsalis "would develop his own sound a few years" after the release of *Black Codes* (Yanow n.d.).

13. For an insightful analysis of jazz criticism, see Gennari 2006.

14. Marsalis has described hip-hop as degrading and compared it to minstrelsy on many occasions, for example, Marsalis quoted in Hewett 2012.

15. Of the 2017–2018 performance schedule for JALC, Giovanni Russonello wrote, "Almost all of the artists set to perform this coming year on Jazz at Lincoln Center's two major stages—the Rose Theater and the Appel Room—are over 50. Most will be playing a kind of jazz that's in close contact with traditional bop, swing or New Orleanian jazz, and many concerts are focused on the repertoire of 20th-century figures like Morton, Thelonious Monk and Benny Goodman."

16. Marsalis tells Giovanni Russonello, "We are a music that is constantly asked to abandon its own identity to become another thing. Why? What's wrong with our identity? We're not going to do that at Jazz at Lincoln Center as long as I'm here" (quoted in Russonello 2017).

17. Robert O'Meally, personal communication with the author, September 2008.

18. The other four members of the Hot Five are Johnny Dodds (clarinet), Kid Ory (trombone), Lil Hardin (piano), and Johnny St. Cyr (banjo). For a critique of this em-

phasis in jazz history on the individual soloist, see Monson (1996) and Taylor (2008). Jacqueline Warwick (2007) also addresses this tendency to focus on the individual artist over collaboration in popular music.

19. Marsalis did not invent the gendered narrative of jazz history, of course. On jazz and gender, see especially Rustin and Tucker (2008). For a cogent critique of Marsalis's lack of female musicians, see Pellegrinelli (2000).

20. Fourteen songs, 26 percent. Jeffrey Taylor (2008) revisits Lil Hardin Armstrong's musicianship. Taylor asserts that rather than perpetuating the story that Lil Hardin Armstrong was vastly inferior to Armstrong's later pianist, Earl Hines, if we listen to her as a group member (rather than a soloist), we can hear that she provided the comping that best complemented Louis Armstrong's playing. Hines was a fantastic improviser, but Taylor argues that his flights of fancy while comping may have contributed to his eventual dismissal from the band.

21. Marsalis's glossy presentation could also be read through Mark Laver's analysis of JALC's new venue in Doha, Qatar. Laver argues that the spread of jazz qua American freedom to a luxurious, new "jazz palace" in Qatar is a "new, corporatized American neocolonialism" in the guise of freedom (Laver 2014).

22. In the 1990s, Marsalis would still bring his laundry home to his mother when he was on tour (Marsalis and Vigeland 2001, 138).

23. Classical pianist and Marsalis's former Julliard teacher, Judith Stillman (106, 115–19).

24. Teal (2014) persuasively argues that this tribute aligned with the overarching theme of jazz as a model of democracy. In this case, jazz is democracy because it allows women.

25. Stephanie Hubbard, Yale music department coordinator, interview with the author, September 14, 2006. The evening's performance was entitled "Newsreel: Yale Remembers World War II" and included the "Star-Spangled Banner" arranged by Igor Stravinsky, "Salute to the Armed Forces," George Gershwin's "An American in Paris," and John Philip Sousa's "Hands across the Sea," among others. The Glenn Miller radio reenactment included: "American Patrol"; "At Last," "The Volga Boatman"; "Rhapsody in Blue"; the Anvil Chorus; the recruitment skit "Uncle Sam's Armorers" from the radio broadcast of June 5, 1943; "In the Mood"; "Moonlight Serenade'" and NBC Radio broadcast, December 1944 (announcing the disappearance of Miller's plane over the English Channel).

26. As was continuously reiterated, the United States needed to heed the lesson from Vietnam: fragmentation leads to defeat. As David Campbell wrote, "In a State Department report, the 1990s were foreshadowed as an era in which divergent political critiques nonetheless would seek equally to overcome the 'corruption' and 'profligacy' induced by the 'loss' of 'American purpose' in Vietnam through 'moral renewal'" (Campbell 1998 [1992], 33).

27. Sherrie Tucker notes how in the Swing Era "skilled women musicians were described as cross-dressers of sorts: 'the female Louis Armstrong' or 'a Gene Krupa in girls' clothes'" (2002, 294). Elsewhere Tucker describes the attempt by Anita O'Day to substitute her

sequined gown with a suit, hoping "that the costume change would result in her being 'treated like another musician' instead of as a 'trinket' to 'decorate the bandstand.'" O'Day had to desist when she "was perceived as sexually suspect and worthy of rumors" (Tucker 2000, 57). On O'Day, see also Erenberg 1998, 200.

28. Harris and Piper address the painful and complicated experience of women of color "passing" as white and being exposed to or asked to participate in derogatory and racist remarks perpetrated by white people. Harris theorizes how "whiteness" takes on valuable property status in racist America, while Piper develops methods to intentionally "not pass," gently alerting acquaintances of her subjectivity as a woman of color who has been injured by their racism.

29. It is important to acknowledge the differences between racial passing and gender passing. Whereas racial passing almost always entails lesser or greater anguish, "gender-crossers" often experience great pleasure in "passing."

30. See McMullen 2007.

31. Songs such as "Kalamazoo" and "People Like You and Me," among many others, represented America as white, middle class, and rural. For more on World War II–era swing music and Department of War information, see Tucker 2000. Like most white bands, Miller occasionally had black arrangers.

32. See McMullen 2006.

33. From the Yale University Band Glenn Miller Recreation Archive, Yale Band Room, Yale University, New Haven, Connecticut.

34. The AAFTTC became the AAFTC when the technical training and the flight training units combined under one authority.

35. This history of Glenn Miller at Yale (presented in this and the following paragraph) is taken from: US Army Air Force 1943, "A History of the 418th Army Air Forces Band of the Technical School of the Army Air Forces Technical Training Command Stationed at Yale University, New Haven, Conn.," Yale University Band Glenn Miller Recreation Archive, Yale Band Room, Yale University, New Haven, Connecticut.

36. US Army Air Force 1943, 21.

37. After decades of speculation about bad weather and improper plane maintenance, new evidence introduced in 1985 suggested that Miller's plane was downed by unused ordnance dropped over the channel by returning Allied planes. See Gustaitis 2001, 74.

38. For "Chattanooga Choo-Choo" in 1942 (Erenberg 1998, 188).

39. Immersed in identity, Duffy remarked that he would *not* fly over the English Channel when the band was in Europe, as if his conjuring were begging the mimesis to unfold of itself. Thomas Duffy, interview with the author, September 18, 2005.

40. For an illuminating examination of the controversy surrounding Maya Lin's Vietnam War Memorial as it relates to universality, plurality, and the "gash that would not heal," see Lowe 1996, 4.

41. Lowe stresses that this applies to other immigrants of color, as well; however, her particular analysis is of the complexities of Asian immigration.

42. Yale students made jokes during rehearsals for a 2004 performance about how the "real" Glenn Miller Orchestra would not display their Yamaha-brand instruments, or as one student remarked tangentially, have any African- or Asian-Americans. Clinton Cave, Yale Band participant in 2004, interview with the author, August 24, 2005.

43. Again, this is a reference to Lowe 1996, 4. (See note 41.)

44. Quoted in Ann Devroy and John F. Harris, "Clinton to Confront Echoes of Reagan on Normandy Trip," *Washington Post,* May 20, 1994, n.p. Clipping taken from Yale University Band Glenn Miller Recreation Archive, Yale Band Room, Yale University, New Haven, Connecticut.

FOUR The Importance of White Women Being Earnest

1. As captured on the DVD *Led Zeppelin* (Caruthers 2003).

2. As one critic wrote, "Paynes' motivation was the fear that Led's spell would evaporate before future generations could discover their music. Her success became every fan's fortune providing original Zeppelin fans a comfortable magic carpet to sit on while happily reminiscing about all those beautiful concerts without reliance on a hazy 60's flashback" (Downing and Reed 2013).

3. The band has been reviewed in numerous newspapers and magazines in the United States and abroad. There is a predictable tenor to most of the mainstream press: first, there is the astonishment that "these girls can really play" and are not "just a gimmick"; second, the comments that they have "got balls" (Reuters 2006) or in some way "lay it down like a man"; and finally, the constant titillation and speculation over the sexuality of the band members.

4. It would seem that an earlier reincarnation of Plant wasn't quite girly enough. Sarah McLellan, the lead singer before Shannon Conley, had to up the femininity, saying, "[Plant] is more feminine than me" (Brandon 2006).

5. The album cover art takes the original art from *Led Zeppelin I* and adds a torso, turning the zeppelin into a giant phallus. The torso could be male or female, but it appears to be female, thus bringing out the "androgynous," gender-mixing titillation the band promotes.

6. Copying exactly, however, also allows the band to take some of their own solos, according to Paynes. In an interview, Paynes said, "We basically decided for the second record to go back to the beginning, Led Zeppelin's first record. . . . But also it has our own flavors on it, too. We took some of our own solos and things like that because the first record, their first record, is like that. So there has to be some breathing room in it." In a move redolent of how she will finesse gender, Paynes takes the template of the recording and, under the aegis of devotional recreation, gives the women in her band some "breathing

room." From an interview with Lez Zeppelin, www.AltarTV.com, accessed June 17, 2013.

7. "The Top Pop Songs of All Time," Rock on the Net, accessed January 2, 2018, http://www.rockonthenet.com/archive/2000/vh1hardrock.htm.

8. Fast is building on the work of Robert Walser (1993) in that section (Fast 2001, 168).

9. Fast critiques Deena Weinstein's characterization of heavy metal as masculine and a site of male bonding (163) and Norma Coates's assertion of rock music coded solely as phallic (164), arguing that such assumptions ignore women's participation in rock's production and consumption. She further criticizes Joy Press and Simon Reynold's book *The Sex Revolts* (1995) (which she also credits, however, as the first book to make gender and sexuality its main topic in a popular music study) for theoretical simplicity that serves only to reinforce rock stereotypes with such over-the-top phrases as "hyperphallic" and "penile dementia."

10. Further, in a musical analysis of "Whole Lotta Love," Fast writes, "Plant's gasps ('ah, ah, ah, ah,' steadily rising in pitch) and ecstatic cries ('love me, love me; no, no, no; luuuuuuuuuuuv . . . luauauauav') are made in response to the washes of electronically produced sound, which begin to occur and are developed before he [Plant] enters. These dominate his voice, which, except for his cry of 'love' near the end of the section, is kept far back in the mix. In their ebb and flow, their movement in and out of the metric framework maintained by the percussion, they suggest a generally very intense but richly varied experience, a sumptuous sexual encounter, one lingered over, not hurried through; furthermore, the electronic sounds create multiple climactic moments in this section, perhaps suggesting a representation of femininity" (197).

11. Lacan, who uses Aristophanes's story to exemplify the subject's primordial longing, has been criticized for centralizing heterosexuality as the sexual norm (see, for example, Butler 2006 [1990], 66–68). It is important, therefore, to remember that nonheteronormative bodies people Aristophanes's story.

12. Concert reviews cited in this paragraph are all available on ledzeppelin.com, accessed January 2, 2018.

13. Smith and Snow were regularly compared to Krupa and Armstrong because of their instruments. Simone was frequently compared to Davis, for example by jazz scholar David Hajdu, who has called her "a female Miles Davis" (Hajdu 2011).

14. These characteristics include "the high range, phrasing that stays away from the beat and was regularly changed in performance, the disjunction of the melodic line . . . , the intensity and volume, [and] the distortion that allows us to hear and feel his body" (Fast 2001, 42).

15. Echols 1999, xvi. "'Robert always wanted to be Janis,' a beaming Jimmy Page told *Rolling Stone* backstage. 'To hear her singing his words—well, he'd be in heaven.'" So wrote Terri Sutton in her imaginative tribute to Janis Joplin in *Trouble Girls: Rolling Stone Book of Women in Rock* (Sutton 1997). Sutton was envisioning Joplin taking Plant's place in

Zeppelin after the male artist "choked on a live swordfish at the Edgewater Inn, Seattle, Washington—malice suspected but not proven." Sutton begins her piece: "I hear your voice all the time these days, Janis. Those boys who clapped for you, they wear your voice now." Sutton here takes what she must assume are obvious similarities between the singers and then imagines a scenario where not Joplin but Plant was lost too young. Other women writers have similarly asserted or assumed that Joplin influenced Plant and other hard rock vocalists. Maureen Mahon writes that Joplin's vocal approach "helped set the template for metal, punk, and grunge vocals in the seventies, eighties, and nineties" (2011, 13). Ann Powers writes that Joplin's "influence surfaces unexpectedly: most often in this decade (1990s), it's found among male singers like Axl Rose and the Black Crowes' Chris Robinson" (Powers 1993). Aerosmith lead singer Steven Tyler is the rare heavy metal vocalist who does make known his admiration for Joplin. In his memoir he writes, "Everybody used to think Mick [Jagger] was my real hero, but I'll confess now ('cause that's what a memoir is for, right?), *it was Janis*. The scarves on the mic, the howl . . . inspired and perspired by pure 180-proof Joplin. She's bone deep and still makes me weep" (Tyler 2011, 66; italics and ellipsis in original). Also, Tyler, 38–39, and Echols, 328, note to p. xvi.

16. See, for example, Jones, Page, and Plant 2012.

17. McMullen 2014.

18. See, for example, Wall 2008.

19. Fast 2001, especially chapter 5.

20. See Alk 1974. Echols also attributes Joplin's hypersexuality to a type of masking of queer desire by overemphasizing her heterosexual or "hippie chick" sexual appetite (Echols 1999, 250–52).

21. For a detailed discussion of Janis Joplin and Bessie Smith in terms of bisexuality, race, and the blues, see Braziel 2004. Listen to Ma Rainey's "Prove It on Me Blues" for an example of centralizing lesbian desire in early popular culture. Echols reads Joplin's overdiscussion of sex in interviews as a "cover" for her bisexuality.

22. *The History of Heavy Metal*, MTV documentary, accessed January 3, 2018, https://www.youtube.com/watch?v=vX2eo011EeA.

23. While in popular discourse the white male origins of rock have been completely naturalized, popular music scholars have demonstrated how rock has been discursively constructed as white and male. For early work on the construction of rock discourse, including the "ideology of rock" with its rock critic "gatekeepers" cultivating a "knowing community," see Frith (1981; 1998). On rock "experts" such as record collectors sharing and guarding "specialized knowledge," see Straw (1997). For the ways in which women become the "other" to rock's authenticity in rock discourse, see especially Coates (1997; 2003). On gender, sexuality, and heavy metal/rock, see Walser (1993); Weinstein (1991); Frith and McRobbie (1990); Fast (2001). For work that addresses the absence of women in rock history generally, with a focus on the normative traditions of rock criticism, see

O'Dair (1999); Brooks (2008); Rhodes (2005); McLeod (2001); McDonnell and Powers (1995). The race and gender narrative of authentic/inauthentic preceded rock criticism in jazz writing. See, for example, the discussion of hot jazz versus commercial "sweet bands" in Erenberg (1998). Kristin A. McGee (2009) traces how female jazz instrumentalists were elided from early jazz history because their production was viewed as inauthentic "mass culture." For pointed analyses of just how rock discourse has written out the contributions of black women, see Mahon (2011) on how privileging the guitar in rock elides vocalist "Big Mama" Thornton's contribution; Wald (2004) on how privileging secular music writes out gospel musician Sister Rosetta Tharpe; and Warwick (2007) on how the myth of the singular, "independent" artist misses the contributions of collaborative projects such as 1960s "girl groups."

24. In his analysis of North American rock criticism, Kembrew McLeod (2001) cites the characteristics that rock critics developed in order to designate "who is worthy of attention." In examining 583 rock reviews and compiling the results in a database, McLeod found that along with authenticity and its correlates (such as "sincerity" and connection with the audience), "originality" is a key factor in deciding whether music is worthy. Originality is an attribute "valorized by rock critics that can be heard repeated numerous times using a variety of adjectives such as 'daring, 'imaginative' or 'singular'" (54). Conversely, those bands that are critically dismissed will be hailed as unoriginal or derivative: "Perhaps the most repeated condemnation by rock critics is based on an artist's perceived unoriginality (these artists are negatively described as following formulas, or being derivative or generic" (55). (In addition (and related) to McLeod's findings I would include Warwick's insight that the "self-contained" artist is prized over collaborative projects.) Kembrew concludes that rock criticism "valorizes serious, masculine, 'authentic' rock and dismisses trivial, feminine, 'prefabricated' pop music" (47). As such, (white) male rockers are more often perceived as authentic ("raw" or "brutal" simplicity) and female acts as inauthentic ("vapid" or "saccharine" simplicity) (55). Men's work is also more likely to be understood as original, whereas women artists are more quickly categorized as unoriginal or interpretative. In 1969 Robert Christgau wrote in the *New York Times*: "For the last five years any rock performer worth his pretensions has written his own songs," and "Song interpretation has been relegated by both performers and audiences to that phony adult world of nightclub theatricality which rock has been striving to destroy for 15 years" (quoted and discussed in Coates 2003, 66). Christgau goes on to assert that this bias made it easier for women (including, Janis Joplin) to continue the practice of song interpretation.

25. These are the common narratives, sometimes asking "Why don't women rock?" and sometimes asking "Why don't blacks rock?" In framing the questions in this way, the contributions of black women are especially elided. Rather than simply stating that rock is "male dominated," I take the same stance as Norma Coates, who writes that rock

becomes "naturalized" as male "in the 1960s and, as a result, women became marginal and/or subservient to men in rock culture and its discursive formations" (67). Coates cites rock critic Richard Fannan's essay at length, which is basically wondering why women (such as Joplin, Slick, Cass, Turner) aren't rocking it like Morrison and Jagger. Fannan's analysis is fraught with complication that Coates brings out, but I reference it as a particular example of how rock critics must wring their hands over women's inability to rock ex post facto—after the discourse has been effectively naturalized as male. As Coates puts it, "Rock masculinity is discursively constructed as to bolster as well as reiterate itself; at the same time, rock masculinity requires the existence, illusory or real, of a subordinate femininity to support it and give it the appearance of 'truth'" (79).

26. In speaking of "Pea Vine Blues," and the Delta Blues style generally, Robert Palmer writes, "If the song is broken down into individual phrases it becomes evident that most and quite possibly all these phrases were unoriginal. They were floating formulas, some of which came from older ballads and spirituals while others were folk sayings or everyday figures of speech . . . Originality in the blues, then, is not a question of sitting down and making up songs out of thin air. Yet a blues singer whose songs consist entirely or almost entirely of borrowed phrases, lines, and verses will claim these songs as his own, and he will be right" (1981, 68–69). One can imagine Robert Plant reading such a definition and feeling justified in his musical borrowing. The statement does not account for how this Delta Blues process, as it enters the mainstream, lends great financial and social advantage to the white men who borrow from black blues artists.

27. Susan Fast primarily counters the moniker of "cock rock" for Led Zeppelin with examples of the band's "feminine side." She also argues that Zeppelin's lyrics can be taken in a variety of ways, sometimes sounding a little too strained in her effort to show that they are "not sexist."

28. Steve Waksman and Philip Auslander (whose chapter on cock rock is refreshingly devoted to Suzi Quatro) have each emphasized cock rock's constructedness and loosened its naturalized connection to maleness (Waksman 1996; Auslander 2006).

29. James Baldwin put it most succinctly when he wrote that the black man in America is perceived as "a kind of walking phallic symbol" (Baldwin 1998 [1954], 269–70). "Blackness" has functioned in the white imaginary as a symbol of hypermasculinity and authenticity, a trope that has obvious significance to understanding the appropriation of black music by white musicians. The hypermasculinity projected onto the body of the black man then extended to music associated with this body. A type of "sonic blackness" adhered especially to the Delta Blues and later electric blues styles that grew out of it and which formed the inspiration for the rock music of the 1960s. See Susan McClary and Robert Walser (1994), Eric Lott (1993), and Ingrid Monson (1995), among others.

30. Unlike Joplin, who made a point of citing her influences and crediting African-American songwriters and vocalists, Led Zeppelin was notorious for not crediting artists

from which they took entire swaths of material, in particular Willie Dixon. "Page's riff was Page's riff. It was there before anything else. I just thought, 'well, what am I going to sing?' That was it, a nick. Now happily paid for. At the time, there was a lot of conversation about what to do. It was decided that it was so far away in time and influence that . . . well, you only get caught when you're successful. That's the game" (quoted in Akkerman 2014, 21). For Joplin's relationship to her musical influences see McMullen (2014).

31. Freud writes that "what had up to then been prevented by [the father's] actual existence was thenceforward prohibited by the sons themselves, in accordance with the psychological procedure so familiar to us in psycho-analyses under the name of 'deferred obedience'" (1995 [1913], 501).

32. Although it is often assumed that Cobain was a direct product of the underground, "hardcore" punk scene, he actually came up through the feminist music scene developing around Evergreen State College in Olympia, Washington. Cobain's understanding of sex and gender was nurtured in the same scene that spawned Riot Grrrl. This is why his "androgynous" look differs from say, glam, or Led Zeppelin. Rocking out in his sundress, Cobain seemed to rebuke the hypermasculinity associated with heavy rock.

33. The term was often used as an insult. It described a music marked by excessive masculinity, associated with less-educated, working-class whites. "Cock rock" could be understood in many ways as the opposite of "progressive rock."

34. He further describes "the cover of an album by MX Machine (Manic Panic, 1988), a picture of a grimacing boy with his fist in the air [and] accompanied by a sticker proclaiming 'No Glam Fags! All Metal! No Makeup!'" (130).

35. Band reviewer Nick Brandon described the idea of the band as "brilliant" (2006).

36. To be specific, I would say aspects of bodies—it is not just that one body is masculine or feminine. This may be where I differ from Halberstam. Halberstam argues that we can have a variety of genders; however, I believe that because the two colors of gender are masculine and feminine, these "various genders" are still made up of the same oppressive definitional materials.

37. As women take over certain professions, those professions become "feminized" and lose prestige. Even in 1995, rock women were negatively described as examples of "female machisma" by Simon Reynolds and Joy Press (1995, 31). Such women were seen as donning a cloak of masculinity, presumably over some true form of womanhood. Other recent feminist rock historians have viewed rock's androgyny of the 1970s as another way to keep women out, viewing it as "femininity without women" (for example, Dibbell 1997, 278). This gender model assumes that femininity provides the depth for women and masculinity for men, and although borrowing can take place, rightful ownership is never questioned.

38. LeCompte's work, being theater, is also described as interrogating the idea of "presence." "The notion of the trace, of the absence of things past that inheres in every presence, seems to resonate throughout the performance of *Poor Theater*." The questions that one

reviewer was stimulated to ask are resonant with the concerns I discuss in this book: "One cannot help but wonder how rigorously this has all, in fact, been choreographed. Despite appearances, is anything actually *happening* now that has not happened before? And if not, is the appearance of liveness in fact the product of sophisticated theatrical illusion?" "Did anyone really see the [original] work itself, on its own terms, or were they always already reading it intertextually, as trace? And is theatre ever truly an experience of presence, or are we just chasing ghosts? (Alas, poor theatre . . .)" (Bottoms 2004, 694).

39. Pacing Nathaneal in "The Sandman" and Freud in his railcar. In our "imaginary projection" we have "indeed imagined everything" (Derrida, quoted in Kroksnes).

40. I'm speaking here of using a category, such as "woman," in a provisional and temporary manner as a strategy to accomplish positive change, as described by Trinh Minh-ha (1989), for example.

Conclusion

1. Trumpeter Charles Tolliver, approached by many of the same funders, re-created the same concert/album with the haunthenticity of Replay. For an interesting comparative review of both, see Ratliff (2009).

2. The Big Bandwagon consists of Moran on piano; Ralph Alessi, trumpet; Walter Smith, tenor saxophone; Logan Richardson III, alto saxophone; Frank Lacy, trombone; Bob Stewart, tuba; Tarus Mateen, bass; and Nasheet Waits, drums.

3. Moran talks about this story in an interview (Carbone 2009).

4. See "Fifty Years of Thelonious Monk at Town Hall," 2009.

5. Derrida's analysis of Kafka's short story "Before the Law" significantly influenced Butler's conception of gender performativity (Derrida 1992 [1982]). In Kafka's story, a man stands before a door to "the Law" guarded by a doorman and asks to enter. The doorman states that the man may not enter, but that "it is possible" he may be able to enter later. Although the door is always open, the man decides "that it is better to wait until he gets permission." The man waits outside the door for years, in fact, until the end of his life—periodically asking permission to enter and being denied, but hoping that one day he will be allowed to enter. As his life nears its end, the man asks why no one else has come to attempt admittance to the Law, since "everyone strives to meet the Law." The doorman, seeing that the man "has reached his end," reveals to the man that the door was made only for him and will now be shut. Significantly, the doorman never tells the man he is permanently prohibited entry. The man is in a state of waiting. Derrida argues that this is our essential relation with "the Law." The Law cannot be found, but gains its power as we stand before it and ask to enter. Both the subject and the Law are in fact brought into being in this relation. Butler applies Derrida's analysis to the operations of gender. Of "Before the Law," she writes, "there the one who waits for the law, sits before the door of

the law, attributes a certain force to the law for which one waits. The anticipation of an authoritative disclosure of meaning is the means by which that authority is attributed and installed: the anticipation conjures its object." Butler suggests that gender is just such an "expectation that ends up producing the very phenomenon that it anticipates." Gender performativity revolves around the ways "the anticipation of a gendered essence produces that which it posits as outside itself." Anticipation, waiting, and expectation attribute and generate the Law, including the law of gender.

6. Contrasted with the performative, which comes from the model that focuses on recognition, described above. For more, see McMullen (2014b).

7. The ability of soldiers to kill in combat is a focus of the recent field of study known as killology. Coined in 1995 by Lt. Col. Dave Grossman in his book *On Killing: The Psychological Cost of Learning to Kill in War and Society* (2009), killology in part involves research into soldiers' reluctance to kill and ways to overcome this reluctance.

8. See note 34 in the Introduction.

9. I am riffing on Morton, who calls for a "less phobic encounter with nothingness" (2015, 250).

BIBLIOGRAPHY

Abbate, Carolyn. 2004. "Music—Drastic or Gnostic?" *Critical Inquiry* 30 (3):505–36.

Abramović, Marina. 2007. *Seven Easy Pieces.* New York: Charta.

Adamian, John. 2004. "Hammer of the Goddesses." *Hartford Advocate* (Connecticut), January 15.

Adorno, Theodor. 2006 [1991]. *The Culture Industry: Selected Essays on Mass Culture.* Edited by J. M. Bernstein. London: Routledge.

Agnew, Vanessa. 2004. "Introduction: What Is Reenactment?" *Criticism* 46 (3):327–39.

———. 2007. "History's Affective Turn: Historical Reenactment and Its Work in the Present." *Rethinking History* 11 (3):299–312.

Akkerman, Gregg. 2014. *Experiencing Led Zeppelin: A Listener's Companion.* London: Rowman and Littlefield.

Alk, Howard. 1974. *Janis: The Way She Was.* MCA/Universal Home Video, VHS, 1993, 96 min.

Anzaldua, Gloria. 2010 [1987]. "La Conciencia de la Mestiza: Towards a New Consciousness." In *Feminist Theory Reader: Local and Global Perspectives,* edited by Seung-kyung Kim and Carole R. McCann, 254–62. New York: Routledge.

Auslander, Philip. 2006. *Performing Glam Rock: Gender and Theatricality in Popular Music.* Ann Arbor: University of Michigan Press.

"Background Lamb." 2007. WiV Entertainment. Accessed March 27, 2018. http://www.wiventertainment.de/.

Baldwin, James Arthur. 1962. "As Much Truth as One Can Bear." *New York Times Book Review,* January 14.

———. 1998 [1949]. "Everybody's Protest Novel." In *Collected Essays,* edited by Tony Morrison. New York: Library of America.

———. 1998 [1954]. "The Black Boy Looks at the White Boy." In *Collected Essays,* edited by Tony Morrison. New York: Library of America.Baudrillard, Jean. 2006 [1994]. *Simulacra and Simulation.* Translated by Sheila Faria Glaser. Ann Arbor: University of Michigan Press.

Benjamin, Playthell. 2006. *Wynton's Hot Fives: Conjuring the Legacy of Louis Armstrong.* Edited by Wynton Marsalis and Louis Armstrong's Hot Fives. New York: Playbill.

Bernstein, David. 2003. "Not Quite the Real Thing but Stars Just the Same." *New York Times,* September 30. http://www.nytimes.com/2003/09/30/arts/not-quite-the-real-thing-but-stars-just-the-same.html.

Bhabha, Homi. 1994. *The Location of Culture.* London: Routledge.

"Björn Thanks Gay Fans." 2011. *ABBA Omnibus* (blog), February 15. https://abbaomnibus.wordpress.com/2011/02/15/bjorn-thanks-gay-fans/.

Boon, Marcus. 2010. *In Praise of Copying.* Cambridge, MA: Harvard University Press.

Bottoms, Stephen J. 2004. "Poor Theater: A Series of Simulacra (review)." *Theatre Journal* 56 (4):693–95.

Boym, Svetlana. 2001. *The Future of Nostalgia.* New York: Basic Books.

Brandon, Nick. 2006. "Out with the Led . . . In with the Lez." *Go and Do Michigan,* March 7. http://www.goanddomichigan.com/stories/030206/hea_girlsrule001.shtml.

Braziel, Jana Evans. 2004. "'Bye, Bye Baby': Race, Bisexuality, and the Blues in the Music of Bessie Smith and Janis Joplin." *Popular Music and Society* 27 (1):3–26.

Bream, Jon. 2015. *Whole Lotta Led Zeppelin, 2nd Edition: The Illustrated History of the Heaviest Band of All Time.* Minneapolis: Quarto.

Breton, André, and Paul Eluard. 1938. *Dictionnaire Abrégé du Surréalisme.* Paris: Gallery of Fine Arts.

Brittan, Francesca. 2006. "Women Who 'Do Elvis': Authenticity, Masculinity, and Masquerade." *Journal of Popular Music Studies* 18 (2):167–90.

Broackes, Victoria, and Geoffrey Marsh. 2013. *David Bowie Is.* London: Vanda.

Brooks, Daphne A. 2008. "The Write to Rock: Racial Mythologies, Feminist Theory, and the Pleasures of Rock Music Criticism." *Women and Music: A Journal of Gender and Culture* 12:54–62.

Burns, Ken. 2001. *Jazz: A Film* by Ken Burns. Paramount Home Entertainment, DVD, 2005.

Butler, Judith. 1997. *Excitable Speech: A Politics of the Performative.* New York: Routledge.

———. 2017 [1988]. "Performative Acts and Gender Constitution: An Essay in Phenomenology and Feminist Theory." In *Feminist Theory Reader: Local and Global Perspectives,* edited by Carole R. McCann and Seung-kyung Kim. New York: Routledge.

———. 2006 [1990]. *Gender Trouble: Feminism and the Subversion of Identity.* London: Routledge.

Butt, John. 2008. *Playing with History: The Historical Approach to Musical Performance.* Cambridge: Cambridge University Press.

Cacouault-Bitaud, Marlaine. 2001. "Is the Feminization of a Profession a Sign of a Loss of Prestige?" *Travail, Genre et Sociétés* 1(5):91 -115.

Campbell, David. 1998 [1992]. *Writing Security: United States Foreign Policy and the Politics of Identity.* Minneapolis: University of Minnesota Press.

Carbone, Bill. 2009. "In Monk's Mind: Jason Moran Gets Inside Thelonious Monk's Music and in Our Heads." *New Haven Advocate,* June 17.

Carpenter, Lorraine. 2005. "The Song Remains the Same: But Lez Zeppelin Tantalizes Dykes and Dudes with Their Gender Switcheroo." *Mirror* (London).

Caruthers, Dick. 2003. *Led Zeppelin.* M: Productions, DVD.

Chernoff, John Miller. 1979. *African Rhythm and African Sensibility.* Chicago: University of Chicago Press.

Chinen, Nate. 2006. "Jazz in America: To the Beat of a Smooth One-Man Band." *New York Times,* August 27.

———. 2010. "Satchmo's Story, Music Substituting for Words." *New York Times,* August 31.

———. 2013. "Sharing a Jazzy Working Holiday: Wynton Marsalis Septet Members, Together Again." *New York Times,* December 28. http://www.nytimes.com/2013/12/28/arts/music/wynton-marsalis-septet-members-together-again.html.

———. 2016. "Wynton Marsalis's 'Spaces,' a Kinetic Series of Zoological Portraits." *New York Times,* April 4. https://www.nytimes.com/2016/04/04/arts/music/review-wynton-marsaliss-spaces-a-kinetic-series-of-zoological-portraits.html?_r=1.

Christgau, Robert. 1976. "Review: Abba's Greatest Hits." *Consumer Guide Review.* Accessed December 23, 2017. https://www.robertchristgau.com/get_artist.php?name=Abba.

———. 1979. "Review: Abba's Greatest Hits Vol. 2." *Consumer Guide Review.* Accessed December 23, 2017. https://www.robertchristgau.com/get_artist.php?name=Abba.

Clayson, Alan. 2006. *Led Zeppelin: The Origin of the Species: How, Why, and Where It All Began.* New Malden, UK: Chrome Dreams.

Coates, Norma. 1997. "(R)evolution Now? Rock and the Political Potential of Gender." In *Sexing the Groove: Popular Music and Gender,* edited by Sheila Whiteley, 50–64. London: Routledge.

———. 2003. "Teenyboppers, Groupies, and Other Grotesques: Girls and Women and Rock Culture in the 1960s and Early 1970s." *Journal of Popular Music Studies* 15:65–94.

Cobb, N. 1969. "Zeppelin Takes off at Carousel." *Boston Globe,* August 21. http://www.ledzeppelin.com/show/august-21-1969.

Cole, Richard. 2002 [1992]. *Stairway to Heaven: Led Zeppelin Uncensored.* New York: HarperCollins.

Collins, Phil. 2004. Tour Programme. Accessed July 10, 2013.

———. 2005. "With Phil Collins in Geneva." Interviewed by Peter Walt. Radio DRS3, February. http://www.peterwalt.ch/radio/srf_3/index.html.

Covach, John. 1997. "Progressive Rock, "Close to the Edge," and the Boundaries of Style." In *Understanding Rock: Essays in Musical Analysis,* edited by John Covach and Graeme M. Boone, 3–32. Oxford: Oxford University Press.

Cusick, Suzanne G. 1994. "On a Lesbian Relationship with Music: A Serious Effort Not to Think Straight." In *Queering the Pitch: The New Gay and Lesbian Musicology*, edited by Philip Brett, Elizabeth Wood, and Gary C. Thomas, 67–84. New York: Routledge.

Davis, Stephen. 2008. *Hammer of the Gods: The Led Zeppelin Saga*. New York: It Books.

Derrida, Jacques. 1991 [1972]. "Signature Event Context." In *A Derrida Reader*, edited by Peggy Kamuf, 80–111. New York: Columbia University Press.

———. 1992 [1982]. "Before the Law." In *Acts of Literature*, edited by Derek Attridge, 181–220. New York: Routledge.

———. 2005. *Rogues: Two Eassys on Reason*. Stanford, CA: Stanford University Press.

Dewing, P. 1977. "Press Review." *MM*, April 15.

Dibbell, Carola. 1997. "Inside Was Us: Women and Punk." In *Trouble Girls: The Rolling Stone Book of Women in Rock*, edited by Barbara O'Dair, 277–88. New York: Random House.

Doggett, Peter. 2012. *The Man Who Sold the World: David Bowie and the 1970s*. New York: Harper Perennial.

Doster, Eve. 2005. "Led Ladies." *Detroit Metrotimes*, August 24.

Downing, Larry, and Jason Reed. 2013. "A Zeppelin Flashback." *Photographers' Blog*, June 6. http://blogs.reuters.com/photographers-blog/2013/06/06/a-zeppelin-flashback/.

Dyer, Richard. 1990. "In Defense of Disco." In *On Record: Rock, Pop, and the Written Word*, edited by Simon Frith and Andrew Goodwin, 410–18. New York: Pantheon Press.

Echols, Alice. 1999. *Scars of Sweet Paradise: The Life and Times of Janis Joplin*. New York: Henry Holt.

———. 2010. *Hot Stuff: Disco and the Remaking of American Culture*. New York: Norton.

Erenberg, Lewis. 1998. *Swingin' the Dream: Big Band Jazz and the Rebirth of American Culture*. Chicago: University of Chicago Press.

Fast, Susan. 2001. *In The Houses of the Holy: Led Zeppelin and the Power of Rock Music*. Oxford: Oxford University Press.

"Fifty Years of Thelonious Monk at Town Hall: Hear the Live, Evening-Length Revival of Monk's Historic Concert." 2009. NPR.org, February 26. http://www.npr.org/templates/story/story.php?storyId=101140318&refresh=true.

Fincher, David. 1989. *Express Yourself*. Burbank, CA: Sire Records and Warner Bros. Records. Music video.

Fink, Robert. 2005. *Repeating Ourselves: American Minimal Music as Cultural Practice*. Berkeley: University of California Press.

Fiske, John. 1994. *Media Matters: Everyday Culture and Political Change*. Minneapolis: University of Minnesota Press.

Foster, Hal. 2001 [1996]. *The Return of the Real*. Edited by Annette Michelson, Rosalind Krauss, Yve-Alain Bois, Benjamin Buchloh, Hal Foster, Denis Hollier, and Silvia Kolbowski. Cambridge, MA: MIT Press.

Freud, Sigmund. 1995 [1913]. "Totem and Taboo." In *The Freud Reader,* edited by Peter Gay. New York: Norton.

———. 1995 [1930]. "Civilization and Its Discontents." In *The Freud Reader,* edited by Peter Gay. New York: Norton.

———. 2003 [1919]. *The Uncanny.* New York: Penguin Books.

Frith, Simon. 1981. *Sound Effects: Youth, Leisure, and the Politics of Rock and Roll.* New York: Pantheon.

———. 1990 [1985]. "Afterthoughts." In *On Record: Rock, Pop, and the Written Word,* edited by Simon Frith and Andrew Goodwin. London: Routledge.

———. 1998. *Performing Rites: On the Value of Popular Music.* Cambridge, MA: Harvard University Press.

———, and Angela McRobbie. 1990. "Rock and Sexuality." In *On Record: Rock, Pop, and the Written Word,* edited by Simon Frith and Andrew Goodwin, 371–89. London: Routledge.

Gabriel, Peter. 2002. "The Musical Box—The Black Show." Accessed June 17, 2018. http://www.usherhall.co.uk/whats-on/musical-box-black-show-celebrating-50th-anniversary-genesis.

Gallagher, Gary W. 2008. *Won, Lost and Forgotten: How Hollywood and Popular Art Shape What We Know about the Civil War.* Chapel Hill: University of North Carolina Press.

Gaskin, Vivienne. 2003. "The Second Coming." *Schnitt.* Accessed December 27, 2017. http://www.iainandjane.com/press/thesecondcoming/index.shtml.

———. 2004. "Space and Time: Live." *Crumb.* Accessed December 27, 2017. http://www.crumbweb.org/.

Gates, Henry Louis. 2014 [1988]. *The Signifying Monkey: A Theory of African-American Literary Criticism.* New York: Oxford University Press.

Geertz, Clifford. 1973. *The Interpretation of Cultures.* New York: Basic Books.

Gennari, John. 2006. *Blowin' Hot and Cool: Jazz and Its Critics.* Chicago: University of Chicago Press.

Gillis, John R. 1994. *Commemorations: The Politics of National Identity.* Princeton, NJ: Princeton University Press.

Ginell, Richard S. 1981. "Review: Herbie Hancock Quartet (1981)." CDBT. Accessed January 15, 2018. http://www.cdbt.hu/.

Gioia, Ted. 1997. *The History of Jazz.* New York: Oxford University Press.

Goehr, Lydia. 1992. *The Imaginary Museum of Musical Works.* New York: Oxford University Press.

Goldberg, Rosalee. 2007. *Performa: New Visual Art Performance.* New York: Performa.

Gordon, Avery. 2008 [1997]. *Ghostly Matters: Haunting and the Sociological Imagination.* Minneapolis: University of Minnesota Press.

Gray, Herman. 2005. *Cultural Moves: African Americans and the Politics of Representation.* Berkeley: University of California Press.

Gregory, Georgina. 2012. *Send in the Clones: A Cultural Study of the Tribute Band.* Sheffield, UK: Equinox.

Grossman, Dave. 2009. *On Killing: The Psychological Cost of Learning to Kill in War and Society.* New York: Little, Brown.

Gustaitis, Joseph. 2001. "Glenn Miller." *American History Magazine* (April):31–74.

Hajdu, David. 2011. "A Spell Deferred: The Revival of Nina Simone: Why Now?" *New Republic,* July 28.

Halberstam, Judith [Jack]. 1998. *Female Masculinity.* Durham, NC: Duke University Press.

———. 2005. *In a Queer Time and Place: Transgender Bodies, Subcultural Lives.* New York: New York University Press.

———. 2014. "Gender." In *Keywords for American Cultural Studies, Second Edition,* edited by Bruce Burgett and Glenn Hendler, 116–18. New York: New York University Press.

Hale, James. 2012. *David Bowie and the Story of Ziggy Stardust.* Narrated by Jarvis Cocker. London: BBC4. Film. 32 min. https://www.bbc.co.uk/programmes/b01koyon.

Hallström, Lasse. 1977. *ABBA: The Movie.* Burbank, CA: Warner Brothers. Film and DVD.

Hancock, Herbie, and Wynton Marsalis. 1999. "Soul, Craft, and Cultural Hierarchy." In *Keeping Time: Readings in Jazz History,* edited by Robert Walser, 55. New York: Oxford University Press.

Harris, Cheryl I. 1993. "Whiteness as Property." *Harvard Law Review* 106 (8):1707–91.

Harris, Savannah. 2016. "Interview: Jason Moran." *A Creative DC,* March 30. http://www.acreativedc.com/blog/2016/3/30/interview-jason-moran.

Harrison, Andrew. 2014. "Why Are Abba So Popular?" BBC.com, April 15. http://www.bbc.com/culture/story/20140415-why-are-abba-so-popular.

Haughton, Hugh. 2003. "Introduction." In *The Uncanny.* New York: Penguin Books.

Hawkins, Gary, and Emily LaDue. 2009. *In My Mind.* Durham, NC: Center for Documentary Studies. Film.

Hegel, G. W. F. 1977 [1807]. *The Phenomenology of Spirit.* Translated by A. V. Miller. Oxford: Oxford University Press.

Hesse, J. 1969. "Led Zeppelin Flies Directly to the Nerve Ends." *Vancouver Sun,* July 26. http://www.ledzeppelin.com/show/july-26-1969.

Hewett, Ivan. 2012. "Wynton Marsalis Interview: It Don't Mean a Thing If It Ain't Got Swing." *Telegraph,* July 5. https://www.telegraph.co.uk/culture/music/worldfolkandjazz/9376790/Wynton-Marsalis-interview-It-dont-mean-a-thing-if-it-aint-got-swing.html.

Hoffman, E. T. A. 1969. "The Sandman." In *The Tales of E. T. A. Hoffman,* edited by Leonard J. Kent and Elizabeth C. Knight. Chicago: University of Chicago Press.

———. 1967. "The Sandman." In *The Best Tales of Hoffmann*, edited by E. F. Bleiler. New York: Dover Publications.

Holm-Hudson, Kevin, ed. 2002. *Progressive Rock Reconsidered*. New York: Routledge.

Holsinger, Bruce. 2005. *The Premodern Condition: Medievalism and the Making of Theory*. Chicago: University of Chicago Press.

Homan, Shane. 2006. *Access All Eras: Tribute Bands and Global Pop Culture*. Berkshire, UK: Open University Press.

hooks, bell. 1990. *Yearning: Race, Gender, and Cultural Politics*. Cambridge, MA: South End Press.

Hoskyns, Barney. 2003. "Been a Long Time: Led Zeppelin." *MOJO*, June.

———. 2006. *Led Zeppelin IV (Rock of Ages)*. New York: Rodale Books.

Hubbs, Nadine. 2014. *Rednecks, Queers, and Country Music*. Berkeley: University of California Press.

Huyssen, Andreas. 2003. *Present Pasts: Urban Palimpsests and the Politics of Memory*. Stanford, CA: Stanford University Press.

Inglis, Ian. 2006. "Fabricating the Fab Four: Pastiche and Parody." In *Access All Eras: Tribute Bands and Global Pop Culture*, edited by Shane Homan. Berkshire, UK: Open University Press.

James, Robin. 2015. *Resilience and Melancholy: Pop Music, Feminism, Neoliberalism*. Washington, DC: Zero Books.

Jameson, Fredric. 2003 [1991]. *Postmodernism: Or, the Cultural Logic of Late Capitalism*. Durham, NC: Duke University Press.

Jankélévitch, Vladimir. 2003 [1961]. *Music and the Ineffable*. Translated by Carolyn Abbate. Princeton, NJ: Princeton University Press.

"Jazz at Lincoln Center Adopts Blind Auditions and New Selection Procedures for Jazz Orchestra." 2016. *Cision: PR Newswire*, August 18. https://www.prnewswire.com/news-releases/jazz-at-lincoln-center-adopts-blind-auditions-and-new-selection-procedures-for-jazz-orchestra-300315206.html.

Jazz at Lincoln Center Orchestra with Wynton Marsalis and Special Guest, Cécile Mclorin Salvant. January 1, 2014. Miami: Adrienne Arsht Center for the Performing Arts. http://www.arshtcenter.org/tickets/calendar/2013-2014-season/jazz-roots/big-band-holidays/.

"JazzGirls Day: A Celebration of Young Instrumentalists." 2016. *JazzBlog*, March 8. https://www.jazz.org/blog/search/?search_terms=JazzGirls+Day%3A+A+Celebration+of+Young+Instrumentalists.

Johnson, Charles R. 2013 [1988]. *Being and Race: Black Writing since 1970*. New York: Scribner.

Jones, Amelia. 2011. "'The Artist Is Present': Artistic Re-enactments and the Impossibility of Presence." *TDR: The Drama Review* 55 (1):16–45.

Jones, John Paul, Jimmy Page, and Robert Plant. 2012. "Led Zeppelin: Rock Legends Get Real about 'the Best Band.'" Edited by Charlie Rose. *CBS This Morning,* CBS News, December 21.

Kaufman, Charlie. 2008. *Synecdoche, New York.* New York: Sony Pictures Classics. Film. 123 min.

Kelsey, Chris. 2006. "Wynton and Louis Armstrong's Hot Fives." *Jazz Times.* Accessed January 10. http://jazztimes.com/reviews/concert_reviews/detail.cfm?article=10412.

Kivy, Peter. 1995. *Authenticities: Philosophical Reflections on Musical Performance.* Ithaca, NY: Cornell University Press.

Kleinberg, Ethan. 2017. *Haunting History: For a Deconstructive Approach to the Past.* Stanford, CA: Stanford University Press.

Klosterman, Chuck. 2005. "She's Got Big Balls." *Spin,* June, 73–78.

Kollectiv, Pil and Galia. 2007. "RETRO/NECRO: From Beyond the Grave of the Politics of Re-Enactment." *Art Papers* 31 (6):44–51.

Kondo, Dorinne. 2000. "(Re) Visions of Race: Contemporary Race Theory and the Cultural Politics of Racial Crossover in Documentary Theatre." *Theatre Journal* 52:81–107.

Kramer, Lawrence. 1995. *Classical Music and Postmodern Knowledge.* Berkeley: University of California Press.

Kroksnes, Andrea. 2001. "Deconstructing Origin Stories." In *For Art: The Institute of Research within International Contemporary Art.* Oslo, Norway.

Lacan, Jacques. [1973] 1998. *The Four Fundamental Concepts of Psychoanalysis.* Translated by Alan Sheridan. Edited by Jacques-Alain Miller. New York: Norton.

Lamothe, Sébastien. 2011. Interview with the author. October 3, Los Angeles.

Larner, Gerald. 2015 [1989]. "John Cage Interview: 'I Gave Up the Notion of Communication as Impractical in My Case.'" *Guardian,* December 8. Reprinted from *Guardian,* November 16, 1989. https://www.theguardian.com/music/from-the-archive-blog/2015/dec/08/john-cage-interview-november-1989.

Laver, Mark. 2014. "Freedom of Choice: Jazz, Neoliberalism, and the Lincoln Center." *Popular Music and Society* 37 (5):538–56.

"Led Zeppelin Bows in with a Roar." 1971. *Oakland Tribune,* Sept. 13. LedZepplin.com, http://www.ledzeppelin.com/show/september-13–1971.

"Led Zeppelin Makes Magic at the Arena." 1969. *San Diego Union,* August 11. LedZepplin.com, http://www.ledzeppelin.com/show/august-10–1969.

Leppert, Richard. 1993. *The Sight of Sound.* Berkeley: University of California Press.

Livingston, Jennie. 2005. *Paris Is Burning.* Santa Monica, CA: Lionsgate. Film. 96 min.

Lorde, Andre. 2007 [1984]. *Sister Outsider: Essays and Speeches.* New York: Random.

Lott, Eric. 1993. *Love and Theft: Blackface Minstrelsy and the American Working Class.* New York: Oxford University Press.

Lowe, Lisa. 1996. *Immigrant Acts: On Asian American Cultural Politics.* Durham, NC: Duke University Press.

Lozano, Lee. 1969. *General Strike Piece.*

Macan, Edward. 1992. "'The Spirit of Albion' in Twentieth-Century English Popular Music." *Music Review* 53 (2):100–125.

———. 1997. *Rocking the Classics: English Progressive Rock and the Counterculture.* Oxford: Oxford University Press.

Mackey, Nathaniel. 1998. "Other: From Noun to Verb." In *The Jazz Cadence of American Culture,* edited by Robert G. O'Meally, 513–32. New York: Columbia University Press.

———. 2005. *Paracritical Hinge: Essays, Talks, Notes, Interviews.* Madison: University of Wisconsin Press.

Mahon, Maureen. 2004. *Right to Rock: The Black Rock Coalition and the Cultural Politics of Race.* Durham, NC: Duke University Press.

———. 2011. "Listening for Willie Mae 'Big Mama' Thornton's Voice." *Women and Music: A Journal of Gender and Culture* 15:1–17.

Manderson, Desmond. 2010. "Fission and Fusion: From Improvisation to Formalism in Law and Music." *Critical Studies in Improvisation / Etudes critiques en improvisation* 6 (1). https://www.criticalimprov.com/index.php/csieci/article/view/1167/1717.

Mann, B. 1972. "Led Zeppelin: Top Heavies Electrify 12,000 at Forum." *Gazette,* June 7. http://www.ledzeppelin.com/show/june-7–1972.

Marsalis, Wynton, and Carl Vigeland. 2001. *Jazz in the Bittersweet Blues of Life.* Cambridge, MA: Da Capo.

McClary, Susan, and Robert Walser. 1994. "Theorizing the Body in African-American Music." *Black Music Research Journal* 14 (1):75–84.

McClintock, Anne. 1995. *Imperial Leather.* New York: Routledge.

McDonnell, Evelyn, and Ann Powers, eds. 1995. *Rock She Wrote: Women Write about Rock, Pop, and Rap.* New York: Delta Trade Paperbacks.

McGee, Kristin A. 2009. *Some Liked It Hot: Jazz Women in Film and Television, 1928–1959.* Middletown, CT: Wesleyan University Press.

McLeod, Kembrew. 1999. "Authenticity within Hip-Hop and Other Cultures Threatened with Assimilation." *Journal of Communication* 49 (4):134–50.

———. 2001. "'*1/2': A Critique of Rock Criticism in North America." *Popular Music* 20 (1):47–60.

McLuhan, Marshall, and Quentin Fiore. 2001 [1967]. *The Medium Is the Massage: An Inventory of Effects.* Toronto: Penguin Canada.

McMullen, Tracy. 2007. "Bands, Orchestras, and the 'Ideal I': The Musical Stage as Constitutive of the 'I' Function." PhD dissertation, Music, University of California, San Diego.

———. 2010. "Subject, Object, Music: John Cage, Pauline Oliveros, and Eastern (Western) Philosophy in Music." *Critical Studies in Improvisation* / Études Critiques en Improvisation 6 (2).

———. 2013. "People, Don't Get Ready: Improvisation, Democracy, and Hope." In *People, Get Ready: The Future of Jazz Is Now,* edited by Ajay Heble and Robert Wallace. Durham, NC: Duke University Press.

———. 2014a. "'Bring it on Home': Robert Plant, Janis Joplin, and the Myth of Origin." *Journal of Popular Music Studies* 26 (2).

———. 2014b. "The Improvisative." In *The Oxford Handbook of Critical Improvisation Studies,* edited by George Lewis and Benjamin Piekut. Oxford: Oxford University Press.Menkes, Suzy. 2013. "David Bowie Brought to Life, in All His Guises." *New York Times,* March 18.

Meyers, John Paul. 2010. "The World According to Marsalis: Difference and Sameness in Wynton Marsalis's *From the Plantation to the Penitentiary.*" *Journal of Popular Music Studies* 22 (4):416–35.

Monson, Ingrid. 1995. "The Problem with White Hipness: Race, Gender, and Cultural Conceptions in Jazz Discourse." *Journal of the American Musicological Society* 48 (3):396–422.

———. 1996. *Saying Something: Jazz Improvisation and Interaction.* Chicago: University of Chicago Press.

———. 2003. "Art Blakey's African Diaspora." In *The African Diaspora: A Musical Perspective,* edited by Ingrid Monson. New York: Routledge.

Moran, Jason. 2008. A Return to Town Hall for Monk. *Guardian,* May 16. https://www.theguardian.com/music/2008/may/16/filmandmusic1.filmandmusic207.

———. 2009. "Glenn Ligon." *Andy Warhol's Interview Magazine,* June 16. https://www.interviewmagazine.com/art/glenn-ligon.

Morgenstern, Hans. 2012. "The Musical Box: Hard Rock Live." *Broward Palm Beach New Times,* May 3. http://www.browardpalmbeach.com/music/the-musical-box-hard-rock-live-may-2-6421557.

Morton, Timothy. 2015. "Buddhaphobia." In *Nothing: Three Inquiries in Buddhism,* edited by Marcus Boon, Eric Cazdyn, and Timothy Morton, 185–266. Chicago: University of Chicago Press.

"The Musical Box: 'The Black Show.'" 2017. The Musical Box. Accessed December 24, 2018. http://www.themusicalbox.net/.Nastos, Michael G. 2009. "AllMusic Review: He and She." AllMusic. Accessed January 8, 2018. http://www.allmusic.com/.

Nicholls, David. 2004. "Virtual Opera, or Opera between the Ears." *Journal of the Royal Musical Association* 129 (1):100–42.

Nietzsche, Friedrich. 1977. *The Portable Nietzsche.* Edited and translated by Walter Kaufmann. New York: Penguin Books.

O'Dair, Barbara. 1997. *Trouble Girls: The Rolling Stone Book of Women in Rock.* New York: Random House.

Oakes, Jason. 2005. "Losers, Punks, and Queers (and Elvis Too): Identification and 'Identity' at New York City Music Tribute Events." PhD dissertation, Ethnomusicology, Columbia University, New York.

Ozment, Elizabeth Whittenburg. 2014. "The Politics of Musical Reenactment: Civil War Commemoration in American Culture." PhD dissertation, Music, University of Georgia, Athens.

Palm, Carl Magnus. 2002. *Bright Lights, Dark Shadows: The Real Story of Abba.* London: Omnibus Press.

Palmer, Robert. 1981. *Deep Blues: A Musical and Cultural History from the Mississippi Delta to Chicago's South Side to the World.* New York: Penguin Books.

Peck, Raoul, ed. 2017. *I Am Not Your Negro: From Texts by James Baldwin.* New York: Vintage International.

Pellegrenelli, Lara. 2010. "The 'Ex-Jazz Lover' Says It's Okay to Be Sad." NPR.org, April 15. http://www.npr.org/blogs/ablogsupreme/2010/04/the_ex-jazz_lover_says_its_okay_to_be_sad.html.

———. 2000. "Dig Boy Dig: Jazz at Lincoln Center Breaks New Ground, but Where Are the Women?" *Village Voice,* November 8–14.

Peress, Maurice. 2004. *Dvorak to Duke Ellington: A Conductor Explores America's Music and Its African American Roots.* Oxford: Oxford University Press.

Phelan, Peggy. 1997. *Mourning Sex: Performing Public Memories.* London: Routledge.

Piper, Adrian. 1986–1990. *My Calling (Card) #1 (for Dinners and Cocktail Parties).* https://adrianpiper.weebly.com/my-calling-card-1986-1990.html.

———. 1992. "Passing for White, Passing for Black." *Transition* 58:4–32.

Pogrebin, Robin. 2006. "New Home for Jazz Gets Mixed Reviews." *New York Times,* January 24.

Powers, Ann. 1993. "Janis without Tears." In *Liner Notes to Janis* [CD box set]. New York: Sony Music.

Ratliff, Ben. 2009a. "Two Approaches to Monk's Historic Night." *New York Times,* March 1.

Ratliff, Ben. 2009b. "Critics' Choice: New CDs." *New York Times,* March 23.

Reddy, Maureen T. 1998. "Invisibility/Hypervisibility: The Paradox of Normative Whiteness." *Transformation: The Journal of Inclusive Scholarship and Pedagogy* 9 (2):55–64.

Reuters. 2006. "Lez Zeppelin: A Band That Flips the Page." CNN.com, January 30.

Reynolds, Simon. 2011. *Retromania: Pop Culture's Addiction to Its Own Past.* New York: Faber and Faber.

Rhodes, Lisa. 2005. *Electric Ladyland: Women and Rock Culture.* Philadelphia: University of Pennsylvania Press.

Robison, Brian. 2002. "Somebody Is Digging My Bones: King Crimson's 'Dinosaur' as

(Post)Progressive Historiography." In *Progressive Rock Reconsidered,* edited by Kevin Holm-Hudson. New York: Routledge.

"A Rock 'n' Roll Suicide." 1998. Iain Forsyth and Jane Pollard. Accessed December 31, 2018. http://www.iainandjane.com/work/live-art/a-rock-n-roll-suicide/.

Rodgers, Daniel T. 2011. *The Age of Fracture.* Cambridge, MA: Harvard University Press.

Ronzello, Robert. 1994. "Concert Notes." Yale Band Archive. Yale Band Room, Yale University, New Haven, Connecticut.

Ross, Ron. 1973. "Genesis at Philharmonic Hall, New York." *Phonograph Record* (May).

Rothstein, Edward. 2007. "Is It Live . . . or Yamaha? Channeling Glenn Gould." *New York Times,* March 12.

Ruby, Jennie. 2005. "Women's 'Cock Rock' Goes Mainstream." *Off Our Backs* 35 (7/8, July):42–44.

Russonello, Giovanni. 2017. "At 30, What Does Jazz at Lincoln Center Mean?" *New York Times,* September 13. https://www.nytimes.com/2017/09/13/arts/music/jazz-at-lincoln-center-30th-anniversary.html.

Salih, Sara. 2004. *The Judith Butler Reader.* Malden, MA: Blackwell.

Schaefer, John. 2006. "Wynton Marsalis Re-imagines Armstrong." *Soundcheck,* September 26. WNYC podcast. https://www.wnyc.org/story/38819-marsalis-re-imagines-armstrong/.

Schechner, Richard. 2002. *Performance Studies: An Introduction.* New York: Routledge.

———. 2006. *Performance Studies: An Introduction.* 2nd ed. New York: Routledge.

Schneider, Rebecca. 2011. *Performing Remains: Art and War in Times of Theatrical Reenactment.* New York: Routledge.

Schuessler, Jennifer. 2012. "Shock Me If You Can." *New York Times,* September 16. http://www.nytimes.com/2012/09/16/arts/shock-me-if-you-can.html.

Scott, Jane. 1969. "Zeppelin Lands to Big Cheers at Musicarnival." *Billboard,* August 2. https://www.americanradiohistory.com/Archive-Billboard/60s/1969/Billboard%20 1969-08-02.pdf.

Seavey, William L. 1969. "Dusk to Dawn—Concert at a Glance: The Led Zeppelin." LedZeppelin.com, January 15. http://www.ledzeppelin.com/show/january-15-1969.

Sebald, W. G. 2011 [2001]. *Austerlitz.* New York: Modern Library.

Shadwick, Keith. 2005. *Led Zeppelin: The Story of a Band and Their Music 1968–1980.* San Francisco: Backbeat Books.

Shaviro, Steven. 2003. *Connected: Or What It Means to Live in the Network Society.* Minneapolis: University of Minnesota Press.

Shawn. 2006. "The Gay Rocker's Code." *hooked.* Accessed May 15, 2007. http://www.hooked-nussu.org/content/view/690/88/.

Sheinbaum, John J. 2002. "Progressive Rock and the Inversion of Musical Values." In

Progressive Rock Reconsidered, edited by Kevin Holm-Hudson, 21–42. New York: Routledge.

Shepherd, John, and Peter Wicke. 1997. *Music and Cultural Theory.* Cambridge, UK: Polity Press.

Shewey, Don. 2001. "Vamp, Bitch, Camp, Kitsch: What Makes *Mamma Mia!* and *The Women* So Gay? And Whatever It Is, Is It Good?" *Advocate,* December 25, 61–62.

Silverman, Kaja. 1983. *The Subject of Semiotics.* Oxford: Oxford University Press.

Smith, Roberta. 1999. "Lee Lozano, 68, Conceptual Artist Who Boycotted Women for Years." *New York Times,* October 18.

Smith, Steve. 2008. "The Musical Box." *Time Out New York,* December 22.

Solis, Gabiel. 2008. *Monk's Music: Thelonious Monk and Jazz History in the Making.* Berkeley: University of California Press.

Sontag, Susan. 2001. *Against Interpretation and Other Essays.* New York: Picador.

Spicer, Mark S. 2000. "Large-Scale Strategy and Compositional Design in the Early Music of Genesis." In *Expression in Pop-Rock Music,* edited by Walter Everett. New York: Garland.

Stanley, Bob. 2005. "Waddya Mean Groupies? We're the Group." *Times of London Online* November 4.

Sterne, Jonathan. 2003. *The Audible Past: Cultural Origins of Sound Production.* Durham, NC: Duke University Press.

Stevenson, Nick. 2006. *David Bowie: Fame, Sound and Vision.* Cambridge, UK: Polity Press.

Stewart, Alex. 2007. *Making the Scene: Contemporary New York City Big Band Jazz.* Berkeley: University of California Press.

Straw, Will. 1997. "Sizing Up Record Collections: Gender and Connoisseurship in Rock Music Culture." In *Sexing the Groove: Popular Music and Gender,* edited by Sheila Whiteley. New York: Routledge.

Sturken, Marita. 1997. *Tangled Memories: The Vietnam War, the AIDS Epidemic, and the Politics of Remembering.* Berkeley: University of California Press.

Sutton, Terri. 1997. "Janis Joplin." In *Trouble Girls: The Rolling Stone Book of Women in Rock,* edited by Barbara O'Dair. New York: Rolling Stone Press.

Tackley, Catherine. 2012. *Benny Goodman's Famous 1938 Carnegie Hall Jazz Concert.* Oxford: Oxford University Press.

Taruskin, Richard. 1995. *Text and Act: Essays on Music and Performance* New York: Oxford University Press.

Taylor, Jeffrey. 2008. "With Lovie and Lil: Rediscovering Two Chicago Pianists of the 1920s." In *Big Ears: Listening for Gender in Jazz Studies,* edited by Nichole T. Rustin and Sherrie Tucker. Durham, NC: Duke University Press.

Taylor, Verta, and Leila J. Rupp. 2014. "For Better—and—For Worse." *Contexts* 13 (2):84–90.

Teachout, Terry. 2009. *Pops: A Life of Louis Armstrong.* New York: Houghton Mifflin Harcourt.

Teal, Kimberly Hannon. 2014. "Posthumously Live: Canon Formation at Jazz at Lincoln Center through the Case of Mary Lou Williams." *American Music* 32 (4):400–22.

Than, Ker. 2005. "Symmetry in Nature: Fundamental Fact or Human Bias?" *LiveScience,* December 21. https://www.livescience.com/4002-symmetry-nature-fundamental-fact-human-bias.html.

Thich, Nhat Hanh. 2003. *Interbeing.* New Delhi: Full Circle Publishing.

Trinh, Minh-ha T. 1989. *Woman, Native, Other: Writing Postcoloniality and Feminism.* Bloomington: Indiana University Press.

Tucker, Sherrie. 2002. "When Subjects Don't Come Out." In *Queer Episodes in Music and Modern Identity,* edited by Sophie Fuller and Lloyd Whitesell. Urbana: University of Illinois Press.

———, and Nichole T. Rustin, eds. 2008. *Big Ears: Listening for Gender in Jazz Studies.* Durham, NC: Duke University Press.

Turner, Victor. 1982. *From Ritual to Theatre: The Human Seriousness of Play.* New York: PAJ.

Tyler, Steven. 2011. *Does the Noise in My Head Bother You?: A Rock 'n' Roll Memoir.* New York: HarperCollins.

US Army Air Force. 1943. Yale Band Glenn Miller Reenactment Archive. Yale Band Room, Yale University, New Haven, Connecticut.

Waksman, Steve. 1996. "Every Inch of My Love: Led Zeppelin and the Problem of Cock Rock." *Journal of Popular Music Studies* 8:5–25.

———. 1999. "Black Sound, Black Body: Jimi Hendrix, the Electric Guitar, and the Meanings of Blackness." *Popular Music and Society* 23 (1):75–113.

Wald, Gayle. 2004. "Sister Rosetta Tharpe and the Prehistory of 'Women in Rock.'" In *This Is Pop: In Search of the Elusive at Experience Music Project,* edited by Eric Weisbard. Cambridge, MA: Harvard University Press.

Wall, Mick. 2008a. "The Truth behind the Led Zeppelin Legend." *Times* (UK), November 1.

———. 2008b. *When Giants Walked the Earth: A Biography of Led Zeppelin.* New York: St. Martin's Press.

Walser, Robert. 1993. *Running with the Devil: Power, Gender, and Madness in Heavy Metal Music.* Hanover, NH: Wesleyan University Press.

Walters, Barry. 2015. "ABBA's Essential, Influential Melancholy." NPR.org, May 23. https://www.npr.org/sections/therecord/2015/05/23/408844375/abbas-essential-influential-melancholy.

Warwick, Jacqueline. 2007. *Girl Groups, Girl Culture: Popular Music and Identity in the 1960s.* New York: Routledge.

Weinberger, Eliot, ed. 1999. *Jorge Luis Borges: Selected Non-Fictions.* New York: Penguin Putnam.

Weinstein, Deena. 2002. "Progressive Rock as Text: The Lyrics of Roger Waters." In *Progressive Rock Reconsidered,* edited by Kevin Holm-Hudson, 91–110. New York: Routledge.

Welch, Chris. 2016 [1998]. *Led Zeppelin: The Stories behind Every Led Zeppelin Song.* London: Carlton Books.

Witkowski, D'Anne. 2005. "Don't Ask, Don't Tell: Just Rock with Lez Zeppelin." *Between the Lines: Michigan's Weekly News for Lesbians, Gays, Bisexuals, Transgenders and Friends* (Ann Arbor), August 25–31.

Wolfe, Tom. 1976. "The 'Me' Decade and the Third Great Awakening." *New York Magazine,* August 23.

Woolfork, Lisa. 2009. *Embodying American Slavery in Contemporary Culture.* Urbana: University of Illinois Press.

Yanow, Scott. "AllMusic Review by Scott Yanow." AllMusic.com. Accessed January 15, 2018. https://www.allmusic.com/album/black-codes-from-the-underground-mw0000188478.

"Young Folks Take Trip at Musicarnival." 1969. *Plain Dealer* (Cleveland), July 21. LedZepplin.com. http://www.ledzeppelin.com/show/july-20-1969.

Zeppelin, Lez. 2007. *Lez Zeppelin.* Emanation Records. CD/Vinyl.

———. 2010. *Lez Zeppelin I.* Hillsborough, NC: Redeye Label. CD/Vinyl.

Žižek, Slavoj. 1999a. "Is It Possible to Traverse the Fantasy in Cyberspace?" In *The Žižek Reader,* edited by Elizabeth Wright and Edmond Wright. Malden, MA: Blackwell.

———. 1999b. "The Spectre of Ideology." In *The Žižek Reader,* edited by Elizabeth Wright and Edmond Wright. Malden, MA: Blackwell.

INDEX

NOTE: Page numbers marked "*fig.*" indicate photos.

MUSIC / CULTURE

A series from Wesleyan University Press
Edited by Deborah Wong, Sherrie Tucker, and Jeremy Wallach
Originating editors: George Lipsitz, Susan McClary, and Robert Walser

Marié Abe
Resonances of Chindon-ya: Sounding Space and Sociality in Contemporary Japan

Frances Aparicio
Listening to Salsa: Gender, Latin Popular Music, and Puerto Rican Cultures

Paul Austerlitz
Jazz Consciousness: Music, Race, and Humanity

Harris M. Berger
Metal, Rock, and Jazz: Perception and the Phenomenology of Musical Experience

Harris M. Berger
Stance: Ideas about Emotion, Style, and Meaning for the Study of Expressive Culture

Harris M. Berger and Giovanna P. Del Negro
Identity and Everyday Life: Essays in the Study of Folklore, Music, and Popular Culture

Franya J. Berkman
Monument Eternal: The Music of Alice Coltrane

Dick Blau, Angeliki Vellou Keil, and Charles Keil
Bright Balkan Morning: Romani Lives and the Power of Music in Greek Macedonia

Susan Boynton and Roe-Min Kok, editors
Musical Childhoods and the Cultures of Youth

James Buhler, Caryl Flinn, and David Neumeyer, editors
Music and Cinema

Thomas Burkhalter, Kay Dickinson, and Benjamin J. Harbert, editors
The Arab Avant-Garde: Music, Politics, Modernity

Patrick Burkart
Music and Cyberliberties

Julia Byl
Antiphonal Histories: Resonant Pasts in the Toba Batak Musical Present

Daniel Cavicchi
Listening and Longing: Music Lovers in the Age of Barnum

Susan D. Crafts, Daniel Cavicchi, Charles Keil, and the Music in Daily Life Project
My Music: Explorations of Music in Daily Life

Jim Cullen
Born in the USA: Bruce Springsteen and the American Tradition

Anne Danielsen
Presence and Pleasure: The Funk Grooves of James Brown and Parliament

Peter Doyle
Echo and Reverb: Fabricating Space in Popular Music Recording, 1900–1960

Ron Emoff
Recollecting from the Past: Musical Practice and Spirit Possession on the East Coast of Madagascar

Yayoi Uno Everett and Frederick Lau, editors
Locating East Asia in Western Art Music

Susan Fast and Kip Pegley, editors
Music, Politics, and Violence

Heidi Feldman
Black Rhythms of Peru: Reviving African Musical Heritage in the Black Pacific

Kai Fikentscher
"You Better Work!" Underground Dance Music in New York City

Ruth Finnegan
The Hidden Musicians: Music-Making in an English Town

Daniel Fischlin and Ajay Heble, editors
The Other Side of Nowhere: Jazz, Improvisation, and Communities in Dialogue

Wendy Fonarow
Empire of Dirt: The Aesthetics and Rituals of British "Indie" Music

Murray Forman
The 'Hood Comes First: Race, Space, and Place in Rap and Hip-Hop

Lisa Gilman
My Music, My War: The Listening Habits of U.S. Troops in Iraq and Afghanistan

Paul D. Greene and Thomas Porcello, editors
Wired for Sound: Engineering and Technologies in Sonic Cultures

Tomie Hahn
Sensational Knowledge: Embodying Culture through Japanese Dance

Edward Herbst
Voices in Bali: Energies and Perceptions in Vocal Music and Dance Theater

Deborah Kapchan
Traveling Spirit Masters: Moroccan Gnawa Trance and Music in the Global Marketplace

Deborah Kapchan, editor
Theorizing Sound Writing

Max Katz
Lineage of Loss: Counternarratives of North Indian Music

Raymond Knapp
Symphonic Metamorphoses: Subjectivity and Alienation in Mahler's Re-Cycled Songs

Victoria Lindsay Levine and Dylan Robinson, editors
Music and Modernity among First Peoples of North America

Laura Lohman
Umm Kulthūm: Artistic Agency and the Shaping of an Arab Legend, 1967–2007

Preston Love
A Thousand Honey Creeks Later: My Life in Music from Basie to Motown—and Beyond

René T. A. Lysloff and Leslie C. Gay Jr., editors
Music and Technoculture

Allan Marett
Songs, Dreamings, and Ghosts: The Wangga of North Australia

Ian Maxwell
Phat Beats, Dope Rhymes: Hip Hop Down Under Comin' Upper

Kristin A. McGee
Some Liked It Hot: Jazz Women in Film and Television, 1928–1959

Tracy McMullen
Haunthenticity: Musical Replay and the Fear of the Real

Rebecca S. Miller
Carriacou String Band Serenade: Performing Identity in the Eastern Caribbean

Tony Mitchell, editor
Global Noise: Rap and Hip-Hop Outside the USA

Christopher Moore and Philip Purvis, editors
Music & Camp

Rachel Mundy
Animal Musicalities: Birds, Beasts, and Evolutionary Listening

Keith Negus
Popular Music in Theory: An Introduction

Johnny Otis
Upside Your Head: Rhythm and Blues on Central Avenue

Kip Pegley
Coming to You Wherever You Are: MuchMusic, MTV, and Youth Identities

Jonathan Pieslak
Radicalism and Music: An Introduction to the Music Cultures of al-Qa'ida, Racist Skinheads, Christian-Affiliated Radicals, and Eco-Animal Rights Militants

Matthew Rahaim
Musicking Bodies: Gesture and Voice in Hindustani Music

John Richardson
Singing Archaeology: Philip Glass's Akhnaten

Tricia Rose
Black Noise: Rap Music and Black Culture in Contemporary America

David Rothenberg
and Marta Ulvaeus, editors
The Book of Music and Nature: An Anthology of Sounds, Words, Thoughts

Nichole Rustin-Paschal
The Kind of Man I Am: Jazzmasculinity and the World of Charles Mingus Jr.

Marta Elena Savigliano
Angora Matta: Fatal Acts of North-South Translation

Joseph G. Schloss
Making Beats: The Art of Sample-Based Hip-Hop

Barry Shank
Dissonant Identities: The Rock 'n' Roll Scene in Austin, Texas

Jonathan Holt Shannon
Among the Jasmine Trees: Music and Modernity in Contemporary Syria

Daniel B. Sharp
Between Nostalgia and Apocalypse: Popular Music and the Staging of Brazil

Helena Simonett
Banda: Mexican Musical Life across Borders

Mark Slobin
Subcultural Sounds: Micromusics of the West

Mark Slobin, editor
Global Soundtracks: Worlds of Film Music

Christopher Small
The Christopher Small Reader

Christopher Small
Music of the Common Tongue: Survival and Celebration in African American Music

Christopher Small
Music, Society, Education

Christopher Small
Musicking: The Meanings of Performing and Listening

Regina M. Sweeney
Singing Our Way to Victory: French Cultural Politics and Music during the Great War

Colin Symes
Setting the Record Straight: A Material History of Classical Recording

Steven Taylor
False Prophet: Field Notes from the Punk Underground

Paul Théberge
Any Sound You Can Imagine: Making Music/Consuming Technology

Sarah Thornton
Club Cultures: Music, Media, and Subcultural Capital

Michael E. Veal
Dub: Songscape and Shattered Songs in Jamaican Reggae

Michael E. Veal and
E. Tammy Kim, editors
Punk Ethnography: Artists and Scholars Listen to Sublime Frequencies

Robert Walser
Running with the Devil: Power, Gender, and Madness in Heavy Metal Music

Dennis Waring
Manufacturing the Muse: Estey Organs and Consumer Culture in Victorian America

Lise A. Waxer
The City of Musical Memory: Salsa, Record Grooves, and Popular Culture in Cali, Colombia

Mina Yang
Planet Beethoven: Classical Music at the Turn of the Millennium

ABOUT THE AUTHOR

Tracy McMullen is an assistant professor of music at Bowdoin College. Her articles have appeared in the peer-reviewed *Journal of Popular Music Studies, Current Musicology,* and *Critical Studies in Improvisation,* and in the edited volumes *Big Ears: Listening for Gender in Jazz Studies* (2008); *People Get Ready: The Future of Jazz Is Now!* (2013); and *Negotiated Moments: Improvisation, Sound, and Subjectivity* (2016).